Perceptions

CULTURES IN CONFLICT

Compiled by	Adrian Kerr
Edited by	Adrian Kerr Paul Hippsley Declan Carlin
Typesetting	Joe Mc Allister
Design	Orla O'Connell
Photography	Jim Cunningham

Acknowledgements

Our thanks to Manus Martin and the Training and Employment Agency for their continued support under the Action for Community Employment (ACE) Programme. Also to Derry City Council's Recreation and Leisure Department for providing generous Community Services Grant Aid which is greatly appreciated.

Special thanks also to the following members of the Press: Danielle Price, Clare McGillan, Nicholas Devlin, Karen O'Leary, Roberta McBride, Sinéad McCarron, Aaron Murray and Marina McGrotty. Also to Rosemary McCloskey, Louise Quigley, Patricia Ann Griffen and Art Byrne for their specialist assistance.

Our appreciation to all those who contributed their thoughts and memories, and to those who provided photographs: Barney McMonagle, Fionnbarra ÓDochartaigh, Willie Carson, Bloody Sunday Justice Campaign, Magee College, Seamus Heaney, Pacemaker Press and Jarlath Kearney.

Thanks also to Derry City Council Heritage and Museum Service; Central Library, Derry; Linenhall Library, Belfast; *Derry Journal* and *Londonderry Sentinel* for reference material; and to Professor Paul Arthur of the University of Ulster for his foreword.

We gratefully acknowledge the financial support and encouragement for this project provided by Ciarán de Baróid and the Northern Ireland Voluntary Trust.

© Guildhall Press May 1996
ISBN 0 946451 32 X

Designed and published by:

GUILDHALL PRESS
COMMUNITY BOOK PUBLISHERS

41 Great James Street
Derry
BT48 7DF
Northern Ireland
Tel: (01504) 364413 Fax: (01504) 372949

Contents

Foreword

Language, history and topography – these are probably our defining characteristics. We are a parochial people (in that positive sense in which Kavanagh hived it off from the provincial). And we believe that we are different. Difference is certainly one of the features of this book. We cannot agree even on a place name. The junior minister at the Northern Ireland Office who suggested innocently that we should counter 'Belfast Is Buzzing' with 'Londonderry Is Leaping' had no idea of the etymological minefield into which he had strayed. He had no sense of (our) history. It was Stephen Gwynn who maintained that no other town in Ireland has had such a vital contact with history as we have had. But, he added tellingly: "Except for its historic associations, there is little reason why any should linger on Derry's prosperous streets."

Pride in place would lead many of us to dispute that judgement. We are as capable as the next of avoiding the despotism of fact by wrapping ourselves in mythologies and ambiguities and self-deceptions. After all, that was one of the themes of Friel's *Translations,* our capacity to adapt to "... a syntax opulent with tomorrows. It is our response to mud cabins and a diet of potatoes; our only method of replying to ... inevitabilities."

Perceptions begins to confront language, history and topography because it enables us to talk *to* rather than *at* each other by acclaiming the richness in diversity. We need to stand outside ourselves and perceive how others see us. In 1982 Paul Theroux was momentarily seduced: "From a distance Derry was lovely and familiar. It looked like a mill-town in Massachusetts – churches and factories pile up on both banks of a river, the same sort of tenements, the same sleepy air of bankruptcy. But up close, Derry was frightful." We want to deny that, and he found enough people who simply asserted the city's 'difference' and who compared it favourably with the awfulness of Belfast's sectarian conflict. What we cannot deny is the record in front of us, especially the vivid photography depicting the destruction and violence of the early period of the troubles.

This book does not pretend to be a dialogue. It is a raw and honest contemporary record. It is necessarily flawed because it is concerned with 'memory' and ... perception. Our most recent visitor, John Ardagh, marvels in our " ... Phoenix-like revival ..." but adds " ... at a price." He quotes Bishop Francis Lagan on the happy fact of the meandering Foyle: "One cannot say it aloud, but maybe the separation of the two populations is needed for a while, as part of the healing process." Ardagh wonders whether this is realism or a council of despair? What cannot be denied is that, as in other divided societies, high fences may make good neighbours. It may not be sociable but it can have the potential to point us in the right direction.

There are many signs that we are on the way. Those of us who live outside the city are conscious of a vibrant cultural life and effervescence missing from most other areas. There is an envy, too, at the economic resurgence and a feeling that the city is the laboratory for a new North centred on new relationships. Let two of our poets serve as our guides from the familiarly haunting history to a brave new world shorn of its opulent syntax. Robert Greacen bemoans a: "City of Walls/City of Siege/Jewel of the North/Maiden of the west/Undone by drums and cymbals." Seamus Heaney offers us a future when he writes of language being both fortification and enrichment. This book can be the first step beyond the fortifications.

Professor Paul Arthur
Department of Politics, University of Ulster

4

Introduction

"In this country perceptions and realities have the same potency."
Irish News editorial 11 May 1996

The idea for *Perceptions: Cultures in Conflict* emerged in August 1995, just before the first anniversary of the IRA ceasefire. Our intention was to document the experiences, beliefs and aspirations of a wide range of Derry people on the troubles, their origins and their aftermath, and how people from different backgrounds, cultures and allegiances perceived those same times.

We began interviewing in early September 1995, covering the period from the 1960s and the emergence of the civil rights movement, through the twenty-five years of the troubles, up to the ceasefires of 1994, the ongoing peace process and beyond. We called for submissions in the local press in December 1995 to allow the general public the opportunity to become involved in this project.

Each interview was conducted at a time and place of the subject's choice, and we assured everyone involved that their stories would not be altered, censored, or commented on in any way. What is contained in this book, therefore, is a totally honest account of each interview and, similarly, each written submission. When the IRA ceasefire ended in February 1996, we decided to offer those interviewed, or who had given us written submissions, during the ceasefire period, the opportunity to update their material which many of them welcomed. We have included as many different sections of our community as possible, but regretfully, due to limited space, we could not include them all and can only hope that those included are a representative cross section of the many viewpoints existing in our society.

We hope that with *Perceptions* we have created a valuable social record of how people from both traditions and cultures feel during this momentous time in our history, a time when the prospects for our future have never been brighter, or darker.

Jack Allen

...to me the Corporation, under the circumstances at that time, were doing a fairly good job. I have statistics at home from one of the papers that indicated that from the end of the war up to 1963 there were some 1500 houses built in the city, and two thirds of those went to Catholics, one third to Protestants.

I was involved in business life in the city in the '60s. They were boom years, with Du Pont and various other industries starting. I had been a Young Unionist, and I was asked to put my name forward for election as a councillor to the Corporation. Prior to the troubles, I was elected and in those couple of years before the troubles the Corporation was looking at many things, including the redevelopment of the Bogside. There was a lot happening, although I do recall members of the public coming and criticising the council for the lack of housing development. But to me the Corporation, under the circumstances at that time, were doing a fairly good job. I have statistics at home from one of the papers that indicated that from the end of the war up to 1963 there were some 1500 houses built in the city, and two thirds of those went to Catholics, one third to Protestants. At that stage, Creggan was the only land within the Corporation boundary available for building houses. The building of houses there was seen as gerrymandering by the Unionists. I didn't see it like that, because there were some 200 families in the Creggan Estate and it was the Corporation that put them there. It didn't give a single vote to Unionists because the South ward, as it then was, had all Nationalist representatives; the North Ward and the Waterside were Unionist. So I believe that under those circumstances we were doing a fairly good job. Also, in those days the money for most of these things had to come from the rate-payers; we didn't have the grants that are available today.

I don't believe there was a need for the civil rights movement bringing people onto the streets. At that particular time, things were on the move as far as business was concerned. Industry was coming to the city, housing was in the pipeline and redevelopment of the Bogside, Lecky Road and Rossville Street areas had begun. Those things were all about to happen, and I believe that some people jumped on the bandwagon at that particular stage. Certainly some of the old Nationalist councillors were involved in the early days, but it should be noted that they soon opted out. Yes, there may have been odd things that people wanted, but in this I believe it was the same the world over, whether it was the UK, England, Scotland, Wales or Dublin. The same thing was happening. There was a demand for houses which couldn't be built quickly enough. The demand right across the UK led to building multistorey flats in Liverpool, Manchester, Glasgow, and the Corporation here was doing just the same as anywhere else. Unionists were criticised for a policy of 'jobs for the boys'. But if you look again across the country, both in the South or in England, it was the custom then in the railways, in the docks, in the mines, that fathers got jobs for their sons. That was the way of life then. So these are things that Unionists have been criticised for which were just a way of life all over the world.

At that stage I don't think there was the same ill feeling between the two sides. And I must say that in Derry, compared with any place else, nobody held any grief or animosity towards people of other religions. Most people, except in a few estates, whether they were Protestant or Catholic, remained good friends.

It's quite difficult for Unionists to talk about Bloody Sunday, not having been there at the time of the events. I think it's difficult for everyone. The preceding months saw the army on the streets. In the early days Catholics in the Bogside welcomed them into the area, but it wasn't long until they turned against the army. I think the problem was the no-go areas of the city and other parts of the province. And the softly-softly attitude of government in Whitelaw's day was also part of the problem. I regret any death throughout the troubles, no matter where, but we were into a confrontation situation at that particular time and who fired the first shot is not for me to say. Therefore I don't want to say that it was wrong or it was right.

The fall of the Corporation in 1969 was a very sore point with the Unionists. The Development Commission came in at that stage; they had endless money to provide houses and provided them very quickly because they were already in the pipeline. We then saw the collapse of Stormont, again something which horrified Unionist people. Events after that were on the basis of trying to get some sort of administration to replace Stormont. From this came the reform of local government and, in 1973, we in the city were elected to a new council to replace the Development Commission. We were at a disadvantage here compared with some of the other twenty-six district councils when the change-over came. For the first six months the Development Commission and ourselves ran the city jointly. And then in October 1973 the first mayor, Dr Raymond McClean, was elected. Unionists found a big change because at one stage we had been the majority. But we didn't become the minority at first and this is one thing that has to be noted. In 1973, it was a split council and it ended up with nine SDLP, nine Unionists and nine others, Nationalists and Alliance, along with a couple of independents. At that particular stage, the SDLP tried to make an agreement with us on a partnership role. We didn't reject that, and in the first year Raymond McClean of the SDLP was mayor and I was deputy mayor. However, when it came to the third year, the SDLP expected to go back in as mayor, but we felt there were other parties involved then and so we supported Ivor Canavan of Alliance to the disappointment of the SDLP. The SDLP have taken a lot of credit for the partnership, but Unionists played a very important role too in being prepared to accept it.

At the time of the UWC strike, being a Unionist, I certainly was against power sharing as it was introduced then. I was always a fairly moderate Unionist and as mayor worked for both sides of the community. Nevertheless, at that particular stage things were being imposed on us by the government that meant the majority no longer had the right in administration. The power sharing imposed meant the minority would be equal to the majority; I couldn't accept that. So as far as the UWC strike was concerned I, like most of my fellow Unionists, had to support it.

The change of the name of the council from Londonderry to Derry was another thing that caused a lot of concern for Unionists. It was harder to take that than the change in the council from a Unionist to a Nationalist majority. To me it was Nationalist triumphalism. In my early days in Derry City or Londonderry Civic Council (not the Corporation), there were attempts by Fergus McAteer and others to change the name, but the SDLP said the time wasn't right. They were prepared, as many other Nationalists were, to accept that Londonderry was the name. It was only when Sinn Féin formed a political party and started fighting elections and the SDLP saw them as a threat that led to the eventual name change.

When it comes to the question of violence, I go back to the point I keep making that the softly-softly attitude of the government in allowing no-go areas enabled the paramilitaries to build up on both sides. I don't believe that there would have been a UVF or UDA in operation had it not been for the IRA. They came out solely to defend the Unionists, or Protestant people, because they felt the British government was not doing enough. But I am against all violence, and there have been too many deaths during the troubles in Northern Ireland.

I don't think the government has used violence against the people of Northern Ireland. They were drawn into a war situation in the early '70s, when the army was called in, but I don't think they were needed at that time. We were in a situation then not of civil war, but of riot. When the troops came in they were welcomed by the Nationalist people. But then, suddenly, they had a job to do to prevent no-go areas. They found themselves in a different situation, and once the first shot was fired the war had started. The army, as far as Protestant people were concerned, were the troops of the country and were there to defend the people of the country.

I was happy when the IRA called a ceasefire, but there was always a doubt as to whether it would last and whether it was genuine. John Hume and Gerry Adams got together and were involved at the top level in the political scene. We feared at an early stage that Gerry Adams wanted to go political, but others wanted to remain in the military end of it. So when the ceasefire came, obviously people felt that there would be a split fairly quickly, that the guns would be out in no time at all. They gave it a month or two months. I am pleased that it has lasted so long. The year of the ceasefire that we have seen so far has been a tremendous boost to the community as a whole, and especially to the business community. The city itself has boomed over the last year. But prior to that, from the reorganisation of local government, I think the one thing that did happen in the city was its rejuvenation and the two communities moved closer together.

I think that at some stage we will get around the table, but it is very hard for Unionists to sit around the table when there are arms under the table. If we sit round the talks table and there isn't decommissioning, the IRA is going to say at every hurdle 'if you don't do this or you don't do that, the talks process is in difficulties'. So they are going to be holding a gun on us sitting round that table.

One other point I think has got to be made. We talked about power sharing in 1974, and I'm in favour of a partnership administration in Northern Ireland. I believe that this has to go for the talks process as well, in that it must be a democratic process. If there ever is a Nationalist majority, I think people will accept it, but I think that we have to talk about the democratic process which will come, I hope, before that. What you are going to have is a position where we get an administration – this year, next year, the following year – a partnership administration according to electoral strength, and this is where

it differs from the previous power-sharing executive. The last power-sharing executive was 'as of right'. There were appointments made to it not necessarily based on electoral strength. Unionists are saying that if we sit down round the table, and if we have an administration, we don't mind sharing power on electoral strength. To define that, we are saying: if you have 30% of the vote you will get 30% of the committees, 30% of the chairmanships, the vice-chairmanships, and so on. We don't have a difficulty with that. But it's going to be very hard for Unionists to sit down round the table when we know that the last talks failed because of the smaller political parties sitting with the same representation as the much bigger Unionist Party. I can't sit down at a table in a talks process with the same representation from Sinn Féin, the UDP, the other Unionist party, and SDLP and Alliance. We have more votes than anybody, and yet we become the minority. I am not asking to be the majority, and we wouldn't anyway with 30% of the votes, but I believe it should be done according to electoral strength.

Having been involved in the talks process in the 1991 period, I would like to see our party put forward proposals for a new administration on a partnership basis and that administration to be involved in the running of Northern Ireland departments as they are at the present time. Departments will be run by a committee-type system in which committees will discuss the various departments. There will be a head of each department who can be a minister, chairman or whatever, and he will report to the assembly and the assembly ratifies his decision. And from that assembly a number of people would be appointed to sit on a committee to discuss areas of common interest, such as agriculture and tourism, with a similar number of people from Dáil Éireann. But not on the basis of giving that particular body executive power because then it becomes a quango. I don't believe the Dublin government would want a few of their members of the Dáil having the right to decide on behalf of the government. So I would like to see something like that, on a partnership basis, and a North-South relationship as far as the economy of the island is concerned. If we have an administration like that, and a relationship with the South like that, then in whatever length of time, and I am not prepared to speculate on the length of time, a Nationalist majority comes about, then... But even if it becomes a Nationalist majority in that administration, I don't think even then the majority of people in Northern Ireland will want to vote for a united Ireland. And we as Unionists believe that if there was a border poll tomorrow the majority of people, and possibly a percentage of Catholic people, would vote to remain within the Union. So even Catholics say that if we get the right type of administration, even if that administration in whatever number of years should become controlled by Nationalists, it will not necessarily mean a united Ireland.

I would like to see political progress on the basis I have indicated. The sooner we get it, the sooner we move on. I believe also that Sinn Féin are keen to a hold out for as long as possible, because the longer they hold out, and that maybe goes for the SDLP as well, the more they are likely to get. Unionists should have had their foot in the door in 1974 or '75, and we would have been back to a better democratic process. The democratic process that we have at the present time is to have civil servants, who are not responsible to the electorate, running the province. Councils have very little power; they clean the streets and empty the bins and bury the dead. So the sooner we get back to a process where the elected representatives are more involved, then the better for everyone.

Ancient Order Of Hibernians

The savage attack by the RUC on peaceful protesters in Duke Street was filmed by worldwide television. This was followed by their treachery at Burntollet, the murder of Sammy Devenney in his home in William Street, and numerous other actions unlikely to endear them to the Catholic population.

Discrimination on a large scale has been practised against the Catholic population since the setting up of the six-county parliament – a parliament described by Premier James Craig as a 'Protestant parliament for a Protestant people'. The Local Government Act, passed in October 1922, abolished proportional representation. This had been included in the Partition Act to protect the voting rights of Catholics. This Local Government Act also gave to the six-county Minister of Home Affairs the power to alter boundaries in the Urban and County electoral areas. This paved the way for the gerrymander of all the electoral areas which contained Catholic majorities. The Special Powers Acts, introduced in 1922 and added to over the years, were used solely against Catholics. The powers given to the RUC and the B Specials, including search without a warrant, confiscation or destruction of property without compensation, imprisonment without trial, the denial of the right of an accused person to see a legal adviser, and numerous other measures, made them – until Hitler – the most repressive legislative Acts to have been passed in Europe. Indeed, so wide-ranging were the powers in these acts, that in later years they were openly envied by the South African government.

From government level down, Catholics suffered from discrimination – and the use of the word Catholic is deliberate, as it was not necessary to be Republican, anti-partitionist, or Nationalist for discrimination to be your lot in life. Periodically in the 1920s and '30s, anti-Catholic pogroms occurred, with no protection or help being given to the victims by the forces of law and order. This was to be expected from the RUC who in 1922, having been given permission to become members of the Orange Order, formed the Sir Robert Peel Orange Lodge. The A and the B Specials had been recruited from the Ulster Volunteers and were often in the forefront in the attacks on Catholics.

During World War Two, the six-county 'Protestant parliament for a Protestant people' asked British Premier Winston Churchill to extend to the six counties conscription which was then in force in Britain. Those in unimportant work or unemployed ie Catholics, would be conscripted, and those doing essential work would not be conscripted. This 'essential' work would include the Specials, many of them now mobilised full time, and the overmanned shipyard and engineering works. The wily Winston was not fooled by this ploy, and the fact that several Victoria Crosses were won during the war by volunteers from the South justified his decision not to extend conscription to the six counties. At the end of the war, Able Seaman McGuinness VC returned to his home in Belfast as holder of the only Victoria Cross won by a resident of the six counties. However, he was a Catholic and discrimination against Catholics extended even to war heroes. Unemployed and broke, he was forced to sell his Victoria Cross.

During all these years, the most glaring discrimination was the gerrymander of the Derry City Council where Protestants, who comprised one third of the population, elected twelve councillors and the Catholic two-thirds elected eight councillors. This gerrymander had been devised by the 'Protestant parliament for a Protestant people' and by its silence, the so-called 'mother of parliaments' was equally to blame. Not only Derry city, but all areas containing Catholic majorities were gerrymandered by the manipulation of the electoral area boundaries, and by a voting system which gave as many as six extra votes to those owning commercial properties whilst non-householders were denied a vote. The overwhelming majority of the latter would of course be Catholics. At the 'Field' on the occasion of the annual 12 July Boyne celebrations, six-county government Ministers regularly made provocative sectarian speeches. Premier Sir Basil Brooke, later Lord Brookeborough, was not one to be outdone when these types of speeches were being made, and in reference to Catholics his advice to the brethren was 'don't give them jobs and don't give them houses'.

In the postwar years, the introduction of the Welfare state by the Labour government helped to improve the lives of Catholics in the six counties. Later, in the fifties, Premier Harold McMillan was telling everyone that we never had it so good. He was of course referring to Britain, where minimum unemployment and good quality council housing probably justified his statement. In these circumstances it was not difficult to attract industry to the six counties. Of course the 'Protestant parliament for a Protestant people' directed this industry to Protestant areas east of the Bann. Meanwhile, high unemployment and poor housing was the norm in Catholic areas. In the early and middle sixties, the policy of directing industry to the Protestant areas created a situation where local labour was not available to staff the expanding factories. Notices now appeared in the Labour Exchanges in Catholic areas offering jobs and houses in Antrim, Larne, and other towns. There were some who accepted the situation, and moved to these areas. Others founded action committees to demand jobs and houses for the Catholic areas. The Derry Unemployment Action Committee was formed, as was the Derry Housing Action Committee. Members of these committees were at times imprisoned, especially when they protested on the occasions of visits to Derry by British government or Stormont Ministers. The siting of the New University in Coleraine instead of Derry

caused bitter resentment and anger in Derry city. This, along with all the other injustices suffered over a long number of years, created what was in effect a time bomb waiting to explode. The civil rights movement hoped to achieve their aims by peaceful protest. This would probably have been possible in a democratic state, but in a six counties governed by a 'Protestant parliament for a Protestant people', peaceful protest was met by violence from the forces of law and order. The savage attack by the RUC on peaceful protesters in Duke Street was filmed by worldwide television. This was followed by their treachery at Burntollet, the murder of Sammy Devenney in his home in William Street, and numerous other actions unlikely to endear them to the Catholic population. With the emergence of the Provisional IRA, after the burning of unprotected Bombay Street in Belfast, the time bomb created by long years of discrimination and injustice finally exploded.

The answer, of course, is that it should have been foreseen and therefore could have been avoided. It would have required acts of fairness and generosity on the part of the Unionist leaders. This would have been difficult for people who appeared to have been locked in a time warp where it was always 1690. The siege mentality was ever present in all government decisions, and was not likely to make any effort to try to bring the two communities closer together. No account was taken of the population changes that were taking place. In the 1960s, population analysts put forward the view that Catholic children would soon be in the majority in primary schools. (This came true in the early '70s and has naturally extended to all levels of education.) However, the six-county government chose to ignore these views. This was an early opportunity to take account of the rising Catholic population and to take steps to end discrimination and injustice. The entrenched backwoodsmen of the Unionist Party were not prepared to grasp the opportunity.

The sectarian murder of Peter Ward in Malvern Street, Belfast, in 1966 caused the British government to become involved in the affairs of the six counties. Three years later came the entry of the British army who, surprisingly, had a brief honeymoon period of good relations with the

Catholic people. This was not to last however, and the army, true to form, began to harass the Catholic people, especially the youths, who were commonly spread-eagled against walls and body searched. Internment and the ill-treatment of prisoners led eventually to Bloody Sunday and the murder by the paras of fourteen innocent civilians. The Widgery whitewash made the situation worse. If the paras, and those whose orders they carried out had been tried and convicted of murder, it is possible that the troubles may have ended sooner. Of course, instead of justice, we got Widgery.

In 1974, following on from the Sunningdale agreement, Brian Faulkner led a power-sharing government in the six counties. This power-sharing assembly, with the possibility of Catholics eventually getting fair treatment, could have resulted in an earlier end to the troubles and may in time have led to a better understanding between the two communities. This was not acceptable to the extreme elements in the Unionist population, and the so-called Workers' Council brought down this enlightened experiment. A weak Labour government stood idly by whilst bully boys blocked roads and closed down the power stations and factories. Masked men armed with cudgels blocked roads in full view of the RUC and the army. The last opportunity for an early end to the troubles had been missed.

Our Order has always sought, and continues to seek, the unification of our country, but only by peaceful means. Had the troubles arose in a situation where Catholics were being treated fairly, we would condemn outright the actions of those who resorted to violence. Sadly Catholics were not being treated fairly, and when they sought, by peaceful protest, to try to get fair treatment, they were savagely attacked by the RUC in Duke Street on 5 October 1968. The violence of the RUC in 1968 and 1969 provoked a reaction from those prepared to use violence to seek to achieve the unification of our country. The Provisional IRA was formed after the burning of unprotected Bombay Street in Belfast. The ill-treatment of those interned without trial, and the murder by the paras of fourteen innocent people on Bloody Sunday, brought increased support to the IRA. That support was sure to increase

with each unlawful action by the forces of law and order. There were many of these actions, including the shoot-to-kill policy, the arming of Loyalist murder squads, and the murders of unarmed civilians by plastic or rubber bullets, fired in many cases at point-blank range. There were of course many more. None of these actions were ever condemned by the government. By their silence they must have believed that these illegal actions were justified. Our Order does not support the Provisional IRA, but taking into account the situation leading up to the troubles and the unlawful actions of the forces of law and order both before and during the troubles, then we would feel that the troubles were justified.

In our submission so far, we have not laid as much blame on the British government as perhaps we should. It is easy to say this or that should have been done, but we feel that it was not a question of what should have been done. Of more importance was when it should have been done. Too little too late has often been the reaction of the British government with regard to the six counties. This is not strictly true however, as the decision to abolish Stormont was certainly not too little, but it was too late. Had Stormont been abolished in the mid-'60s we would have been spared the anguish of the past twenty-five years. When not in power, the Labour Party were inclined to discuss the six counties at their annual conference, but when in government, they chose to ignore what was happening in these six counties. They would have been aware of the gerrymandered electoral areas, such as Derry city, and also of the discrimination and the injustices suffered by the Catholic population. When they were in power from 1964-70, they should have abolished the administration responsible – Stormont. Unfortunately, this corrupt body survived until 1972. Had Stormont been abolished in the '60s, the British government could have passed meaningful laws to end discrimination and injustices practised against the Catholic population in the six counties. In these circumstances, the troubles would not have happened.

This is of course our opinion of what the British government could and should have done. However, after Stormont was abolished, the laws introduced to ensure fair treatment for Catholics have proved to be no more than a charade. In the six counties, before 1972, Catholics were twice as likely to be unemployed as Protestants. Now, after twenty-three years of direct rule, Catholics are two-and-a-half times more likely to be unemployed than Protestants. The senior civil servants who carried out Stormont's bigoted policies are still in positions of power, so perhaps these figures are really to be expected. This will obviously be one of the main issues to be resolved in future all-party talks.

In the Catholic areas where we lived, our members were always aware of the presence of the police and army. This presence would be greatly increased following a bombing or a shooting which could be linked to the Provisional IRA. On these occasions Catholic areas would be completely surrounded, with house searches being carried out on a large scale. Property was often destroyed during these searches. The residents, especially young men, were often body searched. 'Up against the wall, feet apart' was a common command from the police and the army. Dawn raids were almost a way of life. The victims of these raids were often ill-treated and held for several days without access to legal advice. Plastic/rubber bullets were fired by the army at the slightest provocation, and on many occasions without provocation. Children were often targets of the trigger-happy soldiers who were quite prepared to kill – and did. Then of course there were the watchtowers. These ugly structures were seen as an invasion of the privacy of the local residents. This was how life was lived in Catholic areas during the long years of the troubles.

Both communities, of course, suffered grievously at the hands of paramilitaries. Many innocent people lost their lives in so called tit-for-tat murders. Many more were injured in bomb and gun attacks. Following paramilitary bombings or murders, it was Catholic areas which were subjected to large-scale searches. In contrast, Protestant areas were never subject to mass searches, even when the most atrocious murders had been committed on members of the Catholic population. No watchtowers invaded their privacy, no 'up against walls', no house searches on a large scale, no damage to property, no dawn

raids, internment, ill-treatment of prisoners, and no trigger-happy soldiers firing lethal plastic/rubber bullets at children. Indeed in comparison to Catholic areas, life was fairly normal for Protestants. Perhaps this is one of the reasons why the Unionist politicians do not seem to want all-party talks to try to bring about a long-term solution to the problems in the six counties.

We welcomed the ceasefire, and we feel that much credit is due to the two men who did most to bring it about. One, John Hume, risked his political career and his worldwide reputation as a man of peace. The other, Gerry Adams perhaps risked his life if some of the 'hard men' in the Provisionals were not prepared to accept the ceasefire. The ceasefire declared by the Loyalists gave hope that the troubles of the last twenty-five years were over. Credit is also due to the leaders of the political groups who persuaded the Loyalists to declare a ceasefire.

Thankfully the ceasefire appears to be holding, but we feel it is important to get people talking as soon as possible in order to ensure that it holds. The British government has a special responsibility to get all-party talks started. At present, John Major is dependent on the Unionists to keep him in power, especially on some key European issues, when some of his party MPs refuse to vote for him. In this situation, it is obvious that the survival of the Conservative Party is more important than the six counties.

There are many problems to be faced, judging by the expectations expressed, by the opposing groups. How wide the gap is between these groups will not be known until the talking begins. All of these problems must be resolved if we are to achieve the lasting peace that everyone longs to see. As an organisation involved in marches, we have a clear cut policy on the matter. We will not seek to march in an area where we are not welcome. Our two main parades each year are on St Patrick's Day and 15 August, the Feast Day of the Assumption of Our Lady. To march in an area where we might cause offence would not be honouring our patron saint or the mother of Our Lord.

We feel that all-party talks should take place very soon, as only by talking can the two communities be brought closer together. Perhaps 'talks' is not the most apt description of these future all-party meetings. These meetings will be futile if everyone talks and no-one listens. Listening will play a vital part in these discussions. When the Protestant community leaders state that they have a fear of a united Ireland, that their rights as a minority would not be protected, that their standard of living would fall, and various other points, then it is important for the Catholic community to speak of their fears of a return to a 'Protestant parliament for a Protestant people', of discrimination and injustice, of the low standard of living due to Catholics being two-and-a-half times more likely to be unemployed than Protestants, and various other points, then the leaders of the Protestant community should listen very carefully.

The problem of decommissioning of arms, appears to us to be an excuse by the British government to delay all-party talks. The paragraph in the Downing Street Declaration which states that only parties committed to peace can take part in the talks is being quoted as requiring that arms be decommissioned. It is accepted, even by top Unionist politicians, that the Provisional IRA was not defeated, and therefore the surrender of arms, to either the British or Irish governments, is clearly not going to happen. The meaning of the word decommission according to the Oxford Dictionary is 'to take out of service'. The fact that arms are not being used would indicate that they have been taken out of service.

The benefits of the ceasefire, can be seen in the relaxed atmosphere in our city, especially in the shopping areas. Many more people are coming to the recently developed shopping centres. However, the unemployment and housing problems have not been resolved, nor indeed is any apparent meaningful attempt being made to try to resolve them. Unemployment and unfair allocation of houses were two of the main problems which led to the troubles. The Housing Executive, when they were adequately funded, built houses in sufficient numbers to remove the problem of unfair allocation. The large estates of Shantallow, Carnhill, Galliagh, Ballymagroarty etc meant that houses were available fairly quickly to those in need. Presently very much underfunded, the Housing Executive is now building a small number of houses on green areas in the previously mentioned estates. No land has been acquired for future building and this will result in longer waiting lists. There are reports in some newspapers that the Housing Executive may be disbanded and responsibility for housing given to local councils or private groups. This would surely pave the way for a return to unfair allocation.

The unemployed see little hope of getting permanent work, and the Industrial Development Board, having sold off factories and land, is closing down its local office. This same Board is still locating factories in the area east of the Bann. Are we going to see notices appearing again in the Job Market 'jobs and houses available etc'? Surely common sense will prevail and prevent a return to the conditions which led to the troubles.

Clearly, the expectations of the two communities are set much higher than can be achieved. In view of this, the all-party meetings are likely to be long drawn out affairs, possibly spread over a number of years. There may well be at times walkouts and boycotts and threats to end discussion, but despite all of this, the meetings must continue.

Hopefully at the end of all-party talks agreement will be reached on how the two communities can live together in peace. In the short term, genuine efforts must be made to bring factories to the high unemployment areas. At present, factories are locating in areas where the percentage of unemployment is as low as seven or eight per cent. In some Catholic areas unemployment is four times or more this figure. This is totally unacceptable, and cannot be allowed to continue.

Affirmative action to direct factories to these areas of high unemployment should be a priority. British, European, and American funding must be used to offer higher grants and other inducements to these factories. If this problem is not resolved, then, with the cut back in building by the Housing Executive, we will be back to the conditions which caused the troubles. It is possible that some hardliner in the Provisional IRA may not be prepared to accept the outcome of the all-party talks. In a situation where permanent employment and ample housing is available in Catholic areas, then it would be very unlikely that these hardliners would receive any support if they sought a return to violence. However, if high unemployment coupled with lack of housing is still to be found in Catholic areas, then we would be in a very dangerous situation.

Our Order seeks the unification of our country by peaceful means. The Protestant community cannot be bombed, bullied, or threatened into this peaceful Ireland which we seek. Hopefully, conditions can be created where the two communities will learn to trust each other. The culture, the identity, and the flags and emblems of each community must be willingly accepted and respected.

Policing is a most fundamental issue in the six counties. If this is faced honestly and openly then we can begin to solve the problem. The Nationalist community has always viewed the RUC as an instrument of domination and representing a view that it did not share. Interrogation methods used by the police were contrary to the European Human Rights Convention. The police were involved in many other events, such as leaking information to Loyalist murder squads, the shoot-to-kill policy, and recruiting informers among petty criminals in Catholic areas – knowing that these people faced death if discovered. All these events, which occurred over many years, alienated the great majority of the Catholic community. To ensure that this does not continue, a future police force must be acceptable to both communities. The name of the force would have to be changed eg Northern Ireland Police. Recruiting policy for a short number of years should favour Catholic applicants in order to achieve a ratio of approximately 55% Protestant and 45% Catholic. This would be in line with the present population. The members of the RUC, who have themselves suffered in the past twenty-five years, will benefit by becoming a police force that is acceptable to everyone living in every part of this island.

Both communities have suffered terrible atrocities. We must ensure that this never happens again. No community has the right to dominate another community or tradition. To pursue our culture and traditions, our aspiration of a united Ireland, and our religious beliefs, our belief in freedom, these are our fundamental rights. We also respect the rights of other communities to freely uphold their culture, traditions, and religious beliefs. To heal all the past suffering and to learn to forgive will take time. We, as the oldest fraternal society in this country, will use any means at our disposal to help to build bridges and foster good relations with all traditions and beliefs. It is our hope for the future, that we will be able to live in peace, with justice for everyone, in this island that we all love so much.

Apprentice Boys Of Derry

The shutting of the Gates and the siege are not celebrated because the victory guaranteed the Protestant Ascendancy (remember, Presbyterians were never part of that Ascendancy), but rather because it guaranteed civil and religious liberty for all.

The 'Brave 13', a term used by Apprentice Boys all over the world, recalls the action of thirteen brave young men who, in the face of King James's army, closed Ferryquay Gate on 7 December 1688 (as per the old-style calendar, which is 18 December in today's new-style revision) and the stage was set for the siege which commenced the following April and lasted for 105 days. To this day the action of these young apprentices is commemorated by the 'Shutting of the Gates' each year when the four Gates (Ferryquay, Bishop, Butcher and Shipquay) are visited by the General Committee, or a representative body of Apprentice Boys.

The 'Relief of Derry', celebrated on 12 August (28 July, old style), is commemorated with a thanksgiving service held in St Columb's Cathedral which has such memorable links with the siege, and afterwards a very colourful parade takes place through the streets of the city.

Each celebration is heralded by: the firing of a cannon, a replica of the famous siege gun known as 'Roaring Meg' because of its noise; a visitation to the Gates as already mentioned; and then, prior to the Church Service, the ceremony of initiation into the Order of new overseas members. Other members are initiated on a number of fixed days throughout the year, arranged by the Parent Clubs. This act of initiation can only take place inside the Walls of Derry and Apprentice Boys initiated into the Order solemnly vow to honour the two days of celebration, namely 18 December and 12 August.

The celebrations each 18 December commence with a wreath-laying ceremony on the Apprentice Boys' Mound in the Cathedral, fol-lowed by a short parade, after which a large effigy of the traitor Lundy is burned, reminding all of his treacherous conduct during the siege. Prior to the service the Cathedral bells are rung and the Crimson flag flown from the Apprentice Boys' Memorial Hall, St Columb's Cathedral and the Royal Bastion on the Walls. The wearing of the Crimson collarettes by all members recalls the flag flown from the Cathedral during the siege and known as Mitchelburne's 'Bloody Flag' (siege colour).

The governing body of the Apprentice Boys of Derry is called the General Committee and comprises representatives from the eight Parent Clubs which meet within the Walls of Derry, and other representatives from the Amalgamated Committees. The Parent Clubs are named after siege heroes and events and are as follows: Apprentice Boys of Derry Club, formed to commemorate the 'Brave 13'; Walker Club, called after Governor Rev George Walker; Mitchelburne Club, called after Governor Colonel J Mitchelburne; No Surrender Club, named after the city's watchword during the siege; Browning Club, named after Captain Michael Browning who was killed as his ship *The Mountjoy* attempted to break the boom; Baker Club, called after Governor Henry Baker; Campsie Club, called after one of the 'Brave 13' who closed the city Gates; and the Murray Club, called after Colonel Adam Murray, who was born a few miles from the city at Lyng, near Claudy. Each Parent Club has a number of Branch Clubs, which are to be found in Scotland, England, Eire, Canada and Australia.

The above gives but a brief outline of the

Apprentice Boys of Derry and one hopes that those who erroneously cite the organisation as a branch of the Orange Order will see that it is an autonomous body with no links at all, except through a mutual adherence to the truth of biblical Protestantism and the fact that many brethren enjoy membership of both organisations.

"Why do the Apprentice Boys have to march?" ask our ill-informed opponents and certain sections of the media. The answer is that the parades are based on the Trade Guild marches of the past which were held at the time of the organisation's formation, and early Apprentice Boys' marches, like those of the Guilds, ended with a feast which often lasted up to two days. The shutting of the Gates and the siege are not celebrated because the victory guaranteed the Protestant Ascendancy (remember Presbyterians were never part of that Ascendancy), but rather because it guaranteed civil and religious liberty for all.

Until the Glorious Revolution of 1688 when King James was replaced by William and Mary, the British Isles had been classified as an absolute monarchy. After 1688 Britain was established firmly on the road to a parliamentary democracy.

The parades celebrate the Protestant religion and culture and in our remembrance of the events of over 300 years ago we stress the political and cultural links with mainland Britain which guarantees a pluralist society and a tolerance of ethnic and religious diversity.

The first celebrations of the 'Relief of Derry' took place on the Walls on a joyous calm Sunday evening of 28 July 1689 when the starving citizens, who had endured such hardship for 105 days, crowded onto the ramparts to welcome Browning's ships that had just broken the boom across the Foyle.

The first organised celebrations took place on Sunday, 8 August when a thanksgiving service was held in St Columb's Cathedral, thus establishing the pattern for all those which have followed throughout the centuries.

On 1 August 1714, the former Governor and siege hero Colonel Mitchelburne hoisted the Crimson flag, emblem of the city's defiance, on the Cathedral steeple and afterwards formed the club known as the Apprentice Boys. The celebrations continued in one form or another throughout the early 18th century. The resident garrison appear to have taken over the organisation of the events in August and December while the defenders and their descendants participated by attending Divine Service at the Cathedral. *The Londonderry Journal* of 5 August 1772, in just its eighth issue, recorded that the previous Saturday 'being the ever memorable First of August, there were uncommon demonstrations of joy in the city'. The report mentioned processions to the Cathedral and a superb banquet in the Town Hall, along with 'illuminations, firings and other tokens of joy'. In 1775 mention is made in the same newspaper of the Independent Mitchelburne Club and the fact that the same club had participated in the Relief Anniversary of that year when they 'distinguished themselves particularly in this most memorable exercise'. When the centenary of the Relief was celebrated in 1789, Roman Catholic Bishop McDevitt and his clergy joined their Protestant fellow citizens in their thanksgiving services. *The Sentinel*, commenting on the absence of Roman Catholics from the December festivities of 1838, claimed in their editorial that 'until a very recent period Catholics have joined their fellow citizens in commemorating the Shutting of the Gates'.

Early in the nineteenth century the Apprentice Boys' movement began to adopt a more definite role in the celebrations. New clubs were formed, the Apprentice Boys of Derry Club in 1814 and the No Surrender Club in 1824. Plans were drawn up for the erection of Walker's Memorial Pillar and the foundation stone ceremony was held in December 1826 at which the mayor and all leading citizens and military personnel officiated. The first burning from the Walker Memorial Pillar of the traitor Lundy is recorded in 1832. The Apprentice Boys continued to flourish and over the next twenty years, the Walker and Murray Clubs were formed. The celebrations continued to centre around the Cathedral thanksgiving and a banquet in the Town Hall.

In more recent times the terrorist campaign has meant that the Apprentice Boys could not carry out their obligations by walking on the Walls. Until 1994, when a partial walk of the Walls was allowed, and 1995, when a full circuit was made, many Apprentice Boys had never before set foot on the ancient Walls even though they are so much part of the heritage of our illustrious organisation. Governor Walker's fine Memorial Pillar, suffered a sad end when 'mysterious' bombers sealed its fate. The truth has yet to be told about this incident but the Apprentice Boys Memorial Hall still survives despite repeated organised attacks over the years. The foundation stone of this beautiful hall was laid on 12 August 1873 and it was opened on 13 August 1877 at an estimated cost of £3,250. An extension was opened in 1937 at a cost of £30,000 and in 1995 the stonework of this fine example of a baronial 'Scottish style' building was cleaned at considerable cost.

The Hall is the centre of every celebration connected with the siege and all newly-elected candidates for the brotherhood of the Apprentice Boys must be initiated here, within the historic Walls of Londonderry.

Most of the credit for the formation of the Apprentice Boys' Association and the celebrations must go to the siege Governor and hero Colonel John Mitchelburne. To him must be ascribed the distinction and honour of preserving trophies of triumph captured during the siege and placing them in the Cathedral; the erection there of the first tablet commemorating the siege; the giving to the city and the Apprentice Boys their own distinctive Crimson colour and flag; the formation of the first Apprentice Boys' Club of which he was principal organiser and probably first president, forerunner of later governors; the planning of the earliest anniversary celebrations; and the first hoisting of the Crimson flag on the Cathedral tower.

Over the last twenty-five years the Apprentice Boys have witnessed a phenomenal increase in membership and general interest in the history of the siege and the Association. It is obvious that Protestants are rallying to the Crimson colours in troubled times as their forbearers did throughout the centuries. The celebrations of 12 August and 18 December and the Apprentice Boys' Association have encountered much hostility from many sources and the falsehoods written and spoken about the Apprentice Boys are malicious, used with impunity and often without a grain of evidence produced to back them up.

As we approach a new millennium one looks forward to a day when all people can view the parade and no one feel offended. As we await that day, the Apprentice Boys of Derry remain resolute to the principles on which they were founded. We often recall the words of Lord Macaulay in his story of *The Siege of Londonderry*, as contained in his history of England: "A people which takes no pride in the noble achievements of remote ancestors will never achieve anything worthy to be remembered with pride by remote descendants." Likewise we are mindful of the lines from the poem penned by the famous Londonderry hymn writer Mrs Cecil Francis Alexander which serve to show why Apprentice Boys are proud members of an organisation with a historic past and which, with God's blessing, will continue to have a proud and healthy future:

O cold thou must remember,
That bleak day in December,
When the 'Prentice Boys of Derry'
Rose up and Shut the Gates.

Glen Barr

*Both sovereign powers are responsible for the problems we face in Northern Ire-
land. My own political philosophy is kick the two of them out – I am a first-class
Ulsterman not a second-class Englishman, and I have no intention of becoming a
third-class Irishman.*

I was very much involved in the trade union
movement in the late 1960s. I was a trade union official, and held several positions within the
engineering union, including president for seven
years. I was brought up here in the Waterside.
My family were not involved in any political or
religious organisations. I suppose the best way
to describe it was a hard-working Presbyterian
family. It was a very mixed community we were
brought up into, Protestants and Catholics, so
therefore we had a very early education into, I
suppose, divided politics. My own politics would
really be divided along class lines as opposed to
religious lines, they always were, so I wasn't involved in sectarianism, nor did I appreciate the
sectarianism. We lived in a mixed community
and we were *all* poor.

I think there was a lot in the civil rights movement that many of us would certainly have
supported, and I appreciated some of the points
raised. Unfortunately it very quickly deteriorated
into what could then be seen as a fight for Republican rights, and Nationalist rights, and I
suppose a lot of Protestants who had sympathy
with it were very quickly led to believe that this
was another attack on the constitution. It wasn't
really about emancipation and freedom and all
the rest of it, but was instead the start of another
campaign to take Northern Ireland into a united
Ireland, and so people quickly withdrew from it.

Around the time the troubles broke out I was
very much involved in pipe bands. I've always
had a love for traditional music, pipe-band music, and I was in a band from I was
eleven-years-old. We were at the tail end of the
march that day [12 August 1969] whenever the

bottles started coming over from Waterloo Street.
The next thing we knew was that the B Specials
were on the streets, and there were those in the
community who went over and joined in, but the
vast majority didn't bother. They thought it was
just a flash in the pan, that it would die down in a
day or two as it always did. Nobody really thought
it was going to be a long-term thing.

I was totally opposed to internment. When
internment was introduced I publicly disowned
it and publicly disassociated from it. From the
human point of view, from the moral point of
view, I believe it was entirely wrong.

The original story about Bloody Sunday was
that this was part of a campaign, that these people had opened fire on the military, and that
therefore the military were justified in opening
fire on them. Now I don't know. I just don't know
what the stories are, and I don't know if the truth
will ever be told. The unfortunate thing is that
some of the families have allowed themselves to
be tied with the Republican tag, and therefore
that leaves some suspicion in the minds of Loyalists – were they or were they not? And though
you tend to say, well maybe there wasn't anything in it, maybe the army was wrong, maybe
they got scared, maybe they got frightened,
maybe there was a bang, maybe there was a shot,
and everybody opened fire ... it was a tragic event
in the city, and there is no doubt that it was one
of the events that led to the continuation of the
violence. I wasn't there. I don't know the background of it, but I tend to think that there may
have been something from the military that
sparked the whole thing off.

I was angry when Stormont was prorogued. I

was part of a delegation of trade unionists, Protestant trade unionists, from throughout Northern Ireland who had gone to Westminster – it was the start of the old Loyalist Association of Workers (LAW) – and we met Reginald Maudling [Conservative Home Secretary, responsible for NI 1970-72] and he convinced us that security would be intact, and all the rest of it, and then two weeks after that, they prorogued Stormont. I think that basically sums up the then British Prime Minister Ted Heath's whole attitude to everything that he has ever done, even his attitude to the Gulf War and Saddam Hussein. He would be a quisling in anybody's language. I believe that at that stage if he had felt there was something wrong with Stormont, he should have taken action long before, and I think he prorogued Stormont at a time when it certainly needed to be intact to defend itself. Any changes made should have been made because they were changes that needed to be made, and were justified in being made, not because somebody was throwing petrol bombs at you, because that opens a whole different can of worms – that you are prepared to bow to violence. I think this is the thing that Ted Heath showed in his character – that he is prepared to acquiesce to violence and therefore I don't have a lot of time or respect for him. If he had been interested in Northern Ireland he should have examined the whole situation, and should have done something about it long before that.

The UWC strike was justified in as much as Faulkner went forward to represent the people under a false selection – he was elected under a false ticket, and did not represent the majority of the people, and the protest was the wish of the majority of the people. Now there is difference of opinion about what the people wanted at that time. There were those who didn't want Sunningdale because it meant sharing power with Republicans, some who didn't want to share power with Catholics, some who didn't want a Council of Ireland. I wasn't over concerned about that as it was forming good relations with Southern Ireland, which I think is crucial to our future anyway. They don't have to be formalised, or made in a formalised setup, but what we certainly need are good working relationships. However, the most important thing to me was the institutionalisation of divisions in our community. I firmly believe in the evolution of proper politics, in which we must divide socially and economically, and what Sunningdale did was divide us religiously and constitutionally, whereby the evolution of proper politics would never, ever take place again. It was to be written into our constitution that people were to be given jobs because they were Protestant or Catholic, not because they had the ability to do the job. If it had not been written into our constitution that way, it would have been much better because then we could have evolved into proper politics. That was my main objection, and will always be my main objection, to the Sunningdale agreement.

To be brutal about the hunger strikes, I thought that if that's what they wanted to do then it was entirely a matter for themselves. I hadn't a great deal of sympathy with them. Nevertheless, they had a cause and they fought it, and I have always had a sneaking admiration for them because of what they were prepared to endure for what they believed in. They believed in something different from me, therefore I wasn't going to support them on it, but I certainly had a sneaking admiration for their determination. I think that certainly the British made a complete mess of it. To let somebody die over an issue that you then concede later on is the most deplorable thing to do to any human being. I also think that it was probably the single most unifying factor for the Nationalist population. I don't know how Margaret Thatcher feels about it, if she has any conscience about it, but to me, certainly, regardless of who the person is, I doubt if I could sit back and watch somebody dying and not even consider the points they have been making, then, after they had died, you concede. To me that is deplorable.

I think the role played by London and Dublin, I lump the two of them together, has been deplorable. Both sovereign powers are responsible for the problems we face in Northern Ireland. My own political philosophy is kick the two of them out – I am a first-class Ulsterman not a second-class Englishman, and I have no intention of becoming a third-class Irishman. And what I have said quite clearly to the two communities in Northern Ireland is why be second-class Englishmen and third-class Irishmen when we can be first-class Ulstermen? What we need is a new constitution, a new bill of rights, and new political structures which allow everyone to participate in the responsibilities and decisions of the state, and within that, all of us pull together for Northern Ireland. Better to be big fish in a small pond than wee fish in a big pond. At the end of the day, what constitutional rights are we going to have even if we joined up with a united Ireland? I would reckon that if we had a united Ireland tomorrow Derrymen would be crying for independence within ten years as I don't think we have the same type of cultural background as somebody from Dublin, or Cork, or Wicklow. We are a people onto ourselves, and I think we have to realise that. The unfortunate thing is that it has been caught up in religion and culture, and I think if it was given a fair chance, without the influence of the two sovereign powers involved, and what has been inbred in us over the past 300-400 years by those two factions culminating in the two sovereign powers, then I think there's a chance for people to pull together, to unite Northern Ireland, not to unite Northern Ireland with Dublin, or unite Northern Ireland with London.

I've got to make a distinction between all three types of violence, and understand them at the same time. The state has the right to wield violence; that is a God-given right. The state has the right to set up institutions that will protect the state. The problem we face, as far as the RUC and the military are concerned, is that the only way in which you can get support from your people is if they support the institutions of the state. If your people don't support the institutions of the state they will not support the forces of law and order necessary to maintain those institutions. We see state violence in Southern Ireland. I've seen the guards [police] on many occasions knocking the shit out of people on protest, yet nobody complains. The people of Southern Ireland don't complain because they support the Gardaí Síochána, because they are the forces of law and order that have been set up to maintain the institutions they support.

We are in an entirely different situation, so the police have been caught in a cleft stick. I see them as a very bi-partisan force. They are trying to uphold law and order against both sides, and therefore they use whatever violence they think is necessary to uphold the law, and they are forced into taking decisions where they can't win, either from the Republican side or the Loyalist side.

As far as Republican violence is concerned, that's a tradition that I also can understand, in as much as they do not support the institutions of the state, and therefore they want to join up with the Republic. I don't support it. I totally abhor it, and am totally opposed to it, but I can understand it. If that's the way they see it, and have understood that that's the only way to make change, and because they haven't been treated properly by the state, then I feel that they, in their minds, feel justified. And I can understand that. I can also understand the Loyalist side. There are many activities that the Loyalist paramilitaries have been involved in that I have totally condemned, but at the same time I am not going to condemn all of it because I can understand them as well in that they are fighting to defend themselves against being taken into a united Ireland, and they see the forces of law and order not protecting them properly, so they feel a right to defend themselves.

At the end of the day the whole problem of violence comes down to the creation of the institutions of the state, and until we create institutions of the state that can command the support of the vast majority of the people of Northern Ireland, then you will have these fringe groups engaging in violence which their own supporters will find justifiable.

I was aware that the ceasefires were coming, that some moves were taking place, and hopefully I had some influence at some stage in that. I think the Loyalist one probably was the bigger shock in the lengths that it went. I had anticipated that the most we could hope for from the Loyalist side would have been a conditional ceasefire, and when there was a full declaration of a total cessation of all violence, then that certainly came as a shock, but a pleasant shock. The problem I face with the ceasefires now is that we are not making use of them in order to advance any unity of our people and trying to find a solution to the problem. Unless we find a solution to the problems that created the violence in the first place then we will go back into it again.

I totally support the need for decommissioning before all-party talks can take place. I wouldn't be prepared to go to any round-table talks if the guns are held under the table. I won't accept that at all. And yet I accept the Provo line. Why should they give up their guns? They have achieved nothing in twenty-five years, only got around the table. They were around the table at Sunningdale over twenty years ago. If I was a Provo, what would I think? I would think I haven't achieved very bloody much over all of this. A lot of people have died, a lot of people have been blown up, a lot of people have been on dirty protests, they have starved themselves to death, and the person who is going to be walking away with all the prizes is John Hume. What the hell are we getting out of this? We still haven't got our united Ireland. The Brits are still here and we don't seem to have shifted that border one inch. So I can understand where they are coming from. What we should be looking at is a whole new arrangement that allows Republicans to accept that whatever deals are made will be honest, and will be adhered to, and that everybody's opinions will be borne in mind. Therefore the weapons have no need to be used in Irish politics any longer. What do they need their guns for now? At the end of the day, do they think that a united Ireland will be a success if a million Protestants were bombed into it? I am saying no, because what you would have then is the Provos of today in Northern Ireland would be the UDA and the UVF and the UFF tomorrow in an all-Ireland state.

What I would like to see is an independent Northern Ireland. That Northern Ireland would be governed by representatives who had been duly elected by, and represent the opinions of, all the people. I would hope that it would be on a proportional representation basis. There would be no connection with Britain. It would be a totally independent state.

If things started to move the other way, towards a Republican 'victory', then that would be a recipe for civil war. Loyalists would react with force of arms, and I think that would be justified. There are a lot of Protestants at this time who are not prepared to fight to remain British, but who are prepared to die to stay out of a united Ireland.

Jimmy Cadden

...I would have thought that the civil rights movement was the right expression for their problems at the time, but what was first seen as laudable and creditable then became derisory in the eyes of Unionists and the Protestant community in general. It was hijacked in many ways, and many people would say that the latter-day civil rights movement was the early-day IRA movement.

I was quite young in the late 1960s, just before the troubles started. Myself, and people like my family, we were happy. 'I'm all right, Jack' was very much our attitude. You didn't see there was anything wrong. But obviously some people were unhappy. Very much so.

Initially I would have thought that the civil rights movement was the right expression for their problems at the time, but what was first seen as laudable and creditable then became derisory in the eyes of Unionists and the Protestant community in general. It was hijacked in many ways, and many people would say that the latter-day civil rights movement was the early-day IRA movement. That was the perception on this side of the fence. While we would admit today that there was gerrymandering and overreaction by the RUC in Duke Street on that famous Saturday afternoon, we didn't see it like that at the time.

When the situation degenerated even further, around about August 1969, I felt that this was only a temporary thing, that the police would soon sort it out, and even then, when the army came in, that the army would soon sort it out. I felt that these people may have had their gripes, and their moans and groans, but this was no way to go about getting them redressed. As time went on it became less and less about gerrymandering or bad housing conditions or unemployment levels or not being allocated a house or whatever. I think it then became the kernel of a wish for a Republican united Ireland. That began to take over from local issues at the time.

Again with the benefit of hindsight, even the government would admit that internment was a failure. It was a recruiting agent for the IRA more than anything else. But it made sense to me at the time. I remember thinking, these people are causing problems, take them out of the situation then the problems will stop. But obviously that didn't work. For every one they lifted, there were probably another six queuing up to sign on the dotted line as it were.

I remember thinking after Bloody Sunday that if the army said the IRA were shooting at them, and they shot back, then that was the case. Again hindsight has shown that this *wasn't* the case. The Widgery Report was a government response to what was a mad, totally mad, situation at the time. I think it was a cover-up, but it wasn't the last cover-up. They have been doing it ever since, in different fields, different spheres. They had to be seen to be doing something. But, obviously, political strings were pulled there.

As a Unionist, and as a Protestant, the day Stormont fell was a bad day. That was probably the beginning of the Protestant uprising, which then gave itself expression in the UWC strike. I was in total support of the strike because I thought at that time that Protestants just felt 'everything is going one way here, let's flex a few muscles, let's show that we can control the situation as well'. There was intimidation to a certain extent, but I think all those masked people, power things, that's inevitable, it's always going to happen. But I fully backed that strike.

I believed that if the hunger strikers wanted to starve themselves to death, then they should go ahead. You must remember that these were people who were imprisoned for some very bad crimes. At the time, Thatcher was hated because of her dogmatic and insistent attitude, but I saw it as a strength. A lot of things Thatcher did I didn't agree with, but she said 'no, I will not intervene, I will not change my mind, go ahead and die if you want to die'. To me it was no big deal. I could understand why Nationalists/Catholics were getting very uptight about this, but this was a personal decision these people had made, let them go ahead. If you want to die for your beliefs then your beliefs die with you in my mind; so why die for them? I didn't care one way or the other.

I see Loyalist violence as a response to Republican violence, and government/state violence as an excess of a response to both. All three are wrong, they have to be wrong. All three must be condemned. Just because I said that Loyalist violence was a response doesn't water it down, it doesn't mean it is in anyway acceptable. To me, nothing is worth killing for, nothing is worth dying for. This is why the ceasefire is the best thing that ever happened.

My first thought was that the ceasefires would never last, that all we would need was the first opportunity for somebody to say 'let's go back, let's pick up the gun'. And we have had a few times, government inspired, where they could have had a few excuses, where they were given any excuse they needed. Why was there a ceasefire in the first place? I don't know. The Protestant idea was that something has been promised here, that the IRA had been given a promise that further down the line they would get this, get that, get the other. But perhaps the IRA initially called the ceasefire because they realised they weren't going to get anywhere, or because of war fatigue or death fatigue. But I'm happy that it has lasted so long.

I can see the idea that says that arms should be handed in, but I can also see the logic from the terrorist point of view that they are not going to hand over guns until they get what they want. That's their only bargaining tool really. Anyway, what's the point of handing them in? There isn't a stock-list kept where you could tick off every machine gun as it comes in. I think that the government will back down and that we will have talks, but whether the entire Unionist family is

there is doubtful. I don't think the DUP would for one minute sit down with people like Adams. I can't see that happening. Not that it matters because I think the UUP, the bigger of the two Unionist parties, will go ahead, and maybe by being left outside the door for a while, the DUP will eventually have to come in. Personally, I think they should go into talks on the basis that how can you get something until you ask for it? How can you fight your corner, how can you stop something happening unless you protest about it?

I think all the prisoners should be kept in, on both sides. These people are not in for selling sweets, or handing out Bibles at a Sunday school. If they have gone through the due process of the law and been found guilty, then keep them there. I belong to the school of thought that says there is no early release for the people they killed, so why the hell should they have an early release? I firmly, firmly believe that they should do their time and stay where they are and take their punishment. I talked to a few people for stories to mark the first year of the ceasefire – policemen's wives and the families of people who were blown up and shot, whatever – and they don't have their loved ones or their sons or their daughters any more. The one thing they can hang onto is the knowledge that their daughter or son may be dead, but at least the person who did it has been caught and has been punished. To reward them, and it *is* a reward to let them out, would be wrong.

What I would like to happen now is that we just keep going on the way we are with the ceasefire, because as a Unionist I fear what the outcome of talks will be. I can't see the IRA settling for anything less than the promise, no matter how far down the line, of a united Ireland. When the Irish government started to become more involved in Northern Ireland, that's when I began to worry, because the British government has a history over the last few hundred years of saying 'we'll stay and protect the people and the idea of being part of Britain or part of the old empire', and then a few years later they turn around and do exactly the opposite; Hong Kong being the latest example. So when the Irish government came onto the scene, that caused me some concern, and still does. It worries me because then we would have Loyalist violence resuming. If that's not the case, and if the IRA don't get this, or Sinn Féin don't get that, then that's another threat of violence. So at the minute I am quite happy with this no-man's-land of a ceasefire. But obviously that's not going to go on forever.

I personally believe that we are on the road to a united Ireland, and as a Loyalist, in its real sense of the word, and as someone who would class himself as a British citizen, I would not like that, but I am not going to turn around and fight for that not to happen. I don't believe in that. I would make the best of it, but I would worry how others would respond, and that we would then be caught up in a whole new ball game.

I don't think there's any way of avoiding a return to violence at some stage. Once these talks start, and they will, then that's the beginning of the end; because after a few months, even years, of talks, you have to have a point where you make a decision. If that happens it has to be one of two things: staying where we are, or the British government saying that in ten or twenty years we will hand power over to Dublin. Either way we will be back into a state of trouble; I can't see any other outcome. There isn't a solution, because there is a black issue and a white issue, a united Ireland or stay with Britain. There are only six counties left. You can't say 'we'll give them another two and we'll go another fifty years with a new state'. So it's one or the other, a united Ireland or not, which is going to please one half of the community at the expense of the other.

Gregory Campbell

...there's this insidious insistence ... that eventually Unionists will ... be reconciled to their fate. But until we can get to a position where we are treated as equals, not as some sort of inferior, endangered species, or as backward and intransigent bigots who will have to be brought eventually, truculently, to the table; until we can put that sort of belief in the past, and ... move into the twenty-first century as equals ... I honestly have some fears for the future ...

In 1968, the year that the troubles began, effectively, I had just left school and gone into full-time employment. I suppose if I had been five or six years older I might be able to give a more mature account of what things were like then, but because I was only fifteen obviously my views at that time would have been those of a teenager. I wasn't that much concerned about the weighty matters of political evolution, but at the same time I had views, and they were coloured by my own personal experiences and the experiences that all my family and friends and neighbours had. Watching the difficulties that came about with the civil rights demonstrations, and the violence that often followed them, in my community the perception was of being blamed for the wrongs that the Nationalist community were marching about and demonstrating against. Yet when we examined our own background we saw that it was exactly the same as those who were demonstrating. That created a sense not only of injustice, but of antagonism and of indignation. I felt very indignant that these people were marching for rights that I didn't have. I suppose '68, '69 and '70 was a period where all of that indignation was working its way out, and was finding a safety valve in protests on the Protestant side against civil rights.

The fact that the civil rights movement only seemed to care about Nationalist deprivation was part of the indignation. I know that there are those now who say 'well, if you felt that you were deprived why didn't you join the civil rights movement?' But, while I could identify very closely with a campaign that accepted people were deprived across the divide and attempted to get better living conditions and better employment prospects for everyone across the board, I could not support it when it was fronted by people who had previously been involved in campaigns to undermine the state. Protestants simply said, look, the rationale behind this is something we agree with, but we see an agenda here that's nothing to do with jobs and rights and conditions, it's to do with trying to dismantle Northern Ireland and take it into a united Ireland. It's trying to separate those two aims that is the problem. If you take the issue of libertarian human rights for everybody, if you get that on its own, completely divorced from any aspect of the constitutional future, then I think everybody would support that, or at least everybody that I mixed with.

There's no doubt in my mind that I was affected by the sight of violence on the streets, what I saw to be insurrection. But it did not affect me the same way as it did some people who decided that they had to join a paramilitary group. I never felt the need to join a paramilitary group because of what I saw. I never saw any logic in taking it to the point where you join an organisation to kill innocent people. Others did. But it did affect me, it deeply affected me, because I saw this insurrection, I saw this blatant attempt to undermine the state and defy the wishes of the majority of the people and try and take us into a united Ireland, and I reacted against that.

Bloody Sunday is probably one of the better

examples of how the two communities in Northern Ireland look at the same event in a completely and utterly different light. There are scores of examples where people are looking at the same subject matter from a totally different perspective, and Bloody Sunday is one of the more stark. At the time, I remember being involved in the campaign against what became known as the Bloody Sunday parade because it was looked upon as an illegal parade, trying to establish territorial rights, to further the cause of a united Ireland. Now I know that in the Nationalist community there were many who didn't perceive it as that, but that's the way we saw it.

I was in the Guildhall Square that day and as we made our way back to the Waterside reports started filtering through, firstly of shooting, and then eventually of one or two deaths. At the time it was looked on in the Protestant community in a completely different light to the Nationalist community. We felt that there had been an illegal march, there had been prolonged violence in the lead up to the confrontation, and that the soldiers then reacted to that violence. The Protestant perspective was that there were, in all probability, IRA snipers, although we weren't absolutely sure about that. The army then engaged them, and obviously some people died as a result. Some people were innocent, some weren't. But there was no realization, I don't think, in the Protestant community of the depth of feeling in the Catholic community. I suppose now the passage of time has brought about a greater understanding of the Nationalist psyche regarding Bloody Sunday, but at the time there was no conception whatsoever of how deeply it affected the Nationalist community.

I think internment was looked upon as a device employed by a government that was really at sea and not in full control of the situation to try and regain some semblance of control. I think most people in the Protestant community looked at it like that. Instead of being a clear, decisive government responding to a threat, it was a government that was thrashing about, seizing upon any initiative that could be seen to restore some semblance of credibility, and internment was a convenient tool. I imagine that probably the majority of Protestants thought internment was a

good idea. I think at that stage Ian Paisley was out of step with the bulk of the Protestant community because he was the one Unionist leader who opposed internment. He didn't get any great credit for that from the Nationalist community, but he did say that on principled grounds he was opposed to the use of internment. The majority of people eventually came round to his way of thinking, agreeing that it was a tool that could only be used in the most extreme of circumstances.

The fall of Stormont was one of the major events for the Unionist community. A bastion against a united Ireland had been taken away, and by a government that six weeks before had indicated that there was no possibility of such an action. That was a blow to the Protestant psyche, the removal of such a bulwark.

The problem with the Sunningdale arrangement, and with a number of initiatives since, was that any action the British government undertook that was seen to be flying in the face of what the people of Northern Ireland wanted was always going to cause suspicion. Any initiative that is undertaken in any region of the world where there is conflict, if it is seen to be in opposition to a sizable number of people, let alone the majority of people, is always going to fail, or at least flounder. Sunningdale was the first of a number of occasions where the government said 'it doesn't really matter what the Unionist community wants, this is what we think is best for them'. That's the way the Unionist community looked at Sunningdale. There was indignation about it, and particularly over the Council of Ireland aspect. Hugh Logue, a prominent member of the SDLP, described the Council of Ireland as a Trojan Horse that would trundle us into a united Ireland. Understandably, that was the end of any possibility of success for the Sunningdale agreement as far as we were concerned.

I don't think people in Northern Ireland, even the ordinary grass-roots Loyalists and Nationalists, have sufficient appreciation of the huge gulf of misunderstanding that exists between the two sides. I referred to Bloody Sunday as being a prime example, the hunger strike is another one. I know now that the Nationalist community was very, very emotionally affected by it. At the time,

I don't think that the Unionist community understood the depth of feeling that existed within the Nationalist community regarding the hunger strike, nor did the Nationalist community understand the way that Unionists viewed it. The Unionist community view, and I remember how I felt, was that here was a group of people, all of whom had been sentenced – it wasn't a case of remand prisoners taking a protest action, it was people who had been through the due process of law, and had been convicted, many of them of murder – and they were engaging in another campaign to try and discredit the system, and were involved in the most obnoxious, offensive type of behaviour in prison cells [blanket/no-wash protests]. Any sort of outcome that was self-inflicted was, for Unionists, good enough. I remember people in my community being pleasantly surprised whenever the hunger strikers died. They had no perception that Nationalists were appalled at this. Unionists saw murderers going on a hunger strike and eventually dying, and the Unionists reaction was that it was good enough for them. That was the reaction. And there was a universe of difference there, just as far as the east is removed from the west, as the Bible says, and that's an example of the gulf of misunderstanding that existed between the two communities, in relation to the hunger strike, as in so many other things.

If you base your political philosophy on the premise that force is the only way to get your message across, and the use of that force is the most effective weapon you have, then with that particular logic, whoever has the most guns and Semtex wins. But that philosophy is doomed to failure because it's a policy of rearmament, and of continually arming until the other side is completely out-blitzed by the amount of fire power you have. There's no way that this strategy will ever lead to a satisfactory conclusion. The only productive thing to do is to sit round the negotiating table.

I do make a distinction between the different types of violence. I remember at the Pat Finucane sponsored event in Pilots Row in January 1995, with a hostile audience, I suppose I could have simply said all violence is to be abhorred, which it is, and drawn no more distinctions. I could have

taken the easy way out but I didn't feel that would have been honest. I *do* draw a distinction between Loyalist violence and Republican violence. It's not the distinction that one is all right and the other is all wrong – both of them are equally wrong, they can't be justified, they can't be defended and they can't be supported or condoned in any way. But there is a distinction and I've always drawn the distinction. The distinction is that Republican violence has been used as a means to smash the state, smash the system and create a united Ireland. I don't believe that Loyalist violence has ever been used on a proactive basis like that. Their violence was always to stop the IRA, so their rationale was that if there's no Republican violence there's no need for Loyalist violence. I suppose when you look at the ceasefires that proves my point.

State violence just doesn't enter into the equation because I believe that not only is Loyalist violence a reaction to Republican violence, but that all of the measures taken by the state which Republicans took exception to, all of that is a reaction to IRA violence as well. Once it stops, and everybody is certain that it has stopped, then the need for all these measures disappears. If they had stopped killing people earlier there would have been no need for house searches, no need for a Special Powers Act, no need for checkpoints, no need for any of these things. So there are three clear distinctive categories – Republican violence, Loyalist reaction and the state's response to both. I don't wear this idea that violence only came about because of a lack of response to certain demands. You only have to look at the civil rights programme – whether or not you agree with it is largely irrelevant – in the eighteen months from '68 to early '70; all of its demands were met without a shot being fired, and yet people said 'we have to resort to the M60 to get our demands'. That led me to believe there was much more to it, a lot more to it, than a simple demand for civil rights. Those people had an agenda, and they saw it not being met, so they upped the ante, and the Unionist view is that they are still doing likewise.

When the ceasefires were called I felt at the time there was a lot of confusion in my community, a lot of suspicion that hasn't gone away in the intervening fourteen months. Again I suppose the ceasefires are but the latest example of this huge gulf that exists between the two communities. When you looked at the reaction in the two communities on 31 August, in the Nationalist community there was either a sense of euphoria amongst Republicans or a sense of quiet satisfaction amongst what are called constitutional Nationalists that the war was over. In the Unionist community there were variations as well, but different from those in the Nationalist community. It was either relief that it was over, tinged with suspicion that it wasn't; or else a positive belief that, far from being over, it was just a change of tactic. There was a tinge of relief that at least they had stopped murdering people for a while, but how long it lasts we don't know. But there again were those two completely different perspectives of the same incidents.

It's unfortunate to have to say this, but I look upon the problems in the peace process as very much indicative of not only the Republican attitude but also the Nationalist attitude. It's almost as if within the Nationalist/Republican community that there is a view of events moving along in a particular direction; they look upon Unionists as petulant children who will eventually come to an understanding that we, the enlightened Nationalists, have had for years. I find that offensive. But that is the perspective that's growing, not diminishing, in the Unionist community. Take, for example, the attitude to all-party talks. It's almost as if Hume and Adams sit serenely at the top of the pyramid saying 'all-party talks are inevitable, so now all we have to do is get the Brits to convene them and eventually the Unionists will come'. There is this naive and foolish belief that eventually Unionists will reconcile themselves to an attitude that will include all-party talks. There is no understanding that Unionists, particularly the brand of Unionist that I represent, cannot and will not reconcile themselves to sitting across the table from somebody with a mask on and an M60. They won't now, and they won't in the future. And yet there's this insidious insistence which says that eventually Unionists will come to their senses, this patronizing belief that Unionists will eventually be reconciled to their fate. But until we can get to a

position where we are treated as equals, not as some sort of inferior, endangered species, or as backward and intransigent bigots who will have to be brought eventually, truculently, to the table; until we can put that sort of belief in the past, and can move into the twenty-first century as equals, looking at each other as human beings with some sort of dignity, then I honestly have some fears for the future, even though I'm an optimist by nature and I think over the next two or three years there will be many more positive, rather than negative, things to look forward to .

The one thing that gives me hope for the future is that within both Nationalist and Unionist communities there's not only the hope, but the demand, that some form of structured discussions must take place. I think the people are at least as far advanced as the political parties in that they know that there are difficulties, they know that there are deep-seated grievances within both communities. But they're demanding that there be some sort of structured discussions which will lead to a form of government in Northern Ireland which, if not 100%, at least 90% of the people of Northern Ireland can give allegiance to within the next few years. The people are demanding it, and I feel it will come about.

I don't believe enough research has been done into what the projections about a future Nationalist/Catholic majority tell us. Over and over again I've heard this sort of demographic argument indicating that a united Ireland will come about in twenty or thirty or forty years. But the truth of the matter is the opposite. The reality is there is a declining Catholic birth rate. Traditionally it has been much higher than the Protestant birth rate. That is a fact. But the Catholic birth rate, just as in Europe and in the Republic of Ireland, right now in Northern Ireland is plummeting. The myth says it is going up, the reality is that it is going down, so there will not be a Catholic majority. And even if it did come about, there is a sizeable number of Catholics who are not supporters of a united Ireland, who are actually against it. When you add these to the Protestants who are continuously voting to remain within the UK you are going to get an *impasse* in demographic terms. Most realistic predictions point to a Catholic population of around 44% – with about

15% voting to remain within the UK, which means probably 65-70% of the total wanting to remain within the UK.

Only the next twelve to eighteen months will establish whether or not a return of some form of violence is on the cards. I do not accept the theory that because the overwhelming majority of people within Northern Ireland, the Republic, the UK mainland, and the international community want peace that the Provos dare not return to violence. I do not accept that. I accept that there is this huge ground swell of goodwill that demands that there should not be a return to violence. I fully accept that. Where I differ is in my view that if there are sufficient numbers within the Provos who support a return to violence, I believe that it doesn't matter what the Americans say, it doesn't matter what the Europeans say, what the leader-writers in Dublin are saying, or Belfast, or London, they will go back to the bomb. They will decide whether or not they want to go back and whether or not they can sustain a campaign within their own community, not within the corridors of Washington, or Dublin, or anywhere else. If they can win over enough people of their own community to go back to violence then that will be the end of the peace process. I think the next twelve to eighteen months will decide the issue. I have said from the outset of the ceasefires we would need two years or thereabouts before deciding whether or not the peace is here to stay, and I've no reason to change my mind now.

Northern Ireland Civil Rights
ASSOCIATION

A CIVIL RIGHTS MARCH
WILL BE HELD IN DERRY
ON SATURDAY, 5TH OCT.

COMMENCING AT 3-30 p.m.

ASSEMBLY POINT: WATERSIDE RAILWAY STATION

MARCH TO THE DIAMOND

Where a PUBLIC METTING will take place

The original 5 October 1968 poster was printed in red, white and blue in an attempt to attract Protestants to the march. *(Photo: Fionnbarra ÓDochartaigh)*

The RUC arrest a young man in Duke Street in the aftermath of the 5 October march. *(Photo: Fionnbarra ÓDochartaigh)*

Civil rights protests continued unabated after the famous 5 October march. Eamonn Melaugh and Eamonn McCann (above) address a Housing Action Committee protest, and (below) activists stage a sit down protest in Guildhall Square. *(Photos: Fionnbarra ÓDochartaigh)*

John O'Hara, brother of hunger striker Patsy O'Hara, is arrested by police during a civil rights protest at the official opening of the lower deck of Craigavon Bridge, 16 November 1968. *(Photo: Fionnbarra ÓDochartaigh)*

Celebrations for John Hume after his victory in the Stormont general election in February 1969 when he unseated Eddie McAteer as MP for the Foyle constituency. *(Photo: Fionnbarra ÓDochartaigh)*

Joe Cosgrove

In hindsight, internment was a total mistake really, but the error was not with the introduction of internment, the error was with the people they lifted.

Even in the 1960s we all knew that the existing Corporation was very unfair. It was a very depressed time, but things seemed to be changing, to be starting to go well by about 1967 or 1968. Whatever about the Corporation, gerrymandering and all that, I think there was a better feeling between Catholics and Protestants, a feeling of optimism really. True, some people were not feeling that way. But I thought things were beginning to look better.

I was not against the civil rights movement, but I felt at the time that if they started any street protests it was all going to end in sectarian rioting because that is the history of Northern Ireland; anything that starts off with public demonstrations, in the end becomes sectarian. I am not blaming anybody for the violence at the marches. But I thought that people could have learned a little bit from history, and could have been a little wiser. But, in the end, they were all young people and maybe you couldn't expect that from them.

When the troubles started it was a repetition of history, and all you could do was keep your head down and hope for the best. All the angry feelings made the situation worse and made people retire to their own corners.

I don't think there was much trouble in Derry at the time internment was introduced. Most of it was in Belfast. But all the wrong people were lifted. There was no great knowledge of who, if anybody, was actually a danger. In hindsight, internment was a total mistake really, but the error was not with the introduction of internment, the error was with the people they lifted. Internment was introduced by Faulkner simply in order to placate his own extremists after he had banned the 12 August parade in Derry.

I think the bulk of the opinion here in Derry, fair-minded opinion, was that the people shot dead on Bloody Sunday weren't armed. Whether the army knew that or not who can say. I think the Widgery Report was a whitewash, but the whole situation was degenerating so much that you could expect anything.

I don't know whether there was a lot of feeling one way or the other when Stormont was prorogued. I think people just felt that this was another development and not much else.

I don't know if Wilson could in fact have broken the UWC strike by using force. I just don't know about that. He handled it badly anyway. I never really thought he was a very strong man. He was a man who was inclined to backtrack. It was a bit hard to see the power-sharing executive fall because of that, but maybe it was inevitable.

The history of hunger strikes in Ireland has been a bit of a disaster, affecting public opinion and gaining emotional results rather than logical, properly thought-out results.

The alternative to state rule is anarchy and anarchy is the worst tyranny. I think Republican and Loyalist violence are both wrong. They are a fact of life, unfortunately, but generally they don't do any good.

We were already living in a fairly easy society when the ceasefires were called. The violence here was not great, apart from the danger of sectarian shootings developing as at Greysteel. But otherwise there was no rioting, there was only an occasional shooting, an occasional bombing. So as far as the citizens were concerned, things were approaching normality here even before the ceasefire was declared. So locally it didn't strike us as a great development. Yet there was some fear that things were maybe getting worse after Greysteel but for the most part people were fairly relaxed about it all. I dare say if you were living in the Short Strand in Belfast you would have a totally different viewpoint. After a year of the ceasefire, I just don't know how things are going on, although the fact that nothing is happening is a good sign in itself.

To my mind, but I suppose it is idealistic, not practical or pragmatic, there should be no armies in any state apart from those run by the government. That was De Valera's view in the olden days. Theoretically, all arms should be given up unless they are licensed by the state. I don't know about all prisoners being released. I suppose some of their cases should be investigated and maybe some should be released. But to release fellows like the one who shot a man here, outside his own house? The man was a managing director of a firm here and he had no concern with politics. His wife has since been very unwell. It is hard to let someone go who did those kind of things.

I feel there must be a government, and I don't see any other alternative, at the minute, to the way the country is being run now. I wouldn't mind if we eventually did have a united Ireland, if it didn't raise more troubles. But the threat of one has been a constant irritant to the Protestants and a considerable factor in keeping the sectarian levels at boiling point in the North of Ireland. So the promotion of a united Ireland should be soft-pedalled.

As far as I am concerned, and I am too old now to be of any use politically, I am sorry that the Alliance Party did not do better. It seemed to me at the time that it was so obviously the thing we needed, but we didn't allow for the traditional loyalties which people have great difficulty overcoming at the ballot box.

Tony Crowe

The biggest problem of all with the different attempts by the British to find a political solution has been that Protestants felt themselves to be marginalised, and not consulted, and that there was a lot of work going on behind the scenes.

I was probably oblivious to much of the rumblings that were going on in Northern Ireland at the end of the 1960s. I was very much involved in sport and academic life as a young man; I spent much of my time between here and Donegal, then later at university in England. I really wasn't particularly aware of all the nuances. Many of the people involved initially in the civil rights campaign appeared to be very well-intentioned. But the one aspect that really worried me from the very start was that the Protestant working class seemed to be distanced from the mainstream activity, despite the deprivation that existed then, as it does today, among them, and that somehow they seemed to have been passed over. I think that the campaign should have concentrated more on working-class issues. I think that most people, in retrospect, would agree with that now.

When the situation degenerated into violence, I felt it was predictable. But I also felt that there was marginalisation of the minority community in the west bank of the city. I feel that was most regrettable, and the one abiding thing that has come out of the last twenty-five years has been great violence, and a great division within the community, and this violence evoked great fear and alienation in the Protestant working class. The movement of population bore witness to that.

I think that the UWC strike was an understandable reaction to what the Protestant working class perceived as their neglect and marginalisation. They were being passed over by British ministers, and the attention directed to much of the civil rights campaign created a great feeling of being under siege, and of fear, and the UWC strike was a manifestation of that. The feeling was that it was necessary to take their destiny into their own hands. Now, twenty-one years after the strike, there has been much academic work on the subject, and I believe that it shows the strike was an outlet for the reservations of the Protestant working class. The fact is they weren't being consulted, even then. I don't think the vast majority of Protestants wanted anything more than what they should have had, and that was equal citizenship. Although there are perceptions that it was quite the opposite, the vast majority certainly did not, as far as I can recollect, want anything more than that.

On a personal level, I believe that internment by its very nature is ill-conceived and very difficult to manage. It discriminates against all, in that it is without trial, and it can serve nobody's interest because it creates great resentment within the community. Let me assure you that Loyalists suffered as much from internment as Republicans, their avowed enemies. I believe that it creates a very resentful, unhappy state of affairs and doesn't serve anybody. While it may be seen to be expedient in certain very serious situations where it is impossible to use the full procedure of the law, I believe that throughout the world, for example South Africa, it has proven counterproductive. It leaves a great boiling resentment, and certainly that resentment was felt very strongly in the Protestant communities in this city when young people were interned.

In a military campaign one must accept the inevitable fact that, as with Bosnia and other countries very similar in some respects to our own, people perceive themselves to be prisoners of war because they feel that they are at war. The rights and wrongs of their war and what they are doing are entirely beside the point. Consequently, I can certainly identify with the Loyalist notion that they were a defensive grouping, until comparatively recent years, and when they were imprisoned or interned they saw themselves as very much prisoners of a war that was not of their making. I can understand why they would regard themselves as being prisoners of war.

I believe the hunger strikes, as a campaign to get prisoner-of-war status, were counterproductive. I believe that they created a great feeling of estrangement for the minority community here who felt themselves to be at the brunt of the attack. Certainly that was how it was perceived, and perceptions are so much more important sometimes than reality. I don't think the sacrificial nature of the hunger strike has ever been part of the Protestant ethos. It certainly has been in Irish history, with Terence McSwiney and others in the 1920s. I don't regard it as a suitable vehicle for political expression.

The biggest problem of all, with the different attempts by the British and others to find a political solution, has been that Protestants felt themselves to be marginalised, and not consulted, and that there was a lot of work going on behind the scenes. Now there are many reasons for that. People say that Protestants were not prepared to parley with certain people. But don't forget that a war was being waged which seemed to be a war of attrition, a war waged by one people against another, and also that the Southern Irish state would appear to have had a very ambivalent attitude towards it. All these processes did not have the desired effect, because there was a lack of consultation, which created distrust, and some of that distrust has certainly been justified.

Certainly, when the ceasefires were called I shared the common attitude that perhaps I would sit and wait and watch. I'm still very sceptical about the posturing of some of the groupings, particularly since punishment shootings and beatings are still going on. And also the fact that they talk about the peace process with reference primarily to British withdrawal. My notion of British withdrawal is as a forerunner of Protestant withdrawal. That is something that certainly is denied by all of the people who would pay tribute to the peace process. They claim that it is not the case. But the territorial claim to Northern Ireland still stands in the statute book of the Republic. And the interference of the Dublin government has always exacerbated this perception of being under attack and has resulted in greater alienation of the vast majority of the Unionist people.

I don't think you can talk to a grouping if the shadow of the gunman is still there because then you are talking under duress. It's not just paranoia. If somebody still has a stockpile of weaponry then I don't think you are on equal terms. You only talk when there is respect for your tradition and your reservations about their arsenals. I think talks can only take place when there is full decommissioning and when there is full appreciation and respect for each tradition. But if Republicans still claim jurisdiction over the whole of Ireland, and the right to use military methods, then I'm afraid talks are totally impossible.

Republicans have this notion that all guns, the guns in the hands of the RUC, the guns in the hands of the British army, the guns in the hands of any of the crown forces are the guns of the enemy, weapons to be used against the Irish — what they perceive as the Irish Republican people. My perception, and the perception of most Unionist people, would be that that is going too far. Are we not to have any defence at all? We could spend years and years on that very issue alone. If only one could trust that groups weren't stockpiling and that there is not a hidden agenda but that can't be proven. Throughout Irish history we have had repeated insurrections. I have just finished an article for a local magazine on the Apprentice Boys and how its foundation had to do with being under siege in the city. Throughout the 18th century they were really a very liberal grouping and supported the Protestant patriot parliament of Grattan. But whenever pressure came on again at the end of the 1790s, and right into the 1840s, these organisations then became much more militant because they felt that they were under attack. So Protestant history has been dominated by, first of all the great betrayal in the 1640s, then the great siege in 1689, then the deliverance at the Boyne and Aughrim and Derry. These events are still a very strong part of the limited canon of our mythology. There have been numerous examples of betrayal, siege and deliverance. Currently there is a perception that we are under siege awaiting deliverance.

I like to think that the most important thing that has happened recently is the emergence of vibrant young spokesmen within the Unionist community for the first time. And it's very obvious that the Protestant community in general will really have to address their whole sense of belonging and their reaction to the events taking place very rapidly around them. The feeling within the Protestant community has been one of massive sidelining and deprivation. In stark contrast is the regeneration that has gone on in towns like this. This is something that has got to be addressed so that it doesn't create a feeling of disenchantment among Protestants with a myriad of agencies. All that has got to be addressed. Also, there has to be some sort of education to help each group understand what makes the other tick. That's a very vital component of the whole peace process over the next three or four generations. It's a long-term affair, it's not going to happen tomorrow. You can't force people to mate; it has been attempted over this last number of years by some very well-intentioned people, but if you try and force people it's counterproductive. If you leave people with a sense of alienation and disenchantment in this generation, and if they feel sidelined, then trouble will recur in the next generation. The history of Irish Nationalism has proven this, particularly over this past century or so, from Thomas Davis, Young Ireland, right the way through to the Fenians in the 1860s, to the Home Rule campaign, to the emergence of the Irish Republican Brotherhood,

generation after generation, trouble recurring every ten or twenty years.

My ideal future would be somewhere where there was mutual respect, and where people could feel that they could live in a community without alienation, without feeling that they were somehow or other being subjected to hidden pressures. I think there has to be an acceptance that the majority of the people here want the union with England. That has to be accepted. There also has to be mutual respect for tradition and culture. That is a long-term process and a lot of damage has already been done. In fact, I believe the IRA campaign has irrevocably curtailed much of what they would aspire to by the very nature of their campaign which was one of genocide. I think that there's an emerging realisation within the working-class community that there has to be some sort of understanding of each other.

We have always been assured that we would have a very potent role within an all-Ireland unitary state. I don't see that happening, and certainly not in my lifetime. I think there will be a very violent reaction to any notion of a future united Ireland. If it came about through majority rule, my people would have to accept that. In Donegal, and other areas of Ireland, it has proven to be to the detriment of the minority people, and they have become submerged by the overpowering peer culture.

I would hope that much of the work that I'm involved in in this community now, which is for the betterment of all the community, will succeed. We are, in a sense, involved in a rearguard attempt to encourage Protestant people to return to the cityside, and to take an active part, not only politically, but economically and socially in the community.

Derry
Peace Women

I suppose if it saved a life, one life, it was worthwhile, but I think if I had to do it again I wouldn't. We really suffered for speaking our minds

Kathleen Doherty, Harriet Hippsley and Eileen Semple

Before the troubles it was very unfair here, as far as jobs and housing were concerned. When a couple got married they went into a back room or a wee front room in their parents' house. They had no chance of getting their own place, it was really bad. The civil rights movement tried to change all that, and of course we all agreed with it.

KD I got caught up in the violence that happened after some of the marches. My father died on 5 January 1969, around the time of Burntollet. When he was first brought in to Altnagelvin, I saw the crowds all standing around. I didn't know what had happened. I remember passing Irish Street on the way to the hospital and seeing the police standing around there. After we left the hospital that night we had to walk home. I remember going through the Diamond and it was terrible. Later that night we were called back to the hospital because my father was dying, and when we were going up Fahan Street there was a barricade, and I was angry with them for building one there because we couldn't get to the hospital; we had to go out by the Brandywell. There were barricades over there as well. We got to the hospital anyway just before my father died. But one thing was playing against the other; we didn't agree with what was going on, what the police were doing, but we also didn't agree with our own having barricades up because, in our case, we couldn't get to the hospital.

ES I remember they opened a big shed in William Street, when all the trouble started in August 1969. I was in that shed from morning to night. The men from the area came in and give their names, and then so many of them went out

to try and stop the stoning; or the army rang in and said they were stoning somewhere, and the men had to go to that particular place to stop it. That began in 1969, but it went on for nearly a year.

HH I was on the march on Bloody Sunday. I had my young son with me. I remember that day well, everybody was all happy-go-lucky, and it was a lovely day. My mother watched my youngest children to let me go on the march and I had told her that I would call for her when we got to Free Derry corner so she could come along to hear the speeches – we were all great fans of Bernadette Devlin. We were just at Free Derry corner, and I had my son by the hand, when somebody came up through the crowd holding a handkerchief covered in blood. We heard a couple of cracks, and then the crowd all started running, shouting that they were shooting. Everybody was ducking down, as far down as they could get, and running to get home. So I got up into my mother's house which was not very far away, and there were a lot of students there. I don't know how many we brought into the house that day, and they were all terrorised. I still have letters somewhere from them, from Belfast, thanking me for bringing them in that day and even washing their clothes, because some of them had got dye on them and they were afraid to go across the bridge to get the train back to Belfast in case they were arrested. Two of those shot that day, Jim Wray, and Gerard Donaghy, were my mother's neighbours.

KD I remember going up to watch the march with my two youngest children. There were orders that there were to be no tricolours or flags carried on the march; it was a civil rights march and there were to be no political emblems on display, that's the way everybody wanted it. My husband went on it, and the rest of the family, the bigger ones, all went on it. I went straight home as soon as the shooting started to see if my children were all right. Then I heard about the deaths – Michael Kelly, John Young from Westway, William McKinney from Westway, Michael McDaid from Tyrconnell Street, and all the others.

HH The Widgery Report was a disgrace. I remember Mr Wray, who lived just facing my mother's, and I can understand how bitter his family must have felt because everybody was bitter after Bloody Sunday. He put up a board in his front window 'Widgery washes whiter'.

A few months after Bloody Sunday I remember hearing on the radio that a body had been found in William Street, and they described the way he had been shot and all the rest of it. I thought it was terrible, it was our own shooting our own now. I went down to my mother's house that day and everybody was talking about it. They had taken him to the shops in Meenan Park, and there were people there that night who had seen him being taken in with a bag over his head. I said that if I had seen them I would have said something. And people were saying they would have been shot if they had interfered and I said: "If a dozen or a half-a-dozen people had they couldn't have shot you all." And I mean that, I could not have stood by and watched somebody being taken away. I would have had to do something. We heard then it was [Ranger] William Best and why it was and all the rest of it, and I wondered if anybody was ever going to do anything about it.

ES I was going up to mass that Sunday evening and a couple of women from that area told me about it, and I asked could we not have a protest or something about it?

HH I didn't know Kathleen, and I only knew Eileen vaguely at the time. I remember going up to Father Carlin in Creggan and asking him was nobody going to do anything about this? And he said he had been praying that somebody would come forward to do something. He named some women from Creggan and he asked me to tell them that there was going to be a protest about it. While I was up in Creggan I heard that many rumours about what they had done to the young fella, and I went into his house and saw him lying there. As I was coming out I met Willie Carson and he asked me what I thought about it all and I said that something had to be done. I don't really know how everything got started, but the word went round anyway, just word of mouth, that there was going to be a protest down at the shops and when I went down the Lone Moor Road I met some more girls. I think about four or five of us walked over the Moor, and that was the protest.

KD My son was shot a month after Bloody Sunday; shot by the IRA, he was not shot by the army. He had got involved with the IRA through Bloody Sunday. I didn't know at the time, they told me he shot himself, that it was an accident, and of course you believe whatever they tell you. I was going to the cemetery with my husband on the Sunday that young Best was shot. As we were going up Broadway, Father Carlin was coming up in the car. He stopped to give us a lift and he was talking about it. He said something would have to be done but that he couldn't do it so it was up to the people. The next day I was at home and I looked out of the window and there were about four or five women standing across the street. So I went over to find out what was happening, what was wrong, and they said there was going to be a peace march. And I said 'good', and went back to the house to get my coat. Coming down the New Road I saw all these people at the bottom, and I thought it was the IRA waiting on us. And then I saw the flashes of the cameras and realised they were reporters.

HH As we went over the Moor there were only five of us, but when we got over to Westland Street we saw all the girls were running out of the Essex factory to join us. Before that we were ready to turn back. I thought 'thank God we are not on our own now'.

KD We went down to the Official Irish Republican Army offices. They told us to calm down, and I said: "Do you know who I am, I am Kathleen Doherty, Gerard Doherty's mother, you have named this place after my son." That just shut them all up, and everybody turned and looked at me and I said: "If he was alive today he would not agree with what happened at the weekend." We all went home then, but they arranged to meet up again. Later that day a man called at my door and told me that they wanted to meet us up at the centre. We all went up and saw a few people and we had the first meeting in my house. And while the meeting was going on some other women were up in Creggan wrecking cars that belonged to Republicans.

HH Then we got word that some others wanted to meet us to have talks. I knew about Kathleen and her son, and I knew that they couldn't say that she was one sided, and there was another woman, Margaret Doherty, whose brother was killed on Bloody Sunday, who had been on the protest; so we got Margaret and another woman, Mary Barr. The five of us went to meet with them. They had said that Willie Best had been killed in retaliation for what had happened on Bloody Sunday, and because he had been a soldier, and it was all done in the people's name. So we said it was not done in *our* name; maybe there were some people who agreed with them, but we said: "We are letting you know now that *we* don't agree, and that nobody who is here today agrees, so you can stop saying that it was done in the name of the people of Derry." Then we got word that Willie Whitelaw wanted to talk to us in Stormont. It was a couple of days after and we thought it had all died down, and the next thing was we were up in Stormont with Willie Whitelaw.

ES Coming out of Stormont, I said to the policeman: "I hope they didn't go and tell them down the Shankill that we are up here or we will all be shot." Whitelaw met us then in the Guildhall and he promised us that if we got so many signatures for peace he would let so many prisoners out, and he did, he let out three or four hundred. We got a book for the signatures, and Martin McGuinness signed it. Whenever we saw Martin coming we wondered what he was going to do, but he just came in and signed his name and 'peace with justice' after it.

HH Now, when I look back, I feel we were just a tool to be used by politicians. We were a Godsend at the time, because nobody knew where to turn or what to do, even John Hume. Whenever we talked to John he said that we had left the door open now for him to talk to Whitelaw, because nobody was talking to anybody. But I suppose if it saved a life, one life, it was worthwhile, but I think if I had to do it again I wouldn't. We really suffered for speaking our minds. We were accused of being given thousands of pounds. We couldn't even get our walls papered with the money Whitelaw gave us. I had three cars burned outside the door and every window in the house broken; people calling after you in the street 'informer'. I used to say to them that if I was an informer not one of them would be standing there.

ES But then people whose sons were calling after us came looking for our help when their sons were lifted. Three of us used to go to the old RUC barracks, down to Inspector Frank Lagan, to see about them. And then there were others who were across the border and wanted to come back. They thought if they did they would be arrested. We went to see if they would be safe enough to come home, even though some of them were down there and they hadn't done anything.

HH It was the people that put me off, because everybody said they were all behind us but when it came to the crunch we were on our own. And it was our families and our children who suffered. If you were a peace lover then it was a dirty word, and my young ones would come in, they were only seven and eight, and they were asking what a peace lover was because their friends were saying: "Your mammy is a peace lover," and I would say that it was nothing to be ashamed of. But now I suppose it was good they were young, it was not hurting them that much.

When I look back on it, at the way I neglected my home and my husband and my youngsters for other people, to try and bring peace and to have a better community in our town, and got nothing but abuse for it. But through it all I had my family, my mother and my sisters; it wasn't to say that the children didn't get their dinners or the house was not looked after, but when the mother is not in the home it's not the same.

We were driven to Dublin, driven to Belfast, and not fifty pence in our purses; we had no money, and then we were accused of getting thousands of pounds from Whitelaw. We were never offered money, but we were warned not to accept any if we were. The violence in the area at that particular time was getting on people's nerves; that's what brought the women out so much, not the offer of money.

It was arranged for us to meet David O'Connell [Daithí ÓConaill] and some others. We just trusted everybody and set sail to a wee hotel in Dun Laoighaire outside Dublin. We must have waited all day before these boys came, we didn't know who they were, and they asked us were we the Derry women? They only wanted one of us to go, but we decided 'if one goes we all go', so we all got into the car. It took us an hour-and-a-half. We were driven through the back roads of the Wicklow Hills, and then they stopped the car and told us to get out. We thought we were all going to get shot, but they were only checking if it was safe enough to go on. We finally got to the hotel and David O'Connell was there and they introduced a well-known Republican figure as 'Joe Brown'. And I said: "We might look like five idiots but we know who *you* are." So we told him about the shooting and about the gas and our youngsters going to school through it all. I said: "You are sitting here, giving orders that the war has to go on, why don't you come and live down where *we* live? Why don't you come down to the Bogside? Bring your youngsters. I live beside an army base. Your children can stay with me, and they can go out in the street when the bullets are flying over their heads. We will see then if you want the war to go on." Then he said: "My children will be going down to Derry for their holidays in the summer." That was O'Connell. Well, that was twenty-odd years ago and they're *still* not here.

Violence is always wrong, no matter where it comes from. It is all the same, the bullets are all the same, no matter where they come from, so the news of the ceasefire was great, it was marvellous. We used to always think we would never see peace in our day. I couldn't believe it. I used to say to myself when we prayed in mass 'is nobody ever going to listen?' And then the ceasefire was announced and it was all over. John Hume got a lot of stick for meeting Sinn Féin, but when they are talking they are not killing.

I thought it was a joke when I heard the IRA ceasefire was over. I could not believe it. All you get out of people now is 'trust in God that it is not all going to start up again'. I would like to see them all sitting round the table talking, with everybody having their say.

I would like to see peace and normality. Our youngsters are all grown up, and we do not want *their* youngsters, our grandchildren, having to go through the same violence again. This is the third generation coming up now, and if things do not work out another generation of children will be destroyed by it all.

Tony Doherty

...my memories of Bloody Sunday are almost snapshot memories. I was nine at the time; it was my first, and obviously my greatest, traumatic experience. In that respect the snapshots have stayed with me to the present day and they probably will stay until I die.

My memories of Derry pre-1968 are very scant. My first inkling that I wasn't living in a normal society was in 1968 or 1969 when my mother and father took us, as children, to the civil rights marches before the whole scenario got very violent. I attended some of the major demonstrations in Derry at that time. Sometimes I hated the fact that I wasn't ten or fifteen years older in the 1960s than I actually was. I think it must have been a very exciting time given all that was happening across the world. For instance in North Africa, Vietnam and in North America you had several burgeoning campaigns that were broadly anti-imperialist, and that's where I am at politically. I think the civil rights campaigns of the 1960s in the North of Ireland were very necessary and they appeared to have been fairly well organised and thought out.

The violence associated with the civil rights marches was in some respects the inevitable consequence of the nature of the state. Nineteen sixty-nine wasn't the first time the Northern Ireland state responded violently to people asking for civil rights. The structures of the state itself were so bound up in sectarianism and bigotry and discrimination that there was so much to protect – right from the bottom of the scale, from working class right through to the business and professional classes. So being a Protestant and a Unionist was completely bound up with being a 'decent' citizen of Northern Ireland; being a Catholic or being a Nationalist was quite the opposite. Therefore you had these two opposing views colliding, even though there were liberal Protestants who thought that discrimination against Catholics should end.

It was no great surprise that the situation ended up with the violent conflict of the last twenty-five years; that is the way it had to be, unfortunately. The state itself was established to preserve a certain *status quo* for Unionists with practically no reference to the Catholic or Nationalist minority within the state. So I sometimes wonder why it didn't happen to a greater extent prior to the 1960s.

My memories of Bloody Sunday are almost snapshot memories. I was nine at the time. It was my first, and obviously my greatest, traumatic experience. In that respect the snapshots have stayed with me to the present day and they probably will stay until I die. It was such a trauma for myself, and I am sure for hundreds of other people, that a lot of it was blanked out, and all I have is five or six vague recollections of Bloody Sunday, the funerals themselves, and afterwards. I was told by a young boy in the street that my father had been shot. I was nine and the boy, who I was playing marbles with, was also nine. I don't know how he heard about it, if he was down at Free Derry corner or whatever, but he was fit to tell me a good hour, I would say, before anybody else landed at the house or before any relatives started calling to find out what was wrong. So my memories are of being told in the street by a young friend, and of having that knowledge and not imparting it to the rest of my family. I didn't know whether to believe it or not but as the afternoon wore on I remember feeling that what I had been told could well be true, even though I had dismissed it out of hand at the time. So I was stuck with that knowledge for two or three hours until people came back from the hospital, from Altnagelvin, with the news that my father had been shot dead. Apart from that, I remember just snippets of things. I was sent to the shop in Hamilton Street during the wake to get food and the woman in the shop pointed me out to another woman and she gave me whatever messages I had been sent out to get for free. That particular moment in time sort of stands out in my mind for some reason. Maybe it was because I was sent out of the wake house and I was in the street on my own, and I went to the shop on my own.

The only thing I can remember about the funerals was that it was raining very, very heavily, there was muck everywhere, and as I was nine years of age, just two or three-foot high, I was lost in this sea of grown-up bodies. We had congregated around the mouth of the grave, and I remember half-way through the proceedings a man grabbed me by the shoulders and said: "Come you away, you shouldn't be standing here." He had thought I was a stranger to what was going on, and sort of shook me out of the road. But then one of my relatives saw what was going on and said: "No, that's this man's son." Strange things like that stick in my mind rather than the whole event, perhaps because for the most part I didn't really know what was going on.

I had accepted my father's death, years and years ago, but in the last two years or so I have found it more difficult to come to terms with. Maybe it is because I have reached the same age as my father. He was thirty-one when he was killed.

But in some respects what actually happened *after* Bloody Sunday was a more embittering experience than the actual killings. There we were, under the full glare of the world's media; people saw what happened, and attested before courts and tribunals as to what happened. But the final word was that everybody had got it wrong, the media had got it wrong, the people in the street had got it wrong, the relatives had got it wrong, and the only people who had got it right were the Brits. The most galling aspect of Bloody Sunday for me is that denial of the truth. That, more than anything else, has led to extreme bitterness among many Republicans, and even people who

are *not* Republicans, in Derry and throughout the country. I think that experience in itself was one of the main causes of the last twenty-five years of conflict .

I first became involved in protests when I was sixteen or seventeen, around about 1978/79. Then as the blanket protest in the H-Blocks became more and more of an issue during 1979/80, I became involved in the H-Block committee in Shantallow where I lived. By the time of the first hunger strike in 1980, I had become totally involved in the Shantallow H-Block/Armagh committee, and travelled to marches up and down the country. I particularly remember the marches in Dublin around December 1980 as being massive national events.

I felt, given my own experience and what I had gone through, that what was happening to the prisoners was again part of a crude response by the British government; an attempt to say that all that had gone on before 1968 or '69 was normal and that it was the reaction to that 'normality' which was criminal. The British, by trying to portray the Republican struggle as a criminal conspiracy, paved the way for the hunger strikes. Looking at it retrospectively, you can see the hunger strike coming from about 1974 or '75. I remember the situation at the end of the first hunger strike. There was mass confusion around Christmas 1980. I remember Raymond McCartney being on hunger strike because I had been taught by Raymond's brother Jimmy at the Long Tower School. I particularly remember Jimmy addressing rallies in the Guildhall Square that December, and I remember him breaking down a couple of times, and that seemed to touch a raw nerve within myself because I knew the family and knew they were not part of a criminal conspiracy. They were decent people who were dedicated to the Republican cause and critically challenging the conditions in this society. There was a great sense of confusion and of disappointment at the end of the first hunger strike.

By the time the second hunger strike came about I was in Crumlin Road jail myself as part of this so-called criminal conspiracy. But in some respects I can identify more with the first hunger strike because I was approaching it from, I suppose, a civilian point of view. I was sent to C wing in Crumlin Road prison the same day Bobby Sands embarked on the hunger strike, on 1 March, and because my personal circumstances had been so radically altered at the beginning of the second hunger strike, for some reason I didn't attribute the same amount of importance to it as I did the first. I was probably far closer to it but also in some respects I was detached from it because I had to deal with my personal situation changing so much. I knew that I was going to prison for quite a while and I had to deal with all that myself. Retrospectively, I think the impact of the hunger strike on myself has been quite profound, in that I did not know any of the people who were on hunger strike, or who died on hunger strike, but I got to know a lot of the people who were prominent within the prison structure on the Republican side after the hunger strike, after I went to the H-Blocks myself. I could get a greater feel for what the hunger strike really meant, in that I was in the same blocks, I was dealing with the same people, I was appreciating the calibre of the men who died on hunger strike.

I think the hunger strike was a desperate measure. But it was one imposed on the Republican prisoners by a very disingenuous and bull-headed approach by the British. In some respects the ten people who died are heroes, but by the same token it could easily have been another ten people. If I had been in prison before 1981 I could well have ended up on hunger strike much in the same way as Raymond McCartney. So in that sense the word hero doesn't really mean anything because in one sense what happened was very heroic, but at the same time the heroism was on the part of people who were like myself, quite ordinary working-class young men and women.

I think a large measure of the present problem stemmed from the British re-engaging in Ireland in 1969. Northern Ireland wasn't really a part of Britain since 1921. There was independent legislation for Northern Ireland and the Unionists were allowed to 'row their own boat' for fifty years. So Britain had effectively disengaged from Ireland, but allowed the Unionists to maintain the degree of hegemony they did. So when it all blew up again in their faces in the late

1960s, a gulf had opened and the British didn't really know how to deal with it. Not that the way they tried to deal with it did anybody any good. I think that putting the British army on the streets was an utter disaster. I don't believe the British army were brought in to protect Catholics. They were brought into this part of Ireland to maintain the *status quo* in a place which, arguably, was on the brink of civil war in 1969. The initial response from the British government was one of 'put the army in and the army will solve it'. This was part of the imperial mindset that was dominant throughout the British Empire for the best part of the century, and I think it has governed their approach to Ireland ever since. Their main objective has been to defeat Republicans and maintain the *status quo*, whatever that may be, or whatever the Unionists dictate it to be at any given time.

By the same token, the Southern government's role in the whole affair leaves a lot to be desired. They have never taken an active interest. They disengaged just as much as the British did in 1921. They had ample opportunity to investigate employment practices, discrimination, and the whole Unionist hegemony within the state, but they didn't really bother. And even when the troubles blew up again in 1969, their attempts to address the situation were quite crude, and I think even that effectively ended in 1972 with Bloody Sunday. In 1969 they said they wouldn't stand idly by, but that's all they could do, all they were prepared to do.

The question of violence is quite an interesting one, because there are things happening at the moment that make you wonder what is really going on here? For instance, you have three categories of violence, broadly speaking: a Republican campaign to try and destabilize the state, Loyalist violence, and then you have British violence. The Republican campaign was always about what the IRA perceived to be military targets, or associated with military targets; and that was fair enough. You either accept that as a military campaign or you describe it as criminal conspiracy. Broadly speaking, most people agree the Republican campaign was about challenging the British *status quo*. Loyalist violence on the other hand was based on the sectarian issue of killing Catholics. It was really only from about 1990 onwards that the UVF, in particular, started strategically targeting Republicans. Generally speaking, Loyalism and its use of violence has been governed by a hatred of Catholics. It is no surprise that on the Republican side you don't have the equivalent of the Shankill Butchers. It just didn't happen; it is totally inconceivable that it could ever happen. But on the Loyalist side, because of sectarian hatred and bigotry and so on, you could conceive there could be another bunch of Shankill Butchers in ten years time. That is how a lot of people perceive Loyalist violence.

Then of course you have the 'legal' violence of the British state, which was exemplified on Bloody Sunday, and which has been used time and time again since. But it has been put across since the ceasefire, and I think that this is vitally important, that the only group which has not apologized or taken stock of their violence has been the IRA. I think that has to be radically challenged. I am not defending the IRA, just making a straightforward point – the IRA have actually apologized for various acts of violence when and where they saw fit. They didn't apologize for their campaign, which is quite different. The Loyalists apologised for their campaign. They have said sorry for killing all the innocent victims. But if you look at the criteria they have set down for innocence, all the people killed by the Loyalists were innocent victims. Therefore the Loyalists are apologizing for their whole campaign. Not that they are saying they won't start up again, because they will when they see fit. Therefore where does that leave their apology, and what about their new innocent victims? That needs to be challenged; also the fact that the British, because they have made some bland references to sharing and understanding the mistakes in the past, that that somehow gets them off the hook. That is what is coming across at the minute, and that needs to be challenged. Most of the people who were killed by the British were completely innocent civilians. In Derry alone there have been about fifty civilians killed by the British army and the RUC and there hasn't been one successful prosecution. The starkest example of that was Bloody Sunday, and I think until the British actually face up to what they did on Bloody

Sunday, and what they did after in terms of the cover-up, then I really can't see how peace between Ireland and Britain can be brought about.

I was quite relieved when the ceasefire was called, and took part in the street celebrations after the announcement. I think it was a very well-considered and mature approach by the leaders of the Republican movement. There has been a realisation for quite a while that the IRA campaign alone would not remove the causes of injustice and political instability. The Nationalist camp had disintegrated by and large after Bloody Sunday and there was a need for the various factions of that camp, including the Irish government, to re-engage with one another. Broadly speaking, I think the effect of the IRA ceasefire has been very positive.

I think the decommissioning issue is an irrelevant point. The main problem between Britain and Ireland, and I think that it's essentially a British and Irish problem, not a British government and IRA problem, is that the cultural and historical and political gulf that exists between people who perceive themselves to be Irish and perceive themselves to be British is immense. I think that has been demonstrated time and time again, not just throughout the conflict, but particularly since the ceasefire, in that there is no shared understanding of what has taken place in the last twenty-five years, never mind what happened prior to 1969. For that matter, if you go back to the famine, the Great Hunger of the last century, there is no appreciation from Britain's side as to how Irish people feel aggrieved by their handling of that situation. I think all this talk about decontamination and decommissioning is because there exists a massive void that has to be filled; and I think it needs people from the British side to take a reasonable approach to that void. If that happens, you might see many more positive relations between Britain and Ireland.

I am a Republican, I don't make any apology for that, and I see Republicanism as a very positive and forward-looking philosophy. Most people see the word Republican and immediately associate it with killing soldiers and blowing up cities in Britain. Republicanism is a philosophy of freedom and I believe in it; it's about the liberation of the working class, the liberation of women and so on. I wish that everybody was a Republican but that's obviously not the way it is going to be.

I think Britain has to actively encourage its own disengagement from Ireland and by doing so it will force a certain reconsideration within the Unionist mindset. The Unionist mindset is not about looking South, or even looking within the six counties to try and make friends with its neighbours. It is about looking across the water for a friend, a friend which they will very seldom find. I think that within an Ireland context Unionists would have far more influence in political institutions and so on than they have within Britain. They would represent a sizable minority within Ireland, whereas within Britain they are a pinprick. They only have influence if their numbers allow them to give one British political party a majority over the others. Within Ireland they would have much more influence.

Diane Greer

My children won't ever be given one side of the story – they will be encouraged to think for themselves ... form their own opinions and give voice to them, hopefully couched in an appreciation, not a fear, of diversity.

I remember hearing about the civil rights marches when I was younger. I would have been told that 'Catholics are on the march, Catholics are looking for ... Catholics want ...'. I wasn't hearing the other side of that. I didn't know at that stage what they didn't have, or even what they wanted. I remember hearing about Burntollet. People that I knew were there, and were maybe there as oppressors. They told the story, and it sounded like a grand battle. It was told like a folk story. I have a very different view of all that today. I know now that a few Protestants were involved at the beginning of the civil rights movement; I am just sorry they fell away. Some people would say that Sinn Féin hijacked the civil rights movement, and I imagine that is why Protestant participation fell away. It may have been a different story if they hadn't, because there were poor Protestants as well. There were people in the Fountain area who shared the same, or almost the same, levels of poverty as people in the Moor and the Brandywell.

It was a combination of things that caused violence to erupt at many of the marches. Years ago I might have believed that that was just how Catholics did it, that they were a bad lot, and this is how they ended their marches. Now I can see lots of reasons why things happen, how any spark could have started the violence, and I don't particularly point a finger one way or the other. I am aware now that there were two sides to it.

Things had got particularly scary by the second half of 1969. I remember being in my mother's hairdressing business in Waterloo Place on a Saturday and seeing fires burning in the street; it was referred to as the Saturday matinee because it always seemed to happen at the same time. Every Saturday at about two or three o'clock this flared up. My mother's business was burned eventually, but while it was there I was aware of the rioting going on around it. And that frightened me, although I suppose my fears were more for my mother's safety than anything else.

I suppose I had begun to think a lot about things by the time internment was introduced. By that stage I was working in a factory office. A lot of the women in the factory came from the Bogside and the Creggan, and a lot of my own attitudes started to change at that point, because I was already in a tartan gang, spending my Saturday afternoons on Ferryquay Street rioting with the green tartans who came up Butcher Street. When I read in books about the tartan gangs in Belfast, I don't remember ours being as serious or as sinister as it was in Belfast. We simply bought a tartan scarf and put it around our necks and we were in the gang. I had moved through that to a point were I was working with women who came in to the factory at eight o'clock in the morning and talked about their houses being raided the night before and people being taken away. It never ceased to amaze me how women showed up for their work in the morning after having had horrendous nights at home. By quietly listening to people, I began to hear the real human stories and I think that very much influenced my views after that. On one side I was hearing that the arrested men were real bad bastards, that's why they had been taken away; no smoke without fire; they don't lift them for nothing etc and getting the message that everybody who was lifted was guilty of something. I suppose in many ways, looking back, they were only guilty of living in a Nationalist area, or being a Catholic, or being a suspected Republican. But to hear a mother talk about her son and to hear her sobbing with her own friends in what was a safe environment for her, and for me to have the privilege of eavesdropping on that, definitely gave me a whole new idea on what was going on. So as a way to control terrorism I suppose it didn't work and I think we know that. I know Protestants were interned as well but it definitely wasn't to the same extent. It's certainly a way of lifting people out and keeping them under lock and key, but it does not deal with the issue and does not solve the problem.

At the time of Bloody Sunday I still had something in me that was saying they *must* have deserved it, they *must* have had guns, they *must* have deserved to be shot. I don't think I was saying they *definitely* had guns, they *definitely* should have been shot, so even then I suppose I was questioning it at some level. But they were scary times. I would have been socialising at that time and would normally have gone out on the town, but all that stopped, and I felt that people were going back into boxes, they were firmly battening down the hatches.

I can remember something of the atmosphere in Derry. There was a lot of sadness and a real heaviness in the air; it's an old cliché, but you could feel it in the air. But the stories were running mad at the time, that people had guns, and I remember questioning it at some level. It would not have been until much later that I began to be influenced by people I met, people I worked with, who I respected, and believed their story. The Widgery Report, the whitewash, all the rest ... Bloody Sunday had passed a long time by the time I started to look at things like that. I would have to say that I support the Bloody Sunday Justice Campaign and wish those people well in their search for justice. I think this has become clear over the years to some Protestants – it still isn't to many who would still say there were only three shot on Bloody Sunday, the rest were kept in freezers from a battle beforehand etc – and a growing number of people are looking at it and can at least be slightly more objective.

At the time, the fall of Stormont wasn't re-

ally important to me, but there was great discussion and debate and a great sense of strength amongst the Protestants. I didn't really know what was happening there; I didn't think too much about the politics of it. I was quite involved at the time of the UWC strike in terms of supporting the UDA prisoners. That was a time when, within the Protestant community, almost everybody you talked to was either in the UDA or very closely linked with it. I was never a member of the UDA; there was nothing ever signed or any swearing in, but I would have supported the prisoners in various ways. So that was the big issue for them, and there was a big organised street demonstration. There was a huge march in Derry at the time of the UWC strike, and I remember it being a time when I felt clearer about where I belonged and about my identity than I did after that. I am even clearer about my identity now, which is very different to what it was then, but nevertheless I felt part of something major, I felt useful and I felt involved. The day of the big march in Derry was a major turning point for me because I was fairly far forward marching across the bridge. I remember the rioting starting, and then I was at the barricade; it was like looking in at myself, and really scary. Rubber bullets were fired and it was as if I got a still picture for a second, and got a look at what was going on, and I was terrified. I thought 'what am I doing?' If my parents knew what I was doing I'd have been murdered. I was much more afraid of my parents than being shot by a rubber bullet. I think from that moment I eased up in the work of supporting the prisoners.

I suppose what I knew of conditions for prisoners only came from the prisoners I was involved with. When the hunger strike came along I was working in the police station – I worked there for a year as a typist; it was an awful job, but it was a job – and I was there for the end of the hunger strikes. People used to protest outside the station, and at that time, because I was working for the police, I was not socializing anywhere other than places that were safe to socialize in. I wasn't meeting a lot of people who weren't either working for the police or in the police, so I suppose a lot of the conversation was with people who supported the security forces, although I had my own opinion, even then. But I remember the atmosphere, it was serious. I would have to say there was good policing going on, in areas like Juvenile Liaison, but in the main I didn't like what I was hearing; the way people were talking about other sections of the community, it didn't sit right with me. I remember at the time of the hunger strike, particularly the end of it, when people were dying for what they believed in, and there were families and friends supporting them, but there was also the other side of it. On the other side, within the police station on the Strand Road, people were sleeping in corridors; they were doing double shifts for long periods of time; even the canteen staff and the cleaning staff were doing double shifts, and it affected everybody. I watched the stresses within the police station and it always makes me feel how well and effectively people can operate when they are working long hours and long shifts, which helped me understand why other things may have happened when people were clearly not operating on full batteries.

I think any form of violence, wherever it comes from, is a negative thing; paramilitary violence is just as negative as state violence and vice versa. I am a great believer in nonviolent protest and nonviolent methods. There are wonderful examples from around the world of massive nonviolent protests that have worked. I am concerned that a lot of paramilitary violence continues, and it could be said that a lot of state violence continues as well. I am also concerned about punishment beatings, but don't think it's a reason to stop the talking; it's something that we can get down to.

I was more than surprised at my own reaction to the ceasefire. I was coming through Connemara when Gerry Ryan was interviewing a policeman from the North on RTE radio, and the policeman was talking about leaving the force, going away, he had had it. In the middle of this very emotional conversation, Gerry Ryan read out the news of the ceasefire. I get emotional even now just thinking about it, because I had just come over a hill, and the lakes were laid out, all very dramatic, and my kids were in the back of the car and I cried and I cried and I cried, and they could not get over or understand why their mother was crying. But that gives me a glimpse of how important it is for me. There was this feeling at the time of relief, and immense emotion, intense emotion.

I was really pleased on the first anniversary of the ceasefire, pleased that it had held for a year. We were exploring ways in which we could celebrate its first anniversary, but I was away when Sinn Féin were doing something, and I don't know how comfortable I would have felt about going to that anyway. I think I would have felt out of it, but I thought I would maybe think about doing something for marking the second ceasefire, but it didn't come off. But even the talking about it was a good thing, and then when I thought about what I really wanted to do, somebody said to me: "What do you want to say? If you are going to put something in the paper, what do you want to say?" I said it is really simple. It comes from being a mother primarily, just a big 'thank you', a simple big 'thank you' to anybody who had any part to play in bringing this about, and that very much included Sinn Féin, it also included the prisoners etc and I am just really thankful that we have had this time.

Initially I thought, this is going so well here, this is taking a real turn around. I was willing to go with the idea of all-party talks even before decommissioning. I thought 'I don't care about the arms because the issue is nonsensical; I mean, how do we know who has what?' Certainly intelligence will have monitored quite a lot of arms coming in, but they couldn't possibly know all that is held in Ireland on any side, so it's nonsensical to talk about lifting them or decommissioning them. On the other hand I kept thinking, please make a gesture because maybe you will pull the Unionists on board. That would be the only reason I would be looking for them to make a gesture of whatever, a lorry load of Semtex, however they pack it, and to move on to all-party talks now.

I have shifted my thinking because I have had time to speak to some people who have been directly affected ie lost members of their family. I have been talking to people that I didn't know before who have lost members of their family – in the cases that I am talking about it was the IRA who murdered them – and I am thinking, is this too quick for them? Maybe we need to move at the pace of the slowest healers. So part of me is happy to sit for the next year or two, but I know that's maybe not going to be realistic for a certain section of the community, so I don't know what to do about that. I am frustrated at the Unionist leaders, too, who are still saying 'no, no, no'.

I would like to see an agreed Ireland where people who want to remain in the UK can do so, and people who want to belong to a united Ireland can do so. There has to be a mechanism that will allow people to be who they want to be and continue with that. I don't have a problem with a united Ireland romantically, but I may have a problem with a united Ireland economically and socially. I just don't want any more violence and I don't want my kids to grow up with it. I think some of our politicians are too old now and we haven't filled the gap. There is a huge age gap now and we don't have new thinkers emerging. This may not be fair to people who are trying to come through, but I am not aware of anybody, any young people, and I am certainly not aware of any women and I would feel very, very strongly about that. I really think a lot of it could be solved, a different perspective could be thrown on it, if they included more women. Sinn Féin and the fringe Loyalists are trying to so something about that.

I want the British army to withdraw from Ireland; I want reforms in the RUC. People have been psychologically scarred. After twenty-five years, I think people become whatever they need to become in order to be in that war, in order to survive. But I think it would be too hard to undo that in a lot of people who are employed in the security forces. However, I know of good policemen and policewomen who are there, who genuinely want to serve the community – a few

of them happen to be Catholics, and I don't know if that makes a difference, but I suspect it might, in how they interact with people. However, that is a huge task, and it would take years to disband anything; you can't just disband it and then call it something else the next day. The RUC issue needs addressed and I am aware of that, for all the right reasons. I wonder even if it is an impartial force. I actually don't see it as an impartial force if I have to be honest, and I feel there are people in it who are trying to be impartial and having a really hard time with the numbers that maybe are not, so that is cancerous in itself. Just as I believe Sinn Féin are making a genuine effort, I believe there are those in the RUC who are making a genuine effort, but you are talking about correcting attitudes and belief systems, and I don't believe that can be done as it exists, so I think there should be a major 'weeding out' operation. People know who the bigots are. I would love to see greater numbers of Catholics being able to apply, but I think the weeding needs to be done first.

I am sorry I didn't take an interest in politics until quite recently. However, I realise now that I am a Protestant woman living in a minority group in Derry. I have lived my life until now – I do have thoughts, opinions and contributions to make. I am not so arrogant to believe that I speak for Protestant women generally – but I intend to be heard. I am active in the peace process everyday – I am part of it. My children won't ever be given one side of the story – they will be encouraged to think for themselves, form their own opinions and give voice to them, hopefully couched in an appreciation, not a fear, of diversity.

My own journey has been an interesting one, a rich one. I look forward with courage and optimism.

Tension mounts as the annual Apprentice Boys' march approaches Waterloo Place on that fateful day, 12 August 1969. *(Photo: Barney McMonagle)*

Rioting starts in Waterloo Place and soon spreads, the 'Battle of the Bogside' has begun. *(Photos: Barney McMonagle)*

Constituency work for Northern Ireland MPs. John Hume (above) in discussion with a member of the RUC in William Street, 12 August 1969. Bernadette Devlin (below) addresses the crowds from a barricade in Rossville Street. *(Photos: Barney McMonagle)*

13 August 1969 – the morning after the night before – both sides prepare for another day. *(Photos: Barney McMonagle)*

Rossville Street,
13 August 1969,
the RUC regroup . . .

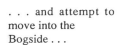

. . . and attempt to
move into the
Bogside . . .

. . . keeping a careful
eye on the high flats,
a favourite vantage
point of the petrol
bombers.

(Photos: Barney McMonagle)

BARRICADE BULLETIN SPECIAL EDITION   No 2 August 14th

BRITISH TROOPS IN DERRY

THIS IS A GREAT DEFEAT FOR THE UNIONIST GOVERNMENT. WE DO NOT YET
KNOW WHETHER IT IS A VICTORY FOR US. A GOVERNMENT WHICH CAN ONLY
BE MAINTAINED BY THE USE OF ARMED TROOPS IS NO LONGER A LEGAL
GOVERNMENT. WHAT WE HAVE TO WAIT AND SEE IS WHETHER WESTMINSTER
IS PREPARED TO ADMIT THIS. FOR THE MOMENT THE FIRST PRIORITY IS
THE SAFETY OF THE PEOPLE OF DERRY. IT IS ESSENTIAL THAT NO-ONE
SHOULD ATTACK THE SOLDIERS. IN THE PRESENT STATE OF TENSION IT
COULD LEAD TO A BLOODBATH. DO NOT LISTEN TO RUMOURS.

At the moment the situation is fluid. It is clear that the
official news reports and comments are not reliable. These are
the FACTS as we know them:

300 SOLDIERS of the Prince of Wales Regiment moved
into the streets of Derry at about 5p.m. today.

They are under the command of the army C.O. At the
moment they are stationed at:the end of the bridge,Guildhall Square,
Waterloo Place, bottom of Great James's Street; they are armed with
sub-machine guns and CS anti riot gas. There is a machine gun nest
on the Ulster Bank building directed at William Street. Barbed
wire barricades have been erected at most of these points.

MEETING WITH THEIR C.O.

The C.O. has seen a deputation and told them that the army is
waiting for reinforcements, that the police have been withdrawn,
the specials have been disarmed. There are no orders for the army
to enter the area.

THE SOUTH

The Irish Army has announced that troops are being moved to the
border to guarantee the field hospitals.

LONDON

The British Home Office has said that the troops were brought in
at the request of the Inspector General of the R.U.C. They make it
clear that the army's presence is a short time operation to restore
law and order. When this is achieved they will be withdrawn. The
British Govt. has also reaffirmed its support for the Government of
Ireland Act 1949 and said that there can be no reconsideration of
the constitutional position unless this is approved by a majority of
the people in both parts of the country.

IMPORTANT

The presence of the troops solves nothing. We must not be fooled
by anyone into taking down the barricades. WE DO NOT GO BACK TO
SQUARE ONE.

It is good that we have a rest from fighting, but at least a token
force must man the barricades tonight. Others must hold themselves
ready to come out if necessary. We do not know what is going to happen.

The barricades must only come down on our terms. The first thing
we must demand is the release of all prisoners taken over the past
four days and a clear and unequivocal statement that there will be
no prosecutions. It would be disastrous tactics for anyone to go out
with the idea of attacking the troops. Anyone setting out on such a
venture should be stopped. But, we stress again WE DEFEND OUR AREA
AGAINST ANYONE.

'BB' is produced by members of the Derry Labour Party

Special edition of the 'Barricade Bulletin', produced on 14 August 1969, to mark the arrival of British troops on the streets of Derry. *(Document: Frankie McMenamin/Seamus McCloskey)*

An early sight of British troops in full combat gear on the streets of Derry, 14 August 1969. *(Photo: Barney McMonagle)*

As direct British involvement increases, Home Secretary James Callaghan visits the Bogside in October 1969. *(Photo: Barney McMonagle)*

John Hume

I put a lot of work into achieving the ceasefire in my dialogue with Gerry Adams which was heavily criticised by a lot of people. But I took the very clear view, as I said repeatedly in public, that since the violence couldn't be stopped by the strictest security laws in western Europe, or by 20,000 soldiers and 12,000 armed policemen on our streets, that if it could be stopped – if a single human life could be saved – by dialogue, then it was our duty to try.

When Northern Ireland was first set up, the border was drawn in a particular manner to ensure that there would be two Protestants to every Catholic in Northern Ireland, assuming that all Protestants were Unionists and all Catholics were Nationalists. It wasn't a natural area, and from the beginning the Unionist mindset was to hold all power in their own hands as the only means of protecting themselves. Of course that led to very widespread discrimination in houses, in jobs and in voting rights. The worst example of that discrimination was the city of Derry where, although they were only 30% of the population, they governed from 1920 right through to the 1970s. My challenge to that Unionist mindset is that, yes, they have every right to their objective, which is to protect their own identity and their own ethos, but their method should be to trust themselves because their own numbers and their own geography mean the problem cannot be resolved without them. So they should come to the table and reach agreement as to how we share this island together.

Central to the origins of our current situation was the very widespread and serious discrimination leading to very high unemployment and appalling housing conditions. I was very well aware of this when I came back from university as one of the lucky ones of my generation, coming from an unemployed background, that I had passed exams and got into university. I got involved immediately, not in politics, but in self-help, to try and resolve the problems of our people by our own means, using our own heads and our own hands, in bodies like the Credit Union and the Housing Association.

The Northern Ireland Civil Rights Association began a campaign for civil rights, but the civil rights movement took on massive dimensions, and particularly international dimensions, when the civil rights marchers were attacked on the streets of Derry on 5 October 1968. That led to a massive reaction, and we immediately met after that and formed the Derry Citizens Action Committee, which became the major civil rights movement in the city and organised a series of civil rights demonstrations. Those led directly to the fall of Derry Corporation, which was the body that controlled the city, and a commission was set up to replace it. That was the first step of the reform process, and of course that work continued.

The SDLP was founded out of the civil rights movement, and the civil rights objectives were central to our whole approach. We secured reforms of the voting system, and we have a democratic voting system now, as reflected in the democratic nature of Derry City Council, for example. We also put a very serious proposal to Jim Callaghan to take housing out of the hands of local authorities, who were abusing that power for discriminatory reasons, and to have the Northern Ireland Housing Executive set up – an independent housing body that has since transformed housing control and allocation throughout Northern Ireland. Side by side with the troubles, the work for civil rights continued at a political level. That also included the setting up of the Fair Employment Agency to take on the problems of discrimination, particularly at public level. But the one area of discrimination that has been very difficult to deal with is employment discrimination because the areas of highest unemployment were also our areas, Derry, West Belfast, Strabane etc. And of course the troubles, of themselves, prevented us from achieving the actions that were required to deal with unemployment, one of which is inward investment, although in recent years, particularly in Derry, we have started to make some inroads into that.

In my opinion you can't stand up seeking civil or human rights if the methods you use undermine the most fundamental human right of all, the right to life. And in addition to that, when you analyse the problem, if your problem is a divided people, then violence is the last method that will resolve that because all it will do is deepen the divisions and deepen the bitterness, and make the problem worse. And it also leads to retaliation and attacks from both sides, the doctrine of 'an eye for an eye' which, as I often say, leaves everybody blind.

When violence of any description takes place from any quarter, it is in itself wrong, no matter who commits it. And we have had experience, tragically, of violence from all sides. We have known about the IRA violence, the terrible tragedies of the Loyalist violence, one of the worst examples being in this area, Greysteel, and of course the worst example of government violence was Bloody Sunday in Derry. Bloody Sunday was a dreadful occasion, it was probably one of the worst days in my own life, and that of itself led to massive recruitment for the IRA; in other words, violence leading to violence.

I put a lot of work into achieving the ceasefire in my dialogue with Gerry Adams which was heavily criticised by a lot of people. But I took the very clear view, as I said repeatedly in public, that since the violence couldn't be stopped by the strictest security laws in western Europe, by 20,000 soldiers and 12,000 armed policemen on our streets, that if it could be stopped – if a single human life could be saved – by dialogue, then it was our duty to try. And therefore I was obviously extremely pleased when we achieved the ceasefire, and of course I think that the ceasefire has had an enormous impact on our whole community, North and South. It transformed the whole atmosphere, and particularly so for young people under thirty who had never known anything in their lives but trouble on the streets and hadn't lived through other periods that the rest of us had. To be able to realise the reality of normality has transformed the whole atmosphere and created a powerful mood among our people for lasting peace. And it has also transformed the attitude of the Irish abroad because it focused their attention on Ireland in a positive way, in a way that it had never done in the past, and all those resources are now available to us to build our new Ireland. And I think that central to that must be a totally peaceful atmosphere, and I am hopeful that there will be a restoration of peace in the near future.

As Gerry Adams and I made clear in our statements throughout the whole peace process, there were two objectives of our process. One was the total cessation of violence. The second was that it would be followed by all-party talks involving both governments and all parties, whose objective would be agreement among our divided people, an agreement that would be able to earn the allegiance of all our traditions. In other words, a political peace process that threatened no section of our community, but challenged both major sections and both major traditions to come together for the first time in a peaceful atmosphere to make an agreement that would respect our traditions and earn the allegiance of both sides. That will, of course, require new thinking on all sides.

However, I was somewhat frustrated by the slowness of moving on to stage two. When you consider that almost eighteen months after the ceasefire, all-party talks still hadn't taken place, and preconditions were constantly being put in the way, I think that on reflection now most people would agree with me that a major opportunity was in fact lost by not moving swiftly to all-party talks. Nevertheless, I hope that, if we can resolve the present situation and get a restoration of the peace process, all-party talks will take place because at the end of the day, until they take place, we cannot achieve the lasting stability that is the basis of lasting peace because lasting stability in any society can only be based on agreement on how you are governed among the people who are governed.

I was deeply shattered when I heard of the ending of the ceasefire, and when I heard that once again innocent people had lost their lives. I thought it was a major setback to our overall situation, but I think also that the mood of the people is even stronger now to secure the restoration of the peace process, and Gerry Adams and I, as we have made clear, are continuing our work to try and ensure that. And I hope that it won't be too long until we do so.

People could put all sorts of interpretations on things that happen, and there has been a lot of speculation about a connection between the bomb exploding at Canary Wharf and the date for all-party talks being announced so soon after. But at the end of the day there has to be all-party talks. I regret very much that that date wasn't fixed quite some considerable time earlier because in my view it's probable we would be very close to lasting peace and stability by now. But, anyway, things that have happened have happened and people will interpret them in different ways, but rather than getting into political arguments about what should or should not have been done, we must keep our eye on the main goal which is how do we achieve lasting stability, and how do we get there? And the way we get there is all-party talks, and I hope that when these talks begin on 10 June that they will begin in a totally peaceful atmosphere, and that a very serious effort will be made by all sides to finally reach agreement.

Myself and my party have made our position very clear on what the government has decided must happen before all-party talks begin. It is an extremely complicated, and in my view unnecessary, road because the simple way of doing so was to call all parties to the table, directly, without elections. All elections will do is harden attitudes and make negotiations more difficult, and there are many other complicated factors. We proposed that the British government simply call all parties to the table without preconditions. If they were sincere about this need for a mandate for peace, the way they could

have dealt with that, which would have been a very strong way of dealing with it, was to let the people speak by having a referendum North and South on the one day. That referendum would ask two questions which are central to the whole peace process: 'Do you want a total cessation of violence?' and 'Do you want all-party talks to negotiate your future?' In my view, had that been done, the biggest turnout in history would have taken place in both parts of Ireland and would have enormously strengthened all sides and all parties involved in the peace process, rather than choosing this complicated method of elections, which are only confusing at the end of the day and not a necessary step towards real negotiations.

What I want to see coming out of all this would be a new Ireland in which there is agreement among the two major traditions that share this island. In order to achieve that, we have to discuss, and it will be the major agenda at any talks, the three sets of relationships that go to the heart of our problem – relations within Northern Ireland, within Ireland, and between Britain and Ireland.

This is not a Northern Ireland problem; this is a British-Irish problem. The failure of Britain and Ireland to sort out their differences in the 1920s was pushed into a corner and called Northern Ireland. It was left sitting there, and rotted away until the events of the last twenty-five years. So, we have to sort out those three sets of relationships, and myself and my party have very clear views as to what we will be putting on the table at such talks. However, when you are going into detailed negotiations like that you don't declare your detailed proposals in advance because if you do you can be sure you won't get them. Solutions must emerge from talks and not seem to come from one side or the other. But the central principle of our approach is that we have to have institutions that will respect the diversity of our community, but at the same time ensure that we all work together for the real interests of our people, bread on our tables and a roof over our heads; in other words the whole economic development.

I am very encouraged, as I have said very often in public, by my European experience of conflict resolution. When you consider that the peoples of Europe slaughtered one and other by the million for centuries, and in this century alone, in the Second World War, millions of people died, yet fifty years later we have a united Europe. The Germans are still German and the French are still French. How did they do it? They did it by building institutions which respected their differences, but allowed them to work together in the common economic interest. We must do the same on the island of Ireland.

Cecil Hutcheon

I remember going into the Guildhall Square on the morning that Bobby Sands died ... There were maybe 10,000 people and there wasn't a word being spoken ... I could see the Brits and the police were moving back because they must have been terrified, not knowing what was going to happen. I thought it was one of the worst periods of the troubles for Nationalists.

I never really knew much about what was going on here before 1968. I was only fourteen at the time and didn't really think about civil rights, about how people were being treated. It was from listening to older people talking about the housing situation that I started to get an idea about what was happening. I supported the civil rights movement because I was living in a Nationalist area and I thought it was a good thing that Catholics in the city, and throughout the North, would get equal rights.

I suppose at the end of the day, violence will come out of things like that. But I put the blame on the RUC and the B Specials and the Stormont government, because they wouldn't let people march for their rights. They knew that in the end Catholics were going to end up having equal rights with Protestants.

I was part of the protest on Bloody Sunday, the civil rights march. I actually called for a boy who was shot dead that day, John Young. He was a good friend of mine. I went up to Creggan to call for John before the march. I got parted from him during the march and the next thing I knew I heard shots. It was just a slaughtering match. I remember lying over in the Bog, behind a small wall, terrified, not realising the extent of what was happening. Running through the back of the flats at the time you could hear bullets buzzing over your head and ricochetting off the walls. People were getting shot in the streets. Although you wouldn't have given much credence to the British army, you wouldn't have thought that they would come in and actually slaughter people on the streets. It made me even more bitter than I had been.

As I said, I was only a young lad, not involved in politics, maybe not really understanding all of it; but from listening to talk about it at the time it was clear that the Widgery Report was a whitewash. There was nobody brought to book for it. They knew people were shot with their hands up, or trying to carry other people away. And the world's media witnessed it. At the end of the day, these tribunals are a waste of time and money because the outcome is always going to be the same. They are not going to charge soldiers here on active service with murder and have them spend the rest of their lives in jail, and that is something which has been proved recently with the release of Lee Clegg.

I remember the morning of internment very well. I lived near the very bottom of Westway in Creggan. It was the time the barricades were up, the time of the no-go areas, and everybody had the feeling that something was going to happen. I remember at about four in the morning, boys coming to the house saying that people were getting lifted, that there was rioting. Boys were put in prison for no reason, without trial. I have a brother-in-law who was one of the first internees, and he told me some of the things that happened; getting thrown out of helicopters six-feet off the ground, being hooded; all these things made people more bitter and made them go and join organisations.

When you are young, and something like the UWC strike happens on the other side of the 'house', you might not take much notice until your lights go out at night and you are left in the dark. Then I realised that they were in the key positions, the key jobs, and able to call a strike. If the Nationalist community had called a strike like that the most we could have done was protest in the street; I don't think we could have left towns and cities without electricity.

The hunger strikes made me feel really sad. The atmosphere was frightening about the town. I remember the morning Bobby Sands died, getting a phone call to the house in the early hours of the morning, going over and knocking different people up and letting them know, and then assembling down the town. The hunger strike made me feel very helpless at the time. There were men dying and there was nothing you could do about it. And the way they were dying must be one of the hardest. I remember going into the Guildhall Square on the morning that Bobby Sands died. There were thousands of people, and it was around 5 o'clock in the morning. I could feel the hair standing on the back of my neck. Everybody was silent. There were maybe 10,000 people and there wasn't a word being spoken. It was really scary. The RUC were there, and there were soldiers surrounding the Guildhall Square, and when they looked at 10,000 people just standing or sitting there in total silence, it was something else. Even now I can remember the feeling. I could see the Brits and the police were moving back because they must have been terrified, not knowing what was going to happen. I thought it was one of the worst periods of the troubles for Nationalists, and for what people went through; for the families, to have to go up to jail and watch their son or their husband dying for what they believed in.

It was good to see that the prisoners got their demands, though it was very sad that ten people had to die before the British government allowed them their rights. The sentences they hand out to political prisoners are ridiculous anyhow. If you do the same in England, say armed robbery, you get about four years. Young boys at seventeen or eighteen were being put in jail who had maybe never done an hour's detention at school, never mind being sent to jail for twenty years. I don't know how people cope with jail. The longest I was held was for five days, over in England

at Paddington Green, and those were the longest five days of my life, so to be told you are going to do twenty years must be a nightmare.

I suppose it was inevitable that the troubles were going to happen, but I don't think people realised it was going to go on so long. Things happened that I agreed with, and things I disagreed with. Even on my own side things happened that shouldn't have happened. I think the Protestants in Belfast, the Loyalist squads, they went out, especially in the early '80s, killing people just because they were Catholic. I don't think the IRA went out and shot people just because they were Protestant. The Loyalists were just slaughtering people in Belfast. At that time I wondered how the people in Belfast coped with such a thing. In Derry you were reasonably safe. There were a few sectarian killings but it seemed to be nipped in the bud right and quick. I think somebody must have been told, somewhere along the line, 'knock it on the head because we know who you are'. But I thought, with some of the things that did come out of the Loyalist side, it must have been terrifying to be a Catholic in Belfast.

A war is a war, and I look at the situation here as a war. It was definitely a war situation when you had to back the RUC with 30,000 troops. So there was a war situation, and innocent people died. There were times when people were killed and you felt bad about it. Maybe I am lucky that nobody in my immediate family has been killed during the troubles. But I think if it had happened I would have been able to accept the fact. Maybe if my brother was a volunteer and was killed on active service, I would accept it better. And I think if one of my family had been killed in an accident, a bombing or walked into a shooting, I think I could have accepted it because in a war situation these things happen.

I started driving a black taxi ten years ago. Then there were places in Derry you couldn't go. You could have gone over to the Waterside if you wanted to but it was dodgy enough. The chances of you getting shot were slight, but the chances of people throwing stones and your window getting smashed were very high. The harassment from the RUC and the British army at the time was on a daily basis. You accepted it because, once you were seen driving a black taxi, they classed you as a Republican right away. But it was funny, there were a couple of English drivers, and there was a Swede or an Italian or something, driving black taxis in Derry. I know people in Derry driving black taxis who were more SDLP minded, but these people were still getting the same harassment. They couldn't understand why they were getting harassed. I think in general most of the drivers accepted it, but you just watched where you were going.

There were a couple of scares in Derry. You had to be careful, watch where you were driving, watch where you were parking, watch if you were working late at night. Around the time Eddy Fullerton was shot dead in Buncrana we were told to be careful where we were going, especially if we used places in the town to stop for lunch or a bite to eat. Somebody knew something was going to happen. They thought somebody in Derry was going to be targeted. So we were just advised to be very careful, especially working at night.

I didn't really like going to the Waterside, but I remember one time I had to go. One of my sons was in hospital when he was young, in a ward of his own, and the hospital phoned and asked me to bring over a TV. I had no other transport so I just took the taxi to the hospital. I remember driving out the link road, and there was a boy walking a dog, and the minute he saw the taxi it was finger up and he started shouting 'you fenian bastard, you IRA bastard'. He was just jumping mad just because I was driving up the link road.

It was just a job, but I think the RUC had a different way of looking at the black taxis. Whatever sort of notion it was they had, I think when the Brits come in around the area, they were told especially to stop hacks. On one occasion a soldier actually told one of the drivers that if there were only two or three people in the taxi, that was the taxi they were to stop. If it was a full load of people, women and children, not to bother, but if it was two or three fellas, teenagers or in their twenties, that was the taxi to stop. I don't know what sort of notion they had in their heads about the hacks, but at the end of the day

it was forty people in Derry driving taxis to make a living. Everything was legal. If you were not legal they would have put you off the road.

It's hard to say how I felt when the ceasefires were called. I mean, there have been ceasefires before. After twenty-five years I am hoping that something will come out of it. But I think people have to be very careful about what's going to happen because of the ceasefire. The first thing that comes to my mind is the prisoners. People are talking about an amnesty, but I remember people talking about an amnesty in 1971 and some of those boys are still in jail. One of the main things is that there are people lying dead in the cemetery who died fighting for a cause they believed in. That cause was a united Ireland, and you have to be very careful that that is still the main objective. Too many have died for that cause, and you can't forget them, or their families, because the last thing you can give is your life, and they have given it.

There were talks going on before the ceasefires, and the Brits knew there was a ceasefire coming, and Sinn Féin and the IRA knew it was going to have to come, that they were going to have to give it a try. But the thing at the minute is that the IRA has stuck by their word, and the only guns you will see on the streets now are the guns of the RUC. I think they are overdoing it with the security now. They should relax a bit, ease up a bit on security. Where I live, Rosemount, there is a seventy-five-foot watchtower which is still being manned twenty-four-hours-a-day, seven-days-a-week. I can't see why there are so many security cameras watching such a small area. The people of Rosemount have a campaign going against the tower. People say to me: "If they would even take the soldiers out of the tower, there's no call for them." I don't think it's enough to just take them out of the tower, it should be removed. All those obstacles of war should be removed. Even the Chief Constable of the RUC, Hugh Annesley, has stated that he believes the ceasefire is here to stay. He must realise the security situation can relax a bit; on border roads etc. People say there are no checkpoints now. There *are* checkpoints, it's just that there's nobody there, standing asking you for your licence. It would only take two seconds to put a soldier back into a checkpoint. On Strand Road they thought they were doing the people of Derry a great service by opening the road again because the barriers had been up for seven or eight years, but two landrovers could block the Strand Road again in two minutes. That's all it would take. If they are talking about peace and ceasefires, then all areas should feel a bit of peace, peace of mind, they should have their privacy. That's one of the main issues in Rosemount. We don't feel we have any privacy at all, our privacy is totally invaded, everyday, for twenty-four-hours-a-day, especially during the last two-and-a-half years.

I hope the ceasefires last, both ceasefires, but I think they need to get round the table and talk. It could be a long time down the road, but I hope it does not take another twenty-five years. I think if the ceasefire ends we will end up with some terrible atrocities. I think a lot people are very worried at the minute. I found on the first anniversary of the ceasefire, on the marches organised by Sinn Féin, that there were a lot of people there who would normally be more supportive of SDLP politics, but they were there because they wanted to show their support for the peace process, no matter what their politics were. I think the British government should look up and see that.

I would like to see a united Ireland. I hope the peace holds. It's hard to say what's going to come out of it. I would like to see the prisoners released. For the people that died, I would like to see them having what they died for. They died for a united Ireland and from when I was a young boy that was always on my mind, a united Ireland. We have fought for twenty-five years and I would like to see us getting what we fought for – to be disassociated from Britain completely. I suppose that it's going to be another while before that happens.

Irish Republican Socialist Party

...that decision ... should not be taken as a threat to anyone. The INLA will only launch any kind of offensive action if our organisation is attacked, or if Nationalist working-class areas are attacked. We see no reason for that to happen at this moment in time ...

Stormont was a corrupt, anti-democratic, sectarian and bigoted regime and the fact that it was allowed to exist at all is one of the reasons why organisations such as ours emerged. Many of our comrades were involved before 1968 in social agitation in Derry, in the Derry Housing Action Committee, and a number of our present members took part in the Burntollet march, for example, and of course the 5 October demonstration in 1968. Looking back at that period of time it was a transition from the corrupt regime, moving towards the total reform or abolition of the Northern state.

When the civil rights movement started, it was a change of strategy which many Republicans looked on at the time with great doubt and hesitation because they had been stuck in the traditional manner of waging war against British imperialism and did not see that there were any benefits to be gained from the use of the nonviolent strategy. On the other hand, many Socialists saw that it was necessary to agitate for rights within the state in order to expose its corruptness, which was precisely what happened. Many organisations existed prior to 1968 campaigning on a number of issues, housing of course being a key one in Derry, but because some Republicans said the only methodology was armed struggle that actually meant that they did not engage in politics. Many people, older Republicans, newer Republicans, Socialists, and people who had no interest in the wider national question in 1968, flocked to the civil rights banner because it was the beginning of politics, it was the beginning of discussion, debate, dialogue, and a better understanding of the nature

of the Northern Ireland state. The civil rights movement itself galvanised Republicans into looking anew at the situation, and that is what caused the split in 1969 within what was originally the one Republican movement.

The eventual emergence of armed struggle was an inevitable consequence of the response of the Stormont regime. As soon as that regime used violence against civil rights supporters, and the Unionist establishment ignored, derided and belittled the civil rights movement, it was always inevitable that someone was going to start to use force against it. I don't think, on reflection, that there was a clearly thought-out strategy at the beginning of the armed struggle phase. It was more a case of people taking up guns to defend themselves, and then, later on, formulating a strategy to bring the struggle forward. On a number of occasions there were attempts to merge armed and civil resistance, particularly in the period after internment, in a genuine people's struggle using any and all means to bring down the Stormont regime.

Bloody Sunday, of course, had a worldwide impact, and eventually forced the British to engage more in the politics and running of the six counties. For Republicans, I think it had a tremendous impact. Many of them, especially former internees, started to analyse the situation. Bloody Sunday showed the naked force of British aggression and caused many comrades who were in the Official Republican movement at that time to believe that it should not move towards a ceasefire and should not continue to support a reformed or democratized Stormont. That caused severe tension with the Official Republican movement, leading eventually to the emergence of our own movement in 1974. Bloody Sunday was a watershed in that I think it marked the beginning of the end of Unionist rule, of one-party rule, in the six counties.

The fall of Stormont was a victory, and has to be seen as a victory. I know there are those who say it was a defeat, and who say it was a democratic forum and therefore we should be calling for its restoration, or its democratization. Republican Socialists don't accept that. The abolition of Stormont was a victory for the previous years of struggle. It was not a complete victory but it was a significant one and gave more hope and encouragement to those who were campaigning towards the goal of a republic.

The removal of Stormont clearly identified that Britain claimed sovereignty over the six-counties. There was now no middle way, no buffer of Unionism. What went on in the six-county state had clearly been the responsibility of the British since 1922, but because of the existence of the Stormont regime they were able, worldwide, to deflect any investigation, interest, or publicity about that six-county state until they were forced by the civil resistance to abolish Stormont. Direct rule has forced the British to govern here openly. Consequently it has brought us to this stage today where they recognise that they have to make some accommodation with the government of the Irish Republic to formulate a new way of ruling the six-county state.

The Irish government played a reactionary role for most of that period. During the coalition government in the late 1970s they hounded and haunted Republicans. They prevented political development of organisations, they harassed anyone who was in opposition to the British regime, a regime which in the late '70s was exercising torture in the six counties. After that period of time, whether it was a coalition or a Fianna Fáil or Fine Gael-led government in the South, there was always an anti-Republican, revisionist, rewriting of history, and a concerted attempt to wipe out any working-class resistance to either of the regimes, North and South.

Republican violence was a response to British rule. It was a response to all the wrongs that existed in the six-county state. For our part, as an organisation we believe that the use of violence is a tactic, not a strategy. It is a tactic to be used in the light of existing circumstances, after a careful evaluation of the situation. As a working-class organisation we have no wish to see violence as a permanent fixture of working-class life. But it is a necessary, and has been a necessary, revolutionary tactic in order to defend working-class areas, and particularly working-class Nationalists in the six-county state, and to force the British to accept that they have no right to be in Ireland. So the use of armed force is a tactic to be used by a revolutionary organisation as circumstances determine.

Loyalist violence has always been a reaction to any progressive movement that developed within the North. It has been turned on and turned off by the British or the Unionist ruling classes at will. Even in the early 1920s, sections of the RUC, in collusion with armed Loyalist gangs, used violence to terrorise progressive movements, both Nationalist and Labour, and since the start of the troubles they have been used in a reactionary fashion. It's a counter-terrorist strategy used by the British and the ruling class in the six counties to terrorise people. Recently, Loyalists themselves have begun to look at their role, and we welcome that. It is encouraging that they are now seeking, to some degree, to be independent of the wishes of their imperialist warlords.

I think everyone welcomed the end of violence. Our movement, however, felt that what was called the peace process was fatally flawed, and we were politically critical of that process. Nevertheless, we took a conscious decision to do nothing that would endanger that peace process, even though we were strongly critical of it.

There are a number of points that we would make in relation to the peace process. Twenty-five years of struggle had involved large numbers of people in both political and military resistance, but they were not consulted, they were not part of the discussions, decisions were taken over their heads. I also believe there was no intent to involve the mass of the people in discussion in the aftermath of the ceasefire as to the next step forward because it was always going to be a case that the British would use every stumbling block to the negotiating table before they would begin to face up to the Government of Ireland Act and their claim to sovereignty. So, yes, we have been highly critical of the peace process, but we are certainly not critical of peace, and we welcome the fact that Nationalists in working-class areas have had a breathing space, which has actually been very good from a number of points in that there is now much more awareness of politics because sometimes the gun, if used solely and exclusively, stifles political discussion.

I think you could make the same criticism in relation to the return to violence as to the calling off of violence; that it was done without reference to, or seems to have been done without reference to, people who have been involved in the struggle for many years, to the mass of the people. We have always made the criticism of the Provisional Republican movement that it is essentially elitist and an all-class alliance. This has been confirmed by their attempt to build a Nationalist consensus involving not only Sinn Féin and the SDLP but the ruling capitalist class in the South, as represented by Fianna Fáil and Fine Gael. They have also created an alliance with Irish America which has influenced the president of the imperialist superpower to get involved in the politics of Ireland. As Republicans we believe that the Irish people have the right to national self-determination and that there should be no interference from outside, including the United States of America. Therefore, the decision to plant the bomb in Canary Wharf we see as being taken in an elitist fashion. However, we understand the anger and frustration that led to that bombing and as Republicans we are certainly not going to condemn it. We understand the frustration that was building up in Nationalist areas and we had, on a number of occasions, warned representatives of political parties in Ireland that the ceasefire was in grave danger because of the negative and reactionary attitude taken by the British, their creation of obstacles, and their total failure to encompass all of the elements that made up the problem in the various stages of the talks process.

There was a marginalisation of the Republican Socialist movement; our prisoners were treated differently in the twenty-six counties, until they were forced to go on hunger strike. The British government still refuses to recognise our existence. Up to now they have banned us from taking part in the elections and talks due in May and June. We regard that as a farce, but we certainly do not accept the right of the British to say which state-sponsored parties are allowed to stand in the elections. I am sure the Natural Law Party, for example, have the right to their politics and their point of view; we would accept their right. We also have a right to exist and we don't need the British government's approval. I think it is symptomatic of the arrogance of the British that they think they can determine who has the democratic right of existence or not; democracy is not determined by what a government says or does. If the system is to be democratic then all shades of opinion should be allowed to express their view.

In May 1995 the INLA released a statement clarifying their position in relation to the cease-fire, and immediately began a process through the Republican Socialist movement of engaging in dialogue with as many groups as possible in order to assess how realistic the British were in their response to the new situation. Through a number of contacts we communicated requests to the political spokespersons of the Loyalist organisations for meetings, without publicity, without preconditions, in order to begin a process which we recognise as dialogue. The only precondition that we had was that we would not talk with the British government because we did not trust them. That stance has not changed since May of 1995. The decision taken recently by the INLA to adopt a stance of defence and retaliation was due to the intransigence of the British and, I have to add, the failure of the government of the twenty-six counties to engage in meaningful dialogue with representatives of the Republican Socialist movement. On a number of occasions we gave clarification to the government of the twenty-six counties, through their civil servants, as to the stance that was taken by our movement. That government accepted our *bona fides* in relation to the whole peace process. However, Dick Spring, the Tánaiste, has constantly refused to meet us despite the fact that he has met spokespersons for the Loyalist organisations on a number of occasions. Our movement has taken no action to endanger the peace process. All the other paramilitary groups have been involved in punishment beatings. In the Loyalist case one of their peace delegation has been convicted of attempting to smuggle guns through Scotland. So our movement is extremely angry and frustrated at the lack of recognition that we are being given because we believe, and have always believed, that those who are part of the problem have to be part of the solution. However, the statement on defence and retaliation, and this was clarified to people, should not be taken as a threat to anyone. The INLA will only launch any kind of offensive action if our organisation is attacked, or if Nationalist working-class areas are attacked. We see no reason for that to happen at this moment in time, and we have put forward a number of proposals by which we believe a situation can be created where the representatives of the armed groups within the six counties could sit down and begin a process of talking to each other. We put forward a suggestion for a labour forum to the Labour Party in the South. Unfortunately, they didn't take it up and we are still pushing those kind of ideas because we feel that dialogue is essential.

Our movement would now like to be included in open-ended, unconditional, all-party talks. Ideally, a consensus will emerge from these talks that will convince the British to begin the total democratization of the Northern state, includ-ing the abolition of the RUC and the creation of a new police service. We would hope to see the extension of equality in all areas, and the solving of the critical question of marching, an explosive issue which at any time could derail the peace process.

We believe that if the British still claim sovereignty, and until such time as that sovereignty is conceded back to the Irish people, they should rule on behalf of *all* the people, until they make a declaration to withdraw and leave the people in Ireland to make a final decision as to what form of government, or what *forms* of government, should be established here.

We believe that the creation of Socialism in Ireland is essential for the wellbeing of the vast majority of its people. Economically, politically, and culturally, partition has distorted and damaged this island. The establishment of a fair Socialist system here would lay the foundations for reconciliation, for working-class unity, and for economic prosperity. The argument about the economics of partition is one which has been going on for many years. But from our point of view, partition has damaged the wealth and economic power of the people in Ireland and has weakened both North and South. A unified state would, we believe, create a prosperous economy from which the vast majority of people in Ireland would benefit. Ultimately we have to persuade people that Socialism and liberation of the working class from capitalism is the only way forward.

Marlene Jefferson

It is the families of the victims of violence who always seem to be forgotten about. That is the tragedy of it because, let's face it, a mother or a wife who has lost someone grieves, no matter what side she is on. All mothers' tears and wives' tears are the same ...

I was bringing up a family of five in the 1960s so I didn't get actively involved in what else was going on at the time. I was always so involved in bringing up my family that I didn't really look all that closely at it. Looking back, I felt afterwards that there was a certain coming together at that time. Coming from quite a strange background, my mother was very Unionist and my father was Labour, I was brought up to be very liberal. I was never brought up to look at people in pockets; people were people.

At the time, I felt that the civil rights movement had something people wanted to listen to, and they wanted to be heard. To be totally honest, I wasn't all that concerned at the time. It seems a very selfish thing to say, but I really wasn't at that time. Then suddenly everything was happening. I remember being very aggrieved that the town seemed to come to a halt when there was a march.

Violence at the marches made me very angry. I lived in the centre of town, in Carlisle Road, and we watched the marches going up and down for maybe a week and then suddenly there were more police in the street and there was a lot of aggravation and violence. That annoyed me simply because I was trying to bring up children and it made life very difficult. Suddenly I found the children totally caged in, if you like, where they weren't allowed to go out; they weren't allowed to do anything. I think that was the start of a very abnormal existence for any children brought up during the troubles.

It seemed quite unreal. I remember having the children down for a few days in a caravan at Benone, and when we came back, we suddenly found the city had become like a siege city, with police and our army on the bridge. I remember my children being very frightened at that time. But like everything else, after a while they seemed to get used to it; it didn't seem quite so frightening, but when they were young it was very difficult. I remember being angry that we should suddenly be under siege.

I was horrified at what happened on Bloody Sunday. I remember being absolutely horrified that people were being shot dead in my city. I suppose it was a very unreal time because, even though you were horrified, you were thankful that you weren't there, that you weren't involved. That's looking at it from a maternal point of view.

It is very difficult to say how I felt about the Widgery Report; I probably accepted it. I think it is very difficult to decide in a balanced way exactly how I felt. Naturally, depending on what side of the problem you were on, that's the way you would have looked at it; I probably felt that it was relatively fair.

Violence to me was violence, and I think one encouraged the other. I used to get very, very angry and annoyed about things. I remember at that time, when things were really bad, when people were being blown up, murdered and shot, and it was terrible. People who say that they have never taken sides are liars as well as hypocrites. I think we have all been guilty of being bigoted about something. I remember one time my daughter saying to me: "Mum, you know, everyone should practise what they preach." They say 'out of the mouths of babes ...'. I remember having to take a very hard look, and I had always considered myself to be very fair and very balanced, but none of us in the troubles has been totally fair and balanced if we are honest about it. Nevertheless, looking at it and giving yourself a shake doesn't do any harm. It didn't do me any harm because it made me look at things perhaps more rationally.

It is the families of the victims of violence who always seem to be forgotten about. That is the tragedy of it because, let's face it, a mother or a wife who has lost someone grieves, no matter what side she is on. All mothers' tears and wives' tears are the same, and I remember thinking at the time that I got involved with Widows' Might, a group of the widows of members of the security forces who had been killed, that here is a group of people who have had to pick up the pieces; get on with it, try to bring up their children as normally as possible; and nobody really knows about them simply because they haven't had time to be vocal. It was the widows themselves who actually decided to do something about it. There was a television programme going out from the Everglades Hotel and they felt that it was so much about those who were involved in violence being killed that they actually picked themselves up, went off to the Everglades and said to the television company: "What about us?" And that's really what sparked off Widows' Might.

The widows themselves were absolutely devastated. Some of their husbands and their children died in horrific circumstances. I can think of one young woman whose husband was a school inspector and a part-time UDR man. He was blown up outside his house and not only did she lose her husband, but she lost her beautiful daughter and her son was very badly injured. What amazed me was that the attitude they had was not violent, there didn't seem to be any hatred there. I found this very hard to take at the beginning because when I started to talk to them, and they were mostly strangers to me, all they were angry about was 'what about our children, what about what has happened to us, does nobody care?' But never once, never once from any of them did the word 'hatred' come into it, and that is really why I decided to become their patron, simply to protect them from the media and the politics of Northern Ireland; to protect them from the harshness and the reality; to try and cushion them. But as time went on, I discovered they didn't need any cushion because they were speaking the truth about how they felt and how they saw things.

I think the day the IRA called a ceasefire was probably the most hopeful day in Northern Ireland since the troubles began. I say hopeful because I remember thinking 'this can't be true, is this really going to happen?' Now, I still believe that it's going to happen. I think that things are very shaky at the moment but I have total faith in the majority of people in Northern Ireland to do their best not to let what has happened over nearly thirty years happen again.

Many people have talked on TV over the last few days about whether things should have moved faster during the seventeen months of the IRA ceasefire; I found that quite thought provoking. I'd have been very anxious at the beginning to get something done but looking back, I think it wise to have waited. We went through nearly thirty years of horror, and why should we suddenly be expected to be able to resolve it overnight? There is no way we can resolve overnight what has been happening in this country of ours. So I am now convinced that it does take time, and I really don't mind if it takes another six months or a year.

The bombing of Canary Wharf was dreadful, it really was. I don't want to be political, but can I say this, and I mean it with the greatest sincerity, I think there are too many people on a hook now and they daren't get off. The people of Northern Ireland over the last twenty-five years, if they have learned nothing else, they have learned to stand up for themselves and speak out and say what they want, not them all but quite a lot of them; people who before would never have made comments are quite prepared to make comment now; and the people who are involved in the peace process, which is quite a lot of people, I feel they daren't get off.

I think the elections are necessary to get representatives there who are put there by the people, and I would like to see a solution where all the people of Northern Ireland can live together. Until we remember that everything begins at home, and until we get our own house in order, and that is one hell-of-a-task, we can't start looking elsewhere.

I would like to see a good, active, political forum in Northern Ireland working for the best for Northern Ireland and creating good community relations with any other country that wants to talk to us. I feel it's important we have dialogue with the South of Ireland and elsewhere, and I think that maybe now is the time for us to look upon ourselves, as well as being people from the North of Ireland, as being Europeans.

Brian Lacey

The late '60s were the days of protest and hope – the worker and student move-ments in France, the Prague spring, the anti-Vietnam War and civil rights movements in America, anti-apartheid, the emerging gay rights movement, the birth of feminism, and all the other similar issues at home and abroad. We saw the civil rights campaign in the North as part of that international agenda, a genuine, worldwide liberating movement quite different from the old National-isms.

The weather was brilliant in Ireland on 31 August 1994. That wasn't the only surprise for me over the next twenty-four hours. The IRA announced its ceasefire to start at midnight and, like a lot of people I know, I celebrated that night and was just about able to get into work on time the following day. I was barely in the door when I had a phone call from London. The Tower Museum had won the award for the United Kingdom Museum of the Year (it was already Irish Museum of the Year). For some reason that morning the news seemed very appropriate. The museum had sort of made its reputation as a place where the stories of the troubles and the historical events which gave rise to them were told in an even-handed way.

Although not born here, I've lived in Derry now for over twenty years. Until I came to work at Magee College in late 1974, and apart from a few visits when I was a child, I was not at all familiar with Northern Ireland and had never spent a night here. The worst of the troubles were over by the time I arrived but I was still to see a great deal of destruction and tragedy and, on a few occasions, even become something of a foot-note to some of these events. When it all start-ed, however, I was living in a very different kind of world.

On 5 October 1968 I was working as a trainee air-traffic-control assistant at Shannon Airport. It was my first real job after finishing the Leav-ing Cert and school in Dublin. You can imagine the sort of life the trainees led. Most of us were still in our teens, away from home for the first time, enjoying whatever limited pleasures Shan-non Airport and County Clare had to offer. More out of luck than skill or aptitude, we managed to avoid contributing to international air-disas-ter statistics. It was a very carefree existence and only once did politics rear its ugly head when a party of Chicago policemen arrived fresh from beating up student protesters at the September 1968 Democratic Party convention. Despite the fact that we were civil servants, expressly for-bidden from taking part in politics, a crowd of us gathered at the terminal building to protest at the visitors.

There was also the famous incident that year when a Pan American (I think) jet en route from Paris to New York was rerouted back to Shan-non after a lunatic passenger announced that he had a bomb in his briefcase. Whatever about the facts, I will always remember this incident as 'the first bomb in Ireland'. There were only about two security officers employed by the airport in those innocent days. All hell broke loose when the plane landed. The Irish army came out from Limerick and, having attached a lead to the brief-case in question, retreated almost back to Limerick again before daring to detonate it. But 'the first bomb in Ireland' turned out to be not a bomb at all, just what we'd all eventually get to know as a hoax.

However, the 'boarding school' high spirits were quenched that famous Saturday night as we incredulously watched the news from Derry on television, especially the well-known shots by RTE cameraman Gay O'Brien. We show that film sequence every day, in fact many times a day, now in the Tower Museum and I often worry about using it – it looks so violent. The paradox of course was that in many ways the incident was hardly violent at all in comparison to what was to follow over the next twenty-five years. Four months later, in January 1969, I myself was batoned by the Gardaí, along with many other protesters on O'Connell Bridge in Dublin, at a demonstration organised by the Dublin Housing Action Committee. I can remember the same cameraman, Gay O'Brien, hanging from one of the ornate lamp standards on the bridge filming the events of that day and thinking to myself that, unlike the Derry police violence, this episode was unlikely to get shown on RTE. It didn't.

The late '60s were the days of protest and hope – the worker and student movement in France, the Prague spring, the anti-Vietnam War and civil rights movements in America, anti-apartheid, the emerging gay rights movement, the birth of feminism, and all the other similar issues at home and abroad. We saw the civil rights campaign in the North as part of that international agenda, a genuine, worldwide liberating movement quite different from the old Nationalisms. By early 1969, I was back working in Dublin and seemed to spend most of my free time going from one demonstration to the other. As the campaign for the Republic's general election that summer gathered momentum, many of us working for the Labour Party thought that revolution was imminent. 'The Seventies will be Socialist' was the slogan. They weren't – instead the troubles began.

History isn't inevitable – the troubles didn't have to happen. The civil rights campaign did not have to become the IRA campaign. But, as we all know, it did. I have no insight into the minds of those directly involved but it seems almost certain to me that nobody foresaw what would happen, nobody planned it, nobody wanted it. A variety of forces such as the slowness of the state to introduce reform and the way it dealt with the crisis through repression (the only way the state seemed to know how) set the troubles in motion and kept refuelling them. By Bloody Sunday I was a student at UCD. I remember how shocked everyone was – the

inconceivable had happened. The university, like everything else in Dublin, closed down on the day of the funerals and there was an absolutely genuine and universally-felt day of 'national mourning'. I was at the British Embassy later that day when it was burned down in protest at what had happened in Derry. Nobody in the crowd objected.

For me, however, the worst period was during the hunger strikes. When Bobby Sands died I was in charge of the archaeological survey of County Donegal. I was staying in a beautiful hotel in the north of that beautiful county, enjoying everything that was best about Ireland: its food, drink, music, conviviality, hospitality, scenery, cultural and environmental heritage – everything that was brilliant about this country and living here. I couldn't help contrasting my experience of Ireland with what I imagined the life of Bobby Sands had been in this same country. And yet he had given his life in the most appalling manner for that Ireland. It still sends shudders down my spine. One thing is totally clear to me. Whether or not a united Ireland is a good thing, it cannot be brought into existence through violence. At best, violence is counterproductive.

A few years ago it occurred to me that I already live in a united Ireland, by which I mean that I live and carry on my life in every part of this island and with every community that lives on it. The border may be a hindrance, but it is not an obstacle and, even as a hindrance, its impact is being lessened every day. I believe that those of us who want some kind of unity can literally imagine ourselves into it – bringing it about through real relationships rather than symbolic ones. I think this is already happening. Growing up in a Nationalist environment in Dublin, I was led to imagine as a child that the unification of Ireland would be a process by which the 'South took over the North' – a process by which 'we got back what Britain had kept from us'. I find it interesting to note that in some respects things are now happening in reverse.

I work in the museum and heritage sector. I am fully aware that, despite the great popular interest in the past in this country, with negative as well as positive results, this is still a fairly marginal, non-central aspect of life. Nevertheless, one or two developments there seem to me to be indicative of the way things are moving. The Ulster Folk and Transport Museum, in the heart of comfortable Unionist north Down, has recently opened a magnificent new railway gallery. The building and exhibition is in effect an Irish national museum of railways. It isn't called that. It couldn't be called that, but that is what it is. The Northern Ireland Museums Council is a new quango based in Belfast. As a paid-for contract from the Irish Museums Association, it organises the all-Ireland museum of the year awards. The patron of these awards is President Mary Robinson who normally presents them at a glamorous ceremony in Dublin (often at Dublin Castle). In effect, a Northern Ireland official institution organises an event involving the president of Ireland.

Similar kinds of joint and cross-border projects are happening all over the place. In the arts, in broadcasting, in the environment, in tourism, in education, in business and commerce. The European situation is changing the picture anyway, as are economic developments and the current technological revolution. Political independence in today's world is a myth. The nation-state, whether we are talking about Ireland or the United Kingdom, is an anachronism (in spite of what is happening in the Balkans and Eastern Europe). Cross-border regionalisation is coming to the fore all over Europe.

For my own part, I find myself less and less concerned about what is called the 'constitutional' or 'border' issue. I don't think it is that urgent and I believe that in the fullness of time politics will solve it. What I *do* think is of greater urgency is the question of policing in Northern Ireland. If every single member of the RUC was a canonized saint, and to say the least they're not, there would still be problems. I believe they have been given a literally impossible job. Whatever about the past, as an existing institution they are part of the problem and are not suited for the new arrangements which must emerge. On two separate occasions the RUC have attempted to pressurise me as a gay man, unjustly if not actually illegally, into acting as an informer for them. On one of those occasions I believe they attempted to blackmail me, organising, illegally, an elaborate scenario for that purpose. If they will try that sort of thing with me I can only shudder about what I know they do with the unemployed, badly-educated, petty criminals from poor backgrounds. If this is the only way they can operate, then they have no business being in existence at all. There must be a new way of policing this society.

I am writing this at a time when alarm bells about the 'peace process' are being sounded everywhere. But there must be such a process and, sooner or later, it will bring about a solution. Hopefully, by the time this book is published, we will be a lot nearer that solution.

Paul Laughlin

Every political party routinely claims to seek peace and reconciliation in Ireland, yet no accommodation can be reached. Clearly, each must employ their own conflicting definitions of peace. There is, therefore, an urgent need to re-establish the meaning of peace.

According to the poet and critic Octavio Paz, writers and the literature they create cannot be separated from the broader social and political context in which they exist. In this, he is of course right. Words cannot exist in a vacuum any more than writers can write in isolation from the events which take place around them. Examining the failure of democracy in Latin America, Paz wrote 'when a society becomes corrupt, what first becomes gangrenous is language. Social criticism, therefore, begins with grammar and the re-establishment of meanings'.

In our own society, language has undeniably grown gangrenous from constant misuse in the pursuit of political advantage. Nowhere has this been more evident than in the use made of the words 'peace and reconciliation'. Every political party routinely claims to seek peace and reconciliation in Ireland, yet no accommodation can be reached. Clearly, each must employ their own conflicting definitions of peace. There is, therefore, an urgent need to re-establish the meaning of peace.

The absence of non-governmental violence is not the sole requisite for peace. Equally, those who merely canonize the will of the powerful, and demand that the dis-empowered and the marginalised should retreat into obedience and passivity, cannot be called peacemakers. Peace can never flourish alongside injustice and it cannot simply overwhelm conflict in some vague and unspecified fashion. Herein lies the essential failure of all those who hope to see a permanent end to violence in this society without rigorously analysing and addressing its underlying causes. An understanding of the con-

flict must, of necessity, preface any wider understanding which might secure a sustainable cessation of war.

The negation of democracy which preceded the enforced creation of a Northern Ireland sub-state remains the wellspring of this conflict. The shaky edifice of Unionist hegemony was built upon that singular act of violence, and thereafter the life of the sub-state could never move beyond a recurring cycle of repression and dissent. While Republicans must bear responsibility for their actions, Unionists cannot easily assume an attitude of moral superiority. The most sustained and bloody period of hostility in the history of this society was heralded by the outrageous suppression of the civil rights campaign. If Unionist misrule may not be seen to justify armed struggle, it most certainly helped bring it into existence.

Unionists now have a responsibility to confront the flawed character of an ideology which would not tolerate a very limited programme of reform in housing, employment and voting rights. The possibility of true reconciliation in Ireland depends as much upon that process of confrontation as on an end to violence.

Like peace, however, the word 'reconciliation' in Ireland has been greatly distorted by its assimilation into the vocabulary of politics. In a strictly theological context, reconciliation is not an absolute principle which must be applied in every case of conflict; each case must be examined in its own particular circumstances. Above all, however, injustice must be removed before reconciliation can take place. Theologians do not, and cannot, expect anyone to reconcile themselves to injustice or to their own oppression. Moreover, reconciliation can only take place following an expression of remorse by those guilty of wrongdoing. In summary, peace cannot exist without justice.

Viewed in this light, Unionism since the ceasefires is manifestly found wanting. No hint of regret has been offered for the long years of Unionist misrule. Where others are seeking through dialogue to create a pluralist society in which all are valued, Unionism bluntly refuses to move beyond a narrow, unachievable vision of an exhumed Stormont under which the Irish identity would again be submerged and uncelebrated. During the war, it was often asserted that violence was the main obstacle to a settlement. Following the ceasefires there are those who assert that violence was the only problem and what is required now is simply a return to majority rule. On the evidence of such thinking, it is regrettably apparent that Unionists have not committed themselves to any process of reconciliation; they merely continue to enunciate an unchanged demand for absolute power.

The pursuit of an unachievable position of supremacy cannot contribute to a durable peace. In articulating such a demand, Unionism demonstrates a failure to recognise the political realignments that have taken place in Ireland and Britain. After sixteen years of Tory rule, driven by monetarist dogma and Little England values, the concept of Britishness which Unionists claim to cherish has quite simply collapsed. Protestantism has become a minority religion to the extent that even the Prince of Wales now finds the link between it and the British crown untenable. The British royal family itself has become an embarrassment on an international scale, while Britain's industrial base dwindles inexorably in the face of foreign competition. The debate on the future governance of Scotland has called into question the constitutional structure and core identity of the UK. As this process of redefining Britain's political identity gathers pace, it becomes increasingly absurd for Unionist politicians to reiterate slogans now most commonly associated with English football hooligans and neo-fascists.

The ceasefires have presented opportunities and challenges to all the political forces in Ireland. A space has been opened in which a process of dialogue and fundamental change must take place. Unionists must decide if they are to be among the shapers or the victims of that change.

Donncha MacNiallais

The hunger strike was a traumatic experience for all of us, both inside the jail and outside. Ten men died, and at the end of the day we did not directly achieve what we considered to be the basis for a solution – the five demands – but what we did achieve was we broke, in the eyes of the world, the British myth that the people involved in the Republican struggle against British imperialism were somehow criminals, or were terrorists or were murderers.

Up until the advent of the civil rights movement I didn't have any real notion of the state. My father was unemployed, as were most Catholic men in the estate where I lived. I was born in the Bogside, raised in Creggan, and the whole situation in relation to nearly everyone in our street was that it was the accepted norm for the men to be unemployed and that many, but not all, of the women had factory jobs. With the advent of civil rights, you started to get a notion that the state was actively opposed to you as an individual, and opposed to the community you came from as a whole. You got the first murmurings of people being afraid of groups such as the RUC, the B Specials etc, and that these were forces that would at best be negative towards you and at worst do you harm.

We had very little contact with the Protestant community. There were Protestants who lived in Creggan, very few, but there were some, and there was never any sort of antagonism, either from them towards us, or from us towards them. We hung about together.

The civil rights movement did concentrate more on Nationalists, but that's because it was Nationalists who were being denied civil and human rights. If the state had embraced the concept of equality for all, then it would not have been seen as something that was Nationalistic. You hear nowadays people from the Protestant community talking about the bad housing they suffered, about the poor wages, about the lack of amenities, and you sort of wonder, well, that was OK, both communities suffered from deprivation;

but why did the Protestant community go on supporting the Unionist clique that ran the state when they were being treated so poorly? The idea that's grown up around us now, that somehow Protestants and Catholics suffered equally badly, is a myth. The simple fact of the matter is that the state looked after what it termed its own. It may not have looked after them the way they should have been looked after, in terms of good housing and in terms of amenities, but it still looked after them, in all sorts of ways.

I was eleven when the troubles began. At the time people felt that their community was being attacked, that their lives were in danger, and that they were going to have to defend their areas and their people with whatever they had, be it stones, bottles or petrol bombs. There was 100% support for that. The fact that it happened is regrettable because it could have been so easily avoided; the history of the state could have been so different if the Unionist government had said 'let's give these people equality'. People were not asking for privileges, they were asking for equality, and if they had received fair play at the time then history could have been so different.

There was a heightened sense of community in the aftermath of internment; people felt that here again was the state attacking the entire Nationalist community, and people were going to pull together. And people *did* do that. They did it in a number of ways: either through a rent and rates strike; joining the IRA, or, in their own small way, resisting any sort of British encroachment on their area. Internment was the thing that taught me what the state was about, and what the state would do in order to protect itself. Even though I was never interned, the introduction of internment would have been one of the greatest influences in my life.

I was in Glenfada Park when the shooting started on Bloody Sunday. I saw a number of people being shot at the barricade just in front of Rossville Street. It was a terrible situation to be in. It left people numbed and disbelieving because all along people really believed, and particularly so in Derry, that you could achieve change through political struggle, through non-violent protest. And the lesson of Bloody Sunday was that the British government would exact a heavy price if you wanted to engage in nonviolent protest, and people paid that price. Looking back on it now, what Widgery was about, what Bloody Sunday was about, was the British trying to show people who was boss in this country. Widgery was an attempt to cover that up and ensure that the British establishment didn't suffer any lasting infamy. The lesson for the future is that things like that don't work. You can shoot people and you can kill people, but there will always be others who will stand up for what they believe in. Some people will take it further and resort to physical force as a reactive measure, and that is increasingly what happened in Derry after Bloody Sunday.

The UWC strike had a minimal effect on us in Creggan. Obviously there was talk about power cuts etc, but I was sixteen at the time and we thought this was great – we are coming to the crux of the matter now, and these people are going to be doing this sort of thing but they are not going to break us. That was our attitude to it. Personally speaking, I did not have any regrets about the executive falling. At the time I didn't lend any support to it. But what it was, in hindsight, was a fascist overthrow of the first ever semblance of democracy within the six counties.

As a prisoner I was directly involved in the blanket and no-wash protests. It was a situation we were forced into by the British government. Most of the people involved in it were in their late teens or early twenties. We didn't, at the

outset of the protest, regard it as being historical. We regarded it solely as a means of achieving what we thought we were entitled to, which was political status. We never regarded ourselves at any time as being criminal, and we resented the fact that the British state was trying to portray us as such. The British then decided to try and break us, and they broke some people, but they didn't break all of us. At the end of the day, because the British were not prepared to be flexible in any way, there had to be a hunger strike. The hunger strike was a traumatic experience for all of us, both inside the jail and outside. Ten men died, and at the end of the day we did not directly achieve what we considered to be the basis for a solution – the five demands – but what we did achieve was we broke, in the eyes of the world, the British myth that the people involved in the Republican struggle against British imperialism were somehow criminals, or were terrorists or were murderers. That was broken once and for all, and in the aftermath of that we then went on to achieve the five demands. And that sprang directly from the hunger strike. The British knew at that stage that no matter what they did, they weren't going to break Republican prisoners.

Loyalist violence is not just a reaction to Republican violence. That is not only a myth, but a barefaced lie. Loyalist violence is fascist and terrorist. It's right-wing. If you look at it on a psychological basis, it's linked very closely to the death squads in South America and South Africa. In any areas of conflict where you have a radical revolutionary struggle you are always going to have a right-wing fascist tendency operating as a sort of secret arm of the state, prepared to carry out what the state does not want to openly carry out, and that is what Loyalists have been doing for years. They have been going out and butchering Catholics, and they are not really interested in whether that Catholic is a member of the IRA, a member of Sinn Féin, the SDLP, a trade unionist, or even a practising Catholic. All they are interested in is that that person is a Catholic, and they are prepared to kill him or her in order to try and terrorise the entire Catholic/Nationalist community into accepting what they want us to accept, which is second-class citizenship in a state that is a gerrymander.

The violence used by the state is obviously the state protecting itself against what it sees as a threat to its existence. Obviously the first threat to its existence since its foundation was the civil rights movement which was asking for equality; the state was founded on discrimination; and because it was founded on discrimination it could not grant equality; and so it had to deal with people who were demanding it. And it dealt with that demand in the only way it knew how, and that was through violence, and that has been the case ever since. The violence which is reactive is actually IRA violence. IRA violence is reactive to the oppression of the state and to the fact that the political process has never worked.

At the time of the IRA ceasefire, I felt very strongly supportive of it. I considered it to be a very honourable and very courageous step to take. Given the history of the last twenty-five years, given that the IRA wasn't defeated, the IRA, by calling a cessation of military operations, was saying to me, to the people that live in this area, to the Unionists, to the people of Ireland as a whole, to the people of Britain, and to the wider European and world communities, that there was another way forward, that it didn't always have to entail armed struggle or armed conflict, and that you could actually make political progress through dialogue and consensus. That was the hope that was contained in the statement of 31 August 1994. Since then, the whole situation, the whole process, has been very backward in terms of British government engagement.

In relation to the Loyalist ceasefire, I remember talking to someone a day or two after the IRA ceasefire, and they asked me what I thought would happen if Loyalist killings continued, and I said that the Loyalists would stop whenever the British told them to stop, and that the British are going to tell them to stop very soon because the British can control what they do, and the Loyalists know that. Whether the UDA and UVF are directly controlled by British intelligence, no-

one knows, but you can bet your bottom dollar they are up to their eyeballs in it.

The ceasefires have presented an opportunity for people – political parties and individuals alike – to reach agreement for the first time in many hundreds of years on how this island is governed. There was never agreement about partition from the people of Ireland, not even from the people of the six counties. Partition was presented as a *fait accompli* by the British government. What we have now is an opportunity to try and reach some form of agreement. We might not all get all that we want out of that agreement, but at least we have an opportunity to try. The only way that can be done is if people sit down and talk. The people who are refusing to sit down and talk, what are they actually saying? What they are saying is that they are not interested in reaching agreement, what they are interested in doing is maintaining the *status quo*. The *status quo* is a failure. It didn't work in the past, it's not working now, and it's not going to work in the future. It has always had to be maintained by force, and what that leads to is a reaction to that force. If that's what the British government and the Unionists want, then I just don't understand them at all.

I'd like to see us all sitting at the table and reaching an agreement. That agreement doesn't have to mean people come away from the table having agreed to some sort of concept or form of government which is going to last forever, but what it does mean is that people can then go away and present their own political viewpoint in a way that maybe can effect change in the future. Because that was part of the problem in the past – people have never believed in the political process, it has never worked, and what we need to do is to positively inject some sort of hope into people's mindsets that the political process can work. If people are not prepared to try and reach that accommodation with each other, then they are sowing the seeds of conflict, and I think that now, regrettably, what we are looking at is renewed conflict at some stage in the future.

An anti-internment march makes its way down William Street on 30 January 1972 – Bloody Sunday. *(Photo: Gilles Perres/Bloody Sunday Justice Campaign)*

Members of the First Battalion, The Parachute Regiment, positioned in the William Street / Little James Street area. *(Photos: Magee College)*

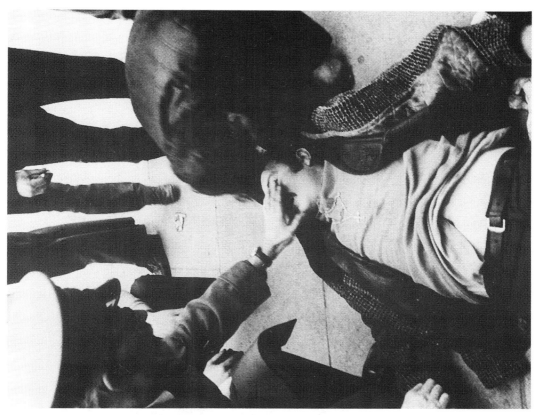

Patrick Doherty, a thirty-one-year-old father of six, shot dead outside the high flats in Rossville Street. *(Photos: Gilles Perres/Bloody Sunday Justice Campaign)*

Jackie Duddy, one of seven teenagers killed on Bloody Sunday, tended by Fr Edward Daly and a member of the Knights of Malta first aid group. *(Photo: Magee College)*

St Mary's Church, Creggan, 2 February 1972. Thirteen coffins line the altar three days after Bloody Sunday. (Photo: Seamus Heaney/Derry Journal)

Pat
McArt

The war was twenty miles up the road, particularly if you lived in Letterkenny, and you were always waiting for what was going to happen next; was a bomb going to go off, were the Loyalists going to come out? We didn't have a role in it, we were only bystanders.

I am from the South, from Letterkenny in County Donegal. I remember coming to Derry in my early teenage years and seeing all the things that reminded me of an English town. Donegal was a very different place from Derry. The border was like the Atlantic Ocean, you had to cross it to get into Northern Ireland. So Northern Ireland for me was a very strange place. It wasn't like Ireland at all. I remember being aware of the tensions in the North and I remember hearing all these things about Catholics and Protestants. I also remember the attitude of the RUC when you were stopped and you were Southern Irish. They weren't particularly nice. It was a different lifestyle, different feel, different aspect of life. I don't know what you would like to call it, but Letterkenny was one way and Derry was another.

I remember watching the TV film of the trouble on 5 October 1968, and saying to myself 'Jesus, that's going on up the road'. That was a major shock. My learning curve took off at an accelerated rate that night. After that, I remember a lot of Derry people coming to stay in and around Letterkenny. The Irish army, after Jack Lynch's famous statement 'we will not stand idly by', also arrived in the area and I remember guys from Athlone and Mullingar who were suddenly moved up into Letterkenny. Older members of my family were in the nursing profession and they told me about lots of young people from Derry coming up to Letterkenny Hospital for treatment after the riots because they wouldn't go to Altnagelvin Hospital.

I totally supported the civil rights movement, and I remember thinking it was grossly unfair that, in this day and age, some people were not allowed to vote while others had two votes be-

cause they owned a shop or something. I took a lot of interest in the situation and felt a great affinity with the Nationalist people in the North in those days. At the time, it was a major issue in Letterkenny. I had a job in a bar and it totally dominated all conversation.

A lot of people were very frightened in the early days of the troubles. The war was twenty miles up the road, particularly if you lived in Letterkenny, and you were always waiting for what was going to happen next; was a bomb going to go off, were the Loyalists going to come out? We didn't have a role in it, we were only bystanders. I remember as well in the early days guys from Letterkenny going in to Derry to take part in rioting and all the rest, there was a bit of 'high jinks' as they would say in some of these marvellous English novels. But by about '70 it got a lot more serious. Up until then the police and troops were raiding houses and beating the crap out of people, but there weren't too many people dying. By about 1971, however, it had become very serious indeed because the death rate was starting to rise.

Internment was easily the worst decision the British government ever made during the twenty-five years of the troubles. The way it was introduced, the way people were arrested, the treatment subsequently meted out to the internees ... that was supposed to be a civilized government? Stories of ill-treatment started to seep back. Some of them could possibly be dismissed as Republican propaganda, but certainly not all. The internees were actually tortured, and the British were later found guilty of inhuman treatment in the European courts.

But I suppose there was another aspect of it

as well. The social instability frightened a lot of people down South. It certainly frightened the politicians. There were a lot of hardline Republicans then, and they started talking about how they wouldn't stop when they got the British out, how they wanted a Republican, or Socialist, Ireland, and I think their uncompromising language and stance, which of course had been shaped by the political situation in the North, alienated a lot of people in the South who didn't like a lot of 'Northerners' coming down and telling them what sort of society they should have.

Bloody Sunday, for me, was nearly inevitable after internment. I think somebody, somewhere, had made a decision that they were going to teach these civil rights people a lesson. Everyone knew, the British army included, that the IRA was not going to use this march as a front. The world's cameras were there, the world's media was there. This was a huge march, they were there to show the depth of feeling against internment. If you watch the television footage, the army claimed they came under attack, but you can see that the soldiers are actually standing out in the open. A professional soldier is taught to take cover. These soldiers are standing out shooting, quite openly. It was quite obvious that nobody was shooting at them. They were certain nobody was shooting at them. The coroner, Hubert O'Neill, who was a former British officer himself, said it was sheer bloody murder. And there is no doubt about it, it *was* sheer bloody murder, and I know one prominent Loyalist in this town who agrees totally that it was murder.

On a personal level, I thought the fall of Stormont was inevitable. I also thought it was a very good thing. I think the Unionist people have a genuine cause, they have been in Ireland for 300 years, and to turn round now and say to those people 'right, clear off back to England', I think that's a bit simplistic and a bit stupid. But there is another side to the story. The native Irish have also got rights which the Stormont government totally ignored for fifty years. There had to be some sort of an accommodation, and Stormont was not, by any stretch of the imagination, an attempt at accommodation. That was sheer domination and it made no attempt whatsoever to

acknowledge the rights of the Nationalist people. As far as I was concerned, Stormont was a cancer in Irish society, or Northern Irish society, and the quicker Stormont went, the better.

I remember there was serious intimidation during the UWC strike, and to this day I always think that had the British government shown a bit more resolve then we would have been on the road to a solution. When I hear people talking now about Sinn Féin and the IRA and about coercion, I didn't see the British government standing up too much to Loyalism, which was a lot more offensive in a way. What was so unfair about giving the 40% Nationalist population a democratic right or say in an assembly in the place in which they lived? That doesn't strike me as being a major concession, it should be a right in any society.

The hunger strikes marked the final alienation of the Nationalist people. Internment, Bloody Sunday, it had all built up, and by the time the hunger strikes came along they weren't going to accept anything to do with the British government. The whole situation got very internationalised after that and I think everybody knew then that there was no turning back.

It's not a very popular thing to say, but I can actually see why people turn to violence. I'm a pacifist, I genuinely am. I've never voted for Sinn Féin for one reason, because of violence. But having said that, I can understand it. If I had grown up in Derry or West Belfast in the late '60s, and had seen what was going on, who knows what I would have done? I have also considerable sympathy for Loyalists, young Loyalists living in places like East Belfast. It's fear and anger that make people turn to violence – that's where politicians are failing. They are all very good at adopting the position they think will keep them elected, not going out on a limb and actually doing something.

I was very, very happy at the time the ceasefires were announced. I don't think violence solves problems, I genuinely don't. It just repeats itself, and repeats itself.

It's over a year now since the ceasefires were announced and I feel that the British government is acting in serious bad faith. It has slowed the peace process, for its own ends, to almost a snail's pace. It needs Unionist votes at Westminster, and holding on to power is much more important than actually finding a solution. This is easily the best chance in a generation to find one. If the ceasefire breaks down we may end up with something close to a Bosnian situation here between Catholics and Protestants. So here is a great chance for a real solution, a chance to make something worthwhile, but, so far, nothing.

The IRA and the Republican leadership have stated categorically that they are willing to make major concessions on decommissioning in the event of all-party talks, but they are simply not willing to go into those all-party talks with this sort of 'surrender' language. In other words, it's the structure, not the substance, of the talks that is the problem. If they dropped the demand for decommissioning you would have all-party talks and the IRA would be talking about decommissioning. It's a procedural row, the substantive issue is not being dealt with and the peace process could go into decline on the basis of that sort of approach. I can understand totally why Martin McGuinness and Gerry Adams are taking this line. There is historical baggage here. There are precedents in Irish history where Irish people have accepted British good faith only to be duped

at a later date. The report of the Boundary Commission in 1924/25 was simply ignored after the six-county state was set up. If you go through history you will find plenty of examples. There is a fear of British bad faith again, especially among Republicans. There is absolutely no real movement whatsoever. They have removed army checkpoints and the Rosemount watchtower, but now they have put up another mast with even more cameras. That is an insult to people's intelligence. Those are not real moves. I was talking to an RUC man I know quite well recently and even *he* thought the British should be moving much quicker.

I would like to see all-party talks, and these stupid preconditions dropped. The Unionists are seriously running away from talks, Trimble and all the rest. They are trying to find an internal solution again with a Northern Ireland assembly. It isn't going to work. I would like to see politicians start discussions and come to some sort of an agreement. That's their job, that's what they are getting their salaries for. Isn't politics the art of the possible? If everyone keeps adopting the stance that they're not going to agree on anything in case it weakens their position, then there's going to be no solution. I am not optimistic.

Nell McCafferty

...even though people are clearly against the ceasefire ending, they are still in that moral dilemma of what do you do about your own people? I was very conscious of it when I was over in Jerusalem recently. Once Hammas started the suicide bombings the Palestinians saw their peace and their prospects for freedom slip away, but found it difficult to turn on their own people. I feel the same way about the IRA.

In as much as I had any feelings at all about what was going on in Northern Ireland when I was young, I knew that I was reared for emigration. That was my future as an educated person from a Catholic background, that there would be no jobs for the likes of me unless I went into the Catholic school-teaching system. Basically I knew, I was reared with the belief, that I would not be spending my life in Derry. Of the people from Queen's who graduated, of my class, my generation from Derry, only a few tried to stay in town. Of all the women I went to Queen's with I was the only one who stayed in Derry, everyone else emigrated to Canada, to America, South Africa, to England and, now that I think about it, all of the men, except for Eamonn McCann. I think it's a very telling fact of growing up in Northern Ireland that we all had to leave home. I wasn't really aware of why this was going on. I mean, I was a happy child, I was a happy schoolchild, I was a happy student, until graduation day, when I looked emigration in the face.

I felt, as regards Northern Ireland generally, it was like looking through a window. On the other side were the Unionists who had nothing to do with me really. I belonged to Derry but not to Northern Ireland, and I didn't belong to Ireland because I was reared to be British. And it nearly worked. When I really began to feel anger and contempt for Unionists was when my brothers and sisters started getting married, and then the search was on for a house for them and I, like all the members of my family, did the rounds of city councillors on their behalf. I went

to Catholic and Protestant, or what were called Nationalist and Unionist, councillors, and got the same hopeless message from them all: join the waiting list, a wait of maybe five or ten years. And then I saw my brother get married and rent a slum flat, and that was to be their future. That was the early '60s.

When the civil rights movement emerged I felt it was a new day dawning. Delighted is too mild a word, I was full of joy that finally we had struck back. At that stage it was the housing crisis which fuelled my emotions, having seen in my own family that once you got married in Derry 'there was no room at the inn', and you would have to pile in on top of your own, and bring your spouse back into your parents' home. It got on all our nerves that several families would be crammed into one house, so I joined the Derry Labour Party which was engaged in housing agitation at the time, and the situation got worse for me because then I really saw slum dwellers and realised that my family was actually very well off in terms of accommodation. So when the civil rights movement started I jumped in and swam around, happy as a fish in a pond.

There was a certain sinister glamour to the militancy of the establishment reaction to the civil rights movement. Police coming down the street with batons ... I felt like a pioneer in the wild west really, I knew we would win. I felt first class for the first time in my life, a first-class citizen and they were the political bums. It was wonderful, it was wonderful to throw stones at what was clearly the enemy. It brought them down out of their ivory towers. I could walk through my own streets at night, in the middle of the night, in my city which I now controlled. It was terrific.

I was a bit frightened at the start of the 'Battle of the Bogside', but not all that much. Within a couple of hours it was quite clear that we could keep them out, and I was really fairly unaware of what was happening in Belfast, we were all so absorbed in our own wee battle which was all we saw. I enjoyed it. I enjoyed seeing the police being put off the streets. I was delighted when I saw the army come in, but then I had to listen to Bernadette Devlin and Eamonn McCann explain why it was a bad thing for the British army to be there. I didn't see why it was bad because we had heard that the B Specials were coming, and I was glad to see the RUC withdraw. The first night the army was there, the first night of alleged liberation, the army put up their own barricades and created a little canvas tunnel through which we had to walk to get out of the Bogside. We had to sign a little book, and a wiser person than I would have realised, would have foreseen the future. I didn't, I was a bit taken aback, and then I treated it as something amusing. I remember signing the book as Constance Markiewicz, then I made a point of going in and out of the Bogside all night and signing my name in Irish or French, thinking that this was easy, taking care of the army. Then internment came, and I was stunned as the repression deepened, but I still thought we would win.

I felt numb after Bloody Sunday. Stunned. Apart from falling in love, it was the single most significant factor in my life, to realise that a government would have its own citizens shot by an army, because at the time we were, after all, British citizens. I still don't understand what happened. I still don't understand why they did it. I would love to know. I just took the Widgery Report as being par for the course. It was, of course, barefaced lies, but by then I understood politics rather better than I had before. I was no longer a political innocent, that all died on Bloody Sunday. I knew then that they would kill, that they would lie, to achieve their own ends.

When Stormont fell I was delighted that it had gone, and full of self-congratulation that it

had only taken four years, less than four years, to bring down the primary institution of the state, of the Northern state that had lasted for seventy-one years. And I regret to say that even then I had, despite Bloody Sunday, some innocent hope that Britain would now do what the Unionists had not done, would give us all first-class citizenship. How wrong I was.

The British government suffers from a multitude of handicaps. Depending on the situation at the time they have been shown either not to know what is going on, or not to care what is going on, or to be manipulative and devious. This is very strange language to use about a government, allegedly your own government, that the people who rule you are people who will murder you, lie about you, put you in jail if necessary. The people of Northern Ireland, particularly Nationalists – the Unionists don't seem to have cottoned on to this – the Nationalists of Northern Ireland are a people marked apart in this world, as are the blacks in South Africa, as are the Palestinians, as were the Jews, we are special people. Our government would kill us at the drop of a hat to serve its own ends. It is an amazing thing to state that and to realise that that is part of what you are and who you are. We are marked, we are special, we are different.

Up until recent times the Dublin government has stayed apart. I could see why; they didn't really believe that Northern Ireland belonged to them and they didn't know who to shoot, so they stayed offside. And I think also we didn't help them. I was part of the Socialist school in Northern Ireland and I suppose the Republican school which went around singing 'take it down from the mast, Irish traitors'. It's one of the great ironies of the situation that those of us who had decided that the only answer was a united Ireland treated the people and the institutions of the Free State with such contempt, and still do. Just as we say the British government doesn't understand us it is quite clear that we don't understand the South either. The ignorance in Northern Ireland about the Republic of Ireland is vast, there is a huge gulf between the two, and while insisting that Ireland should be united in some form we are doing to the South what Unionists are doing to Northern Ireland Nationalists, what the

British are doing to *all* the people of the North. We would like the country but without the people in it. But lately the Southern government, now that the fighting is over and they have had twenty-five years experience, they are behaving, on the whole, quite well, or they were until the ceasefire broke down, when they ran for cover again.

I am not a pacifist. People have the right to defend themselves, or to go on the offensive. I think the IRA campaign was legitimate, although it took me all of seventeen years to acknowledge that to myself and to confirm it in public. In the early '70s I was deeply opposed to the IRA. I thought we could have continued with unarmed struggle, the civil rights way, and the IRA that I knew then was, to my mind, a bunch of young macho cowboys, and I saw them behaving as such; mainly the Official IRA, I have to say, as I was more in contact with them because they shared some kind of alleged Socialist perspective. But I opposed them, and then as the conflict deepened and I got drawn in, as Britain behaved with more and more repression and refusal to grant us proper citizenship, absolute refusal to grant our reasonable demands, I came to the conclusion that armed struggle was justified. One of the reasons I say that is because, again with my Socialist background, I had been adopting this dodgy position of, I think it's called critical support. Certain activities of the IRA were justified, and others were not. It is acceptable that one can kill a British soldier but unacceptable to plant bombs or to shoot Protestant working men, as happened at Teebane when eight were killed in 1992. But then I decided that was an immoral position to take, that once you put a gun into someone's hand, or give them the right to use a gun, then you must accept responsibility for what they do, both good and bad, moral and immoral, or whatever the words are that apply in the Geneva Convention, and I decided that the Socialist view was immoral, and that you had to take responsibility for everything the IRA did, and so I did.

I wouldn't even dignify the claim that Loyalist violence is just a reaction to Republican violence with a discussion of their point of view. They are an extra-military arm of the state, be

that state a Unionist state or a British government state. I would always admit that they frightened the life out of me. The one thing I dreaded all through the troubles was ever to fall into Loyalist hands, not because I was in any way a prominent figure, but just as a person who had been reared in the Catholic culture. I dreaded being caught by Loyalists, especially the Shankill Butchers. They put the fear of God in a person the way they would torture you. They were the single most frightening element in the last twenty-five years of the troubles. I was relieved when the IRA shot a few of them, and when the rest of them went to jail.

Technically speaking, the British were wrong to shoot the IRA in Gibraltar, and technically speaking they were wrong in Loughall, but you expect these dirty tricks in a war. The one thing the British did which put themselves beyond the pale of civility was Bloody Sunday. That was unadulterated, unambiguous state terror. It stands out above all the things the British ever did.

I felt wonderful when the ceasefire was called. I had believed for a couple of years that armed struggle at that stage was becoming counterproductive, that the British were ready now to do the deal, and that help was at hand in the pan-Nationalist front. It was a wonderful day when the ceasefire came. I thought it was a very brave thing for the IRA to do, and visionary of Sinn Féin. They couldn't have done it of course without the help of the man himself, John Hume. I, like thousands of others, have had years of harmless pleasure in criticising John, but I salute him now, where would we be without him? It was a great day, the day of the ceasefire, and I understood that of course they couldn't declare it permanent, you can't speak for the next generation, you can't even surrender yourself in advance, but I believed it was. I knew tactically why the IRA wouldn't say that it was permanent, but I believed they would never shoot again. Wrong as ever, brilliant political analyst that I am.

After the ceasefire I thought we were going to have to learn to swallow every insult. We have been down that road before, with the Unionists, we are going to go down that road now with the British, we will have to take the long-term view and be patient. I believe the British want to disengage, that there will be an agreed Ireland, and that one day the British will force the Unionists to the negotiating table. We should have been patient.

I burst into tears when I heard that the ceasefire was over. In the succeeding forty-eight hours, in the succeeding week, a close friend took me aside and told me I was being hysterical, literally hysterical. She told me that I should go into a dark room and lie down for a week, that this would pass, that we would not be going back to full-scale war. I was interested in the moral dilemma because, although most people were against the IRA action, they couldn't go out into the streets and protest against them because then we would be marching in support of David Trimble and John Major. We couldn't very well, on the other hand, stay at home, because that would be giving tacit support to the IRA, so I talked about it a lot with people; what are we going to do? We can't let the IRA dictate our lives, especially if we think they are wrong, and I think even though people are clearly against the ceasefire ending, they are still in that moral dilemma of what do you do about your own people? I was very conscious of it when I was over in Jerusalem recently. Once Hammas started the suicide bombings the Palestinians saw their peace and their prospects for freedom slip away, but found it difficult to turn on their own people. I feel the same way about the IRA.

Having thought about it for a while, I am now getting it clear in my mind, I am now going to say publicly that the IRA are wrong. A new ceasefire should be instituted straight away. They don't have to say it is permanent. The bomb was wrong, it was a disaster, it was foolish. But then of course when it became clear that the London bombing had actually worked, and had forced Britain to give a date for the start of talks, then I said 'wasn't I wrong again, weren't the IRA right to break the ceasefire?' Isn't Northern Ireland full of ambiguous delights? Having got their date, they should have reinstated the ceasefire at once. The date for talks should have been announced the day after the ceasefire was first called, but there you are, you are dealing with Britain. It beholds us to know our history well, that these things take time.

I think the IRA should immediately declare a new ceasefire. The language of the British is interesting and clever at this stage, and careful. They are not saying that they want the next ceasefire to be declared permanent, they use vague phrases like 'for good'. I think the IRA should reinstate the ceasefire at once. Republicans should enter into the negotiations on 10 June, accept that it is going to take another fifteen years of political torture and turning of the screw, and be confident the outcome will be an agreed Ireland. Another big reason I would have for welcoming a ceasefire and immediate all-party negotiations is that the sooner all those *men* are locked away in a room chattering amongst themselves, the sooner the rest of us can get on with shaping an Ireland that will reflect our heart's desire, in other words the day of the woman will have come, and we can all then take over the North and co-operate with the South and with Britain ... the feminist dimension, such as has obtained in the South since 1970.

I wish you had asked me how I felt as a woman through all of this. A few days after the first civil rights march was batoned off the streets in Derry a meeting of all the city elders, and youngers, was called on the Monday night, and out of that the Derry Citizens Action Committee was formed. The 5 October march had been staged by the Derry Labour Party, under Eamonn McCann, so they all gathered for a meeting in the City Hotel, and it was understood that women were not invited. It was not that we were told *not* to come, but we weren't *asked* to come, and I remember standing outside the hotel with a friend of mine, also a school teacher, a woman, and we were too shy to go in. We were trying to rev each other up, saying we had as much right to go in there as anyone else, but such was the climate of those times, those days of long ago, that a woman would have looked odd and out of place, so we didn't go in, and I felt lonely outside as I watched people who were politically illiterate, pillars of the establishment, the Catholic establishment, troop up the steps. Men, all men, including my own comrades from the Derry Labour Party, with whom I had worked, and nobody ever said to me 'are you coming in?' It was understood to be a male-only club. I think there was one woman there that night who may have been there as a wife, Sheila McGuinness, but good for her, at least she stuck her neck out, and she was given the job, because she was an artist, of designing the civil rights logo. That was the only tangible contribution of women there, even though women were heavily involved at all levels, either as marchers, as fighters, as activists, as members of political parties in Derry. We were back-room people.

And thus it has continued in the last twenty-five years. To rephrase Churchill's great statement about 'the waters receding and the dreary steeples emerging, the integrity of their quarrel intact', the integrity of Northern Ireland male chauvinism has remained intact despite the fact that throughout literally the rest of the globe, feminism has changed the mind of the world. Northern Ireland has remained relatively impervious to it. Not because it is a backward place, but because we don't have proper political institutions here which can be influenced or made to pass laws outlawing discrimination against women, for various reasons which I won't go into here.

Northern Ireland has remained untouched by feminism, but the women's groups are starting up, are there, are in place, they just haven't had a chance to raise their banner. Once the all-party talks start those women will come to the fore. They have already made the links with the South and they are conscious of what is going on in Britain. I have spent the last twenty years in Dublin working, even though I am in Derry all the time, and I haven't been as lonely as I might have been had I remained living in the North looking through the window at feminism around the world.

Eamonn McCann

I was not in favour ... of the alternative to the armed struggle which was put in place ie the alliance between the Republican movement, Sinn Féin, the Dublin government and corporate America. I saw it as one which was inimical to work-ing-class interests, and one which was going to lead to political compromise of a sort which was unnecessary ...

In the period leading up to the emergence of the civil rights movement, it seemed to a lot of people, including myself, that the whole nature of Northern Ireland politics was changing, and that the question of the border was becoming increasingly irrelevant. The Catholic community had instead begun to see its future as finding equal citizenship within the state. It also seemed to many of us that the whole attitude of Britain to the North was undergoing a fundamental change; that Britain was no longer simply taking the Unionist line and defending partition, as a result of serious economic changes mainly; with investment in the South of Ireland, the declining nature of the Northern economy and so forth. It appeared that Britain was now more inclined to balance between the Orange and the Green rather than just line up with the Orange side. It seemed to many of us that there was an opportunity of breaking the sectarian logjam here, and that the issue of equal rights, civil rights, for the Catholic community could be a key question which would transform the nature of Northern politics and end the sectarianism.

At Queen's University, where I had been in the early '60s, there were very large numbers of Protestant students who were quite enthusiastic about this project and who genuinely had no time at all for the sectarianism of the Unionist Party and the Orange Order. So the coalition that vaguely came together was one representative of the Catholic community with radical young Protestants, and also, very importantly, the trade union movement which had begun to get more involved in these issues. It was a time of great

hope and expectation, fuelled by Terence O'Neill having become Prime Minister and seeming to promise some sort of change.

It's difficult to tell in retrospect at what point it began to become clear that this whole project for transforming Northern Ireland into a more rational political society, through the aegis of the civil rights movement, was becoming unstuck. It ought to have been obvious from a fairly early stage that, even physically, the demonstrations came to be located in the Catholic community, and that the reaction of the police was to drive them back into the Catholic community. So even physically you could see the re-sectarianising, if there is such a word, of political struggle happening before our eyes, and I don't think anybody was prepared for it. Certainly I wasn't, and the Socialist optimism of a lot of people like myself was very speedily disillusioned. I suppose by about 1969, the truth was beginning to seep into a lot of people, but I don't think that ideologically, or in terms of our political perspectives at the time, we were capable of actually handling the way things were changing.

I think the state has to bear the major responsibility for pushing the civil rights movement into a Nationalist cul-de-sac. You can also blame all the people involved in the leadership of the civil rights movement, including at that period myself, for not seeing more quickly what was happening and not being more ready with a response when it did happen. There is no doubt at all that the instinctive response of the state was to treat the civil rights movement as a movement of Catholic militancy, and the slogan 'CRA equals IRA', which began to appear on gable walls, reflected not just the attitude of Paisleyites at the time but also the official attitude of the state in the shape of the Home Secretary, William Craig, for some of that period, and also the RUC. The RUC was nakedly sectarian and they clearly made no differentiation between students marching for 'one person one vote' and decent housing and all the rest of it, and people who were out to destroy the state and create a united Ireland.

I was ambivalent about the outbreak of violence, I suppose, like most of the other people who were around at the time. I wasn't a naturally violent person, and it has to be remembered of course that while street riots and exchanges of CS gas on one side, and petrol bombs and stones on the other, may seem small beer from the perspective of 1995 because we have come through a war in which over 3,000 people have died, at the time it was very traumatic and certainly was more vivid violence than anything that we had witnessed in our lifetime. And therefore it was shocking, it was frightening, but it also was, for me, exhilarating. It was extremely exciting to be involved in the war zone because as nobody had died at that point, at least in the initial riots, the idea that this might lead to actual death, and grief, and the shattering of happiness that would go with that didn't occur to us, so you could have the excitement of being involved in mass violence without, at that stage, the consequences which we now know were to flow from it. But I also took the view in August '69, especially since what was happening was an attempt by the RUC, with Loyalist civilians mingling among them, to invade the Bogside and to do violence to the people there, that they were very simple issues.

However much we didn't want the thing to take the sectarian shape of the communal divisions of Northern Ireland society, nevertheless a simple question which was posed was the right of the Bogside community to defend itself against physical attack. I had no problem about doing that for the Bogside. Neither had I a problem politically, and more generally, of saying that in those circumstances we had to stand by and be involved with the people of the Bogside in resisting this aggression against the community. So,

like everybody else, I joined in the defence of the Bogside and the rioting associated with it. Again, the consequences of it, which now appear to be obvious looking back, I don't think occurred to many of us at the time, even as late as the end of 1969 when British soldiers were already on the streets and there had been a number of deaths and so on. It was still only a tiny minority of people, who were disregarded at the time, who were forecasting that this was going to lead to the type of all-out horrendous struggle that we saw in subsequent years.

The first thing about Bloody Sunday itself was that, even as you observed it happening, it was difficult to believe. Even somebody like myself, who would have styled himself as a Socialist revolutionary at the time, and who had talked about the ruthless and murderous nature of imperialism and so forth, had never quite anticipated seeing this sort of thing on the streets where I had been brought up. And also on the day, it seemed ludicrous that the British army were actually killing people, because absolutely nothing had happened that day to justify this in any terms whatsoever. There was the makings of a standard-issue Derry riot, of which we had seen dozens in the previous couple of years, but the idea that they were actually prepared to shoot people and kill them seemed too weird to take seriously. I can recall even lying in Rossville Street, and I actually saw a couple of people being shot outside Rossville flats, and at the time it simply didn't occur to me that what was happening was that these people were being killed. So I was numbed by the sheer awesome extent of the British army's violence for a time. After that, the immediate reaction of the days following wasn't a rational political response in many ways; it was a reaction of grief and tremendous rage and a thirst for revenge, and an understanding that this had transformed things utterly. I think that everybody knew in the area, and I think perhaps in the world, that something of a most tremendous significance had happened in and around Rossville Street that day. The appointment of Widgery two days after Bloody Sunday – Widgery was, after all, the Lord Chief Justice of the land and the highest legal figure who could have been appointed to carry out an inquiry –

seemed to indicate to some that the British were taking it seriously, and at the very least we should wait for Lord Widgery's Report before drawing final conclusions about the role of the British state in the killings and the reaction of the British state to the killings.

The Widgery Report itself was as politically significant as the actual events of Bloody Sunday, in the sense that until Widgery published the report it was possible to say that Bloody Sunday had happened as a result of the parachute regiment going berserk, or the parachute regiment acting in a way which didn't reflect the overall British attitude to the civil rights movement and to the crisis in Northern Ireland. But Widgery came out and whitewashed what had happened and, in effect, exonerated the Parachute Regiment, and once that report was accepted by the British parliament, then it was quite clear that there was no point in seeking redress for the grievances of the Bogside and of the Catholic community generally, and for politically disadvantaged people generally in the North of Ireland. There were no rational grounds for believing that you could seek that sort of redress within the constitutional process laid down by the British state. This was the Lord Chief Justice of the land, there was no appeal against that in the parliament of Britain which had accepted his report. So when people said 'behave within the rules and seek a constitutional solution for your problems', it wasn't just an atavistic response or an emotional response on the part of the people who said 'no, we now want to bring down the state'. It was actually a perfectly rational response to what had happened. It may not be the *only* possible rational response, but the point I'm making is that joining the IRA in the aftermath of Bloody Sunday and the publication of the Widgery Report was a rational, intellectual response to what had happened on the streets of Derry. In that way Bloody Sunday and the Widgery Report transformed the whole axis of the political discussion in the North of Ireland and we are living with that still.

The UWC strike was a very interesting event, rich in political lessons, not all of which were as they have been drawn. There is one lesson which isn't usually drawn in the North of Ireland, and

it's to do with the power of the working class. It has to be remembered that the UWC strike is the one instance in the whole of the last twenty-five years when some group of people here managed to change, radically change, official British policy in the North. Official British policy in the North, supported by all parties at Westminster, was that the power-sharing executive, with the Council of Ireland, was the best way forward, and all the majesty and might of the British state was deployed, supposedly, to uphold that policy. In eleven days the UWC strike forced the Wilson government to abandon that policy, to abandon the power-sharing executive and to abandon the Council of Ireland, and the entire strategy of the British government, negotiated of course with the Southern government, collapsed because the British state proved unable to withstand this mass industrial action. It was mass industrial action brought about, partly at least, by the use of vicious intimidation of Protestant workers. It was straight-forward intimidation which brought out Coolkeeragh Power Station. In Belfast the UDA actually threatened people, so it wasn't that the entire Protestant workforce suddenly decided to stop work as a tactic. They were forced out. Nevertheless it was that withdrawal of labour, for whatever reason, and under whatever pressures, which actually forced a change in British government policy. It's interesting that armed struggle has never done that, and parliamentary activity has never done that either. So there is a message there about where *real* power lies to change government policy.

The other point is that the attempt to compromise the constitutional position, which was involved primarily in the establishment of a Council of Ireland, united all factions within Unionism behind the policy of 'not-an-inch'. The UWC refused to have anything to do with the Council, and it was really the beginnings of what since has been a stalemate in Northern Ireland. There have been, in fact, two communal vetoes involved, and nothing can be done really which the Catholic community here is adamantly unwilling to accept, and nothing can be done either which the Protestant community is adamantly unwilling to accept. Therein lies the reason for the insolubility of the Northern Ireland question, when it's posed in communal terms. I think also the other lesson I remember from the time was that the readiness of constitutional Unionist politicians to associate themselves with paramilitaries, and to march with masked paramilitaries, also exposed constitutional Unionism for what it is, not a legitimate political formation in the sense of European democracy but the leadership of a particular community whose interests it is ready to defend by whatever means are necessary. Whether they really represent the interests of that community, of course, is an entirely separate question.

The success of the UWC strike was specifically as a result of sectarian patterns of recruitment. The workforce in the power industry was overwhelmingly Protestant which was absolutely crucial to the strike. The fact that they were able to pull out Ballylumford, Kilroot and then Coolkeeragh – the major power installations in the North – was absolutely crucial to them. It meant, for example, that many people in the third and fourth days of the strike joined it not because they had taken the decision to, but because their factories simply closed down, and therefore the UWC said that those factories were joining the strike. The enormous potential power of workers positioned in key industries, particularly so in power generation, was shown. The fact that they had an overwhelmingly Protestant workforce was absolutely crucial to the way the strike worked.

It's interesting, though it's not directly relevant to this, that when the Tory government privatised power in Northern Ireland and got rid of an awful lot of those jobs, there wasn't a strike. The workers themselves didn't draw the lesson that 'we don't have to accept this; we can stop this, we did it before'. It's a rather sad commentary on the nature of Northern Ireland politics that while they were willing to use that power for rotten reactionary reasons in 1974, they proved unwilling to do it – and the union leadership has got responsibility for that too for not inviting them to – when it came to their own jobs, and a lot of those jobs don't exist any more.

The hunger strike was a long time coming, of course. The abolition of political status was introduced in March 1976 by Merlyn Rees [Secretary of State for NI, 1974-76]. I viewed it, as many other people did then, as an attempt to criminalize what was going on here. And that's exactly what it was. It was an attempt to depict people who were in prison because of their involvement in the struggle here, or in any way in the events here, as common criminals rather than politically motivated people, and that had to be resisted. I think that almost everybody who was around at that time, and politically active on the anti-imperialist side, must feel slightly uneasy about the fact that it wasn't until people went on hunger strike that a mass movement was generated in support of their campaign.

What I really think, looking back on the hunger strike, is that while on the face of it the hunger strikers didn't win and Thatcher didn't climb down, they actually *did* win comprehensively really because after the hunger strike it was no longer possible to criminalize the hunger strikers – all over the world people just knew that whatever these people had done, and whatever about the history of Northern Ireland, that these people were not criminals. Criminals don't behave like that, criminals do not starve themselves for seventy-four days, and one after the other go to their deaths for a principle. The hunger strikers absolutely, comprehensively, defeated the attempt to criminalize the struggle in the North of Ireland, and in that sense, the important sense, it was an absolute success. Having said that, of course, ten people died, and there was an enormous amount of suffering, inside and outside the prisons, because of it, but you can see the hunger strikes as one of the key turning points in the Northern Ireland struggle, and one particularly in the international perception of the Northern Ireland struggle. People all over the world understood that this was something awesome in its dedication, and that these people, whatever they were, weren't common criminals.

The easiest thing in the world to do is simply to say 'I am against all violence, and we must all be peaceful people', and at various times virtually everybody involved in the events in Northern Ireland has made statements like that. In human terms that's understandable, but it's not realistic. The first thing we have to under-stand is that the state is, by its very nature, violent. I remember when the IRA mortar-bombed Downing Street there was an outcry in the British press about this being an attack on peaceful politics because here were these peo-ple with mortars that were actually bombing the headquarters of a constitutional government. But what was happening in Downing Street that day was a meeting of the war cabinet. This was at the time of the Gulf War, and they were sitting there actually planning mass destruction. Peo-ple like Major and Kenneth Clarke and so forth are steeped in blood from head to foot, and al-ways have been. It's probably true that there isn't a moment of any day, of any year, when there are not people somewhere in the world being killed with guns supplied by the Western pow-ers, and quite frequently by organisations and groups which have been funded and encouraged by Western governments. So the hypocrisy of the state in relation to violence is absolutely to-tal. And also they are better at it, and they are bigger players in the violence game than either Loyalist or Republican paramilitaries; so I see them as the most violent people of all in this situation.

The IRA grew out of a genuine struggle of a genuinely oppressed group of people ie the Catholic community in the North, and the strug-gle which grows out of a fight against oppression has a legitimacy about it which cannot be con-ferred upon the violence of the Loyalist paramilitaries who objectively grew out of an attempt to maintain a *status quo* which involved the oppression of another community. To that extent, IRA violence has been relatively progres-sive and the violence of the Loyalist paramilitaries has been relatively reactionary. That's a very important distinction that has to be made. It is also reflected in the pattern of vio-lence. Nobody can minimise the pain and the grief inflicted by the IRA, and it would be wrong to do so, but any objective analysis of the violence, and there have been exceptions, there are excep-tions to all these things, will show that in general terms the IRA's violence has not been as sectar-ian and has not been as vicious, in that there are very few instances of IRA units actually taking

open pleasure in killing and inflicting suffering. I don't know what is in people's innermost thoughts, but the records seem to show very few cases of that, and no equivalent at all of the sort of the gleeful torture of innocent Catholics by the Shankill Butchers and by elements of the UDA and the UVF down through the years. So even in that broad moral way you have to make a distinction.

While all the people in Northern Ireland in-volved in violence can to some extent be described as victims of the troubles in that they were sucked into it by the political system, nev-ertheless they weren't all sucked in to the same extent. There are certainly very few Republicans sucked into psychopathic violence in the way that people like Johnny Adair from the Shankill and Lenny Murphy and the other notorious torturers actually were. So there are a lot of distinctions to be made, and it's very easy to be too broad and too glib about condemning violence. Having said that, I was never in favour of the armed struggle as a tactic, but that's a political question, and on the question of violence we must make distinc-tions.

I was very pleased there was a ceasefire. As I said, I had always been against the tactic of armed struggle, because as someone who sees the key to progress as being the involvement of the mass of the working class for their own liberation, I saw that there were serious limitations in the tac-tic of armed struggle however understandable it was after Bloody Sunday, and however rational the decision to join the IRA was in many in-stances. Nevertheless, armed struggle, by its nature, can involve only a relatively small number of people, for security reasons apart from any-thing else. There is no point in arguing that you can have a mass democratic form of armed strug-gle; you could, but it would last about three weeks. Also, of its nature it is elitist, in the sense that it is not controlled by the people in whose name it is conducted. So I was in favour of the end of the armed struggle to that extent. I also simply couldn't understand how many of the Re-publican actions in the years leading up to the ceasefire were supposed to advance the cause that they were pursuing. You can look at some things, the bombing of the Baltic Exchange being an obvious example, where you can see particular things that may have sent a shudder through the British government and got a response. But certainly the attacks on members of the UDR and people who work for the RUC and so forth, while some can argue they were legitimate targets, though I think that's questionable, how exactly such attacks were supposed to advance the cause of getting the British out of Ireland and creating a non-sectarian society was certainly a mystery to me, and I think increasingly a mystery even to people in the Republican movement. So I was in favour of the ceasefire in that sense.

However, I was not in favour, and said at the time, and still say so, of the alternative to the armed struggle which was put in place ie the alliance between the Republican movement, Sinn Féin, the Dublin government and corporate America. I saw it as one which was inimical to working-class interests, and one which was going to lead to political compromise of a sort which was unnecessary, and I believe there ought to have been much more discussion and analysis within the Republican movement of what other alternatives to armed struggle might have been available rather than simply going for the pan-Nationalist alliance which they did go for, and which in my view is going to end in tears. I'm not in favour of a return to the armed struggle but I don't think that the strategy which the Republican leadership has adopted as an alternative to the armed struggle is going to lead to the liberation they wish for.

I think the problem of the prisoners is one that transcends the peace process. Even before the ceasefire I would have argued, and did argue, for the unconditional release of *all* prisoners in the North because, for a start, I don't acknowledge the right of any British government to imprison people for political reasons since the British government is the major source of the political problems here. So that is one broad point about the prisoners. Having said that, of course, it is quite clear the prisoners are now being held as hostages, and everybody knows there can't be a settlement which does not involve the release of prisoners, and the British are being extremely slow and grudging and sour in relation to the release of prisoners, and I think that a case could

be made that some assurances on the prisoners should have been obtained before the ceasefire. Once the ceasefire was called it was difficult to see what direct pressures could be brought to bear on the British government to move faster on the issue, and on arms and decommissioning and all the rest of it.

Decommissioning is a phoney issue. All the arguments put up by the Republican leadership seem to me to be quite sound arguments, within the limits of what they are arguing, that decommissioning has never been asked for in the past in comparable struggles. The notion that the IRA should have to hand over guns as some sort of token before Sinn Féin is brought into talks just seems to me to be ludicrous, and the British are taking a political stand on it.

I think there is a bigger issue underlying decommissioning – the issue of consent ie whether the Republican leadership now believes that Northern Ireland shall remain part of the United Kingdom for as long as the majority of people within the North want it that way. I believe that if they have arrived at that conclusion then they should say so openly, and I think it's the fact that they are *not* dealing with that issue which explains the intractability of the decommissioning issue.

To hand over weapons to the British would be to acknowledge the legitimacy of British authority in the North, directly to acknowledge it, and it wouldn't matter a hoot if some international commission, headed by Jimmy Carter or Senator Mitchell or whoever, supervised it. It is the British government which would have to be satisfied that the arms had been handed over or destroyed, it would still set the criteria for the acceptance of Sinn Féin into talks, and then determine whether the criteria had been met, so all this about international commissions and intermediaries doesn't really change the nature of it.

What the issue is here, with the decommissioning of arms, is the issue of consent. What would be talked about if there were round-table talks in the morning, all-inclusive all-party talks? The interesting question arises of what would they say to one and other – what are their negotiating positions? As long as there aren't talks because they are held up over the issue of decommissioning, we aren't getting to that point. And we won't because it's being done the wrong way round. What people should be dealing with now is the issue of consent. If the Republican movement has accepted that Northern Ireland will remain part of the United Kingdom while the majority of the people here want it to – and a lot of people in politics, in the media and so forth are convinced that it has – then it should say so openly and then the decommissioning issue might solve itself very quickly. However, these are very deep questions that go right to the heart of what the Republican struggle has been about, not just in this generation, but for a long time past, and I think that while we have reached a crisis in the peace process, there is also a crisis in Nationalist politics underlying it, which may be incapable of resolution in Nationalist terms. We live in interesting times in that regard.

What I would like to see in the future is a situation emerging in which working-class people in the North identified themselves with politics other than by reference to the religious community to which they, so to speak, belong. That would lead to an end to the sectarian shape of politics, and I think that there are opportunities for trying to pursue that ancient Socialist dream even now.

One of the strange things about Northern Ireland which recently occurred to me is that Catholics and Protestants in the North have never been more alike. The cultural background of people on the Shankill and the Falls has never been as close to one and other as it is now. That's part of the globalisation of culture, the Americanisation of world culture, as well. While there are still distinct elements to the cultures of the two communities, nevertheless they share an awful lot. Ninety per cent of what could probably be defined as culture is common in our society – soccer and pop music and literature not coming from within Ireland, but from outside. It's also true that the workforce has never been more integrated, for all sorts of reasons, not just to do with legislation but to do with the changing pattern of the ownership of industry in the North, which is increasingly owned by foreigners – multinationals and corporations who don't

give a hoot about who is a Catholic and who is a Protestant, rather than Orange businessmen who used to have a direct interest in only employing Protestants. The economic divide, while still there, is smaller now than at any time before, and for great numbers of people, people and families entirely dependent on state benefit, it's exactly the same – you don't get more in child benefit on the Shankill than you get on the Falls. So in economic terms and in cultural terms, strangely enough, Catholics and Protestants have never been closer. And it is happening at a time when the political divide is at least as wide as it ever was. There is a contradiction here which eventually will have to be resolved, and my hope is it will be resolved in a way that brings people together rather than pushes them apart.

I can't actually see the possibility of a united Ireland which is not a Socialist Ireland, and I think that when I referred earlier to the crisis in Nationalist politics, I think that it's not going to be possible under capitalism. That's my interpretation of the peace process; that what we have seen is the Republican movement looking for the strongest Nationalist allies it can get, and obviously the strongest Nationalist allies are the SDLP, the Church, the Dublin government, Irish America and so forth, and they have put that in place. There has never been a stronger Nationalist alliance in an attempt to move towards a united Ireland. That will have been done at the expense of giving up, in effect, on many Socialist issues. You can't fight for Socialism while you are arm-in-arm with Albert Reynolds, or John Bruton, or John Hume, or Cardinal Daly and so forth. What we are seeing now, therefore, is that the Nationalist project has been effectively brought to a halt because no capitalist government in the South, is going to break with Britain. It's not going to cut itself off from Britain, for all sorts of economic reasons, nor is it going to break with the United States, therefore the price you pay for putting in place the strongest possible Nationalist alliance is, really, to give up on driving the British out of Ireland. This may seem like a paradox, nevertheless it seems to me that if you just look at what's happening this is true, and it's interesting that Sinn Féin no longer uses the slogan 'Brits Out'. It's 'All-Party Talks' now. The slogan 'Brits Out' has not decorated a Sinn Féin platform for a long time now because if it did, they certainly wouldn't get Fianna Fáil front benchers, as they have got recently, onto their platforms. They wouldn't get Bill Flynn, the Irish-American multimillionaire to join in the chorus of 'Brits Out' and so forth, but he is in favour of all-party talks. And there I think you see in practical terms the contradiction between the all-class Nationalist alliance on the one hand, and achieving the goal of a united Ireland on the other. The conclusion I draw is that if we are going to move towards unity the people of the South will have to rise up as well to overthrow their capitalist government which is in alliance, effectively, with the British government, and corporate America, and all the rest.

I don't see the choice as being between Socialism and a united Ireland. I don't believe there is ever going to be a united Ireland which is not Socialist. By the same token, I don't think you are ever going to have Socialism in any part of Ireland while Ireland is divided. It would be ludicrous to imagine a Southern Irish state in which the working class was in power while you had this little slum still existing up here. It would be ludicrous to imagine Northern Ireland having a different social order and a different system of economic organisation to the South. So the two parts of Ireland have to move together, and I think when the people of the Bogside, for example, look for allies in the South, they are going to have to come back to the old Socialist dictum that you don't look to the people who are ruling in the South, but look to the people there who are fighting back against their rulers, and establish a thirty-two-county movement which is aimed against both Irish states. So I see the future of Socialism as bright over the next few years. I don't see a capitalist united Ireland ever existing in my lifetime, or in anybody else's lifetime.

Creggan 1970: Handkerchiefs soaked in vinegar and/or lemon juice were used to counter the effects of CS gas. *(Photo: Barney McMonagle)*

A typical Sunday afternoon in the Bogside, circa 1971. *(Photos: Barney McMonagle)*

Changing faces of the British army, Bogside and Brandywell, 1971. *(Photos: Barney McMonagle)*

John Hume, soaked by a water cannon, is arrested after a demonstration in Laburnum Terrace, 26 August 1971.
(Photo: Willie Carson)

Waterloo Place in the summer of 1973. *(Photo: Willie Carson)*

Ferryquay Street, 15 May 1973. *(Photo: Willie Carson)*

UDA patrol in the Waterside in the mid-1970s. *(Photo: Willie Carson)*

Raymond McCartney

Ten people dying, ten people you knew, ten friends, ten comrades is a big price, it was a massive price. There's absolutely no doubt about it. But in a historical context, what came about as a result of the hunger strikes was that a major thrust by the British government to defeat Republicanism was itself defeated. I think Gerry Adams best sums it up when he says that the British government tried to criminalize Republican prisoners, but Republican prisoners ended up criminalizing the British government.

By the time I was about fifteen or sixteen, I think, like a lot of Nationalists of my age, I realised there were injustices, but there seemed to be an inability to do anything about them. But because those injustices were so blatant, it was only a matter of time before the right group of people came along to confront the issues. Through a combination of events that group emerged in the late 1960s.

If you look at the history of the six-county state, it's based on domination, and that domination over many years was either by the threat, or actual use, of force. So in 1968 when people came out to expose the nature of the state, it could only react in one way; no longer could it just use the threat of force, now it had to implement it.

When you look back on the way the state toppled, you could say it was inevitable. No state that dominates gives up power easily. It would have been great if the Unionist government or the British government had realised in the late 1960s that there was injustice and had sorted it out properly. But the reality is they didn't, so when the state was exposed, street resistance was inevitable and, in a sense, that was necessary.

Internment, prior to the 1970s, appeared to work. Each time the Unionist government and the British government had employed internment, it seemed to defuse whatever sort of resistance that occurred on the streets of the six-county state. So you can look at it from the Unionist point of view, and you can say, well, here we have another attempt to bring down the state – how did we deal with it in the past? We dealt with it by the use of internment, so let's use internment again, it should work. But by this stage, things had moved on. Nationalist and working-class resistance was more co-ordinated, with wider demands. In the past, the demands were mostly on the constitutional issue, but by this time people placed more emphasis on the search for equality. Internment, therefore, this time around, wasn't going to have the desired effect. I think people sometimes perceive any oppressive acts by the British government in Ireland as a recruiting sergeant for a, b, c and d. I think that's a failure to tackle the real problems. In other words, is the use of internment right or wrong, is the British presence in Ireland right or wrong, was the shooting dead of fourteen people on Bloody Sunday right or wrong? It's not down to whether they shouldn't have done it because it increased recruitment to the IRA, because the British government could then say, well, as long as it's not going to recruit people for the IRA, let's do it. So I think it's a false premise in the first place, and I think it's people trying to absolve themselves from tackling the real problems.

I was seventeen at the time of Bloody Sunday. I went on the march, like most members of my family, and I witnessed the events of that day, and there's no doubt that it had a great impact on my life. My cousin was one of those shot dead, and I can remember how it affected his family who had seen their eldest son being killed. I saw the impact it had on his parents, on his brothers and sisters, and even on us, his wider family. I believe the British are always looking to absolve themselves, and their excuse then was that the IRA fired first. Even if this was true, it's irrelevant. The British government conceived an operation, and they sent in the paras to teach the people of Derry a lesson. That was their plan.

In the aftermath of Bloody Sunday, any doubts and fears that I had about committing myself to the IRA disappeared. I remember expressing that thought to a very senior member of the IRA at the time, and he told me – obviously having experienced a lot of people at that particular time expressing the same wish to him – not to allow emotion to influence what was a very important decision. He asked me to go away and reflect on it, and take a couple of months before making up my mind. I did eventually make that decision, and I joined the IRA.

When you look back at the Widgery Report, it actually exposes our political naiveté at that time; there was an expectation that a British judge was going to examine the facts, as everyone here knew them, and that Britain would be painted as murderers. But the opposite happened. And I have heard even the relatives of the victims on Bloody Sunday saying that Bloody Sunday was bad but the day the Widgery Report was published was worse. There was a widespread belief in the city that those who did the shooting were only the minions, but it was the establishment who dictated the whitewash that was the Widgery Report.

I think that, symbolically, Stormont had represented fifty years of Unionist repression, so its removal was obviously seen by Nationalists, and Republicans like myself, as a great bonus. After the fall of Stormont the British could no longer remain detached. Up until 1972 they could use the excuse that the Unionist government, and the Unionist Party, were effectively in control. So after that they were always trying to look for ways to deal with the conflict in an internal way, and Sunningdale, despite its small Irish dimension, was such an attempt. But because it tackled the nature of the state, even to a small degree, it led to a reaction from the British establishment. It spread the idea that a Unionist mass movement brought Sunningdale down, but in reality it was brought down by elements within the British establishment, and in particular the British army, who just didn't want to know.

The prison protests, and the hunger strikes, again have to be placed in a historical context. Sunningdale, the convention, all had failed, so the British were again trying to devise a plan to resolve the conflict. Underlying British attempts to resolve the 'Irish problem' has always been the defeat of Republicanism. So in 1975 they devised a plan which was known as Ulsterisation. Basically, that meant removing the British army visibly from the streets and putting the RUC in primacy. Running alongside that was a heavy play on 'normality', that this was just an internal 'United Kingdom problem'. Another aspect of the policy was criminalization. Since the hunger strike in 1972, Republican and Loyalist prisoners had political status. The British removed this in 1976 because they couldn't sell the idea that it was an internal problem if there were political prisoners. So, immediately, Republicans resisted this attempt to portray them as criminals, and the history of the prison protests is well documented. Basically, men refused to wear the prison uniform and go to work. It escalated because of the brutality and the repressiveness of the regime, resulting in what became known as the no-wash protest. You had attempts by Cardinal ÓFiaich and Bishop Daly and Fr Alec Reid, with Atkins [Secretary of State for NI, 1979-81] and Alison [Minister of State, NIO, 1979-81], to try and resolve the prison dispute. The prisoners were always saying to them that the British weren't willing to tackle the problems, but they tried for eighteen months, until eventually they themselves admitted that the British weren't going to move on the issue.

On the many occasions that we, the prisoners, debated the protest, we always had that feeling that prison protests in the past had always come to a head through the use of hunger strikes once every other means had been used. We found ourselves in that position from 1979 on. By 1980, people in jail were arguing very strongly with the leadership of the movement outside who were totally against the use of the hunger strike. The leadership finally agreed, and in October 1980 the first hunger strike started.

At the end of that hunger strike [18 December 1980], the British government produced a document to the prisoners' OC that contained the basis of a settlement by which the prison protests could have been resolved. It would have taken a lot of careful negotiation, but the basis was there. But the British government, once the hunger strike was over, once it felt that the street protests and the mass movement were defused, then hardened its position. The British didn't think that the protesters, the blanket men, could go back on hunger strike for a second time. They made a massive miscalculation. Ten people dying, ten people you knew, ten friends, ten comrades, is a big price, it was a massive price. But in a historical context, what came about as a result of the hunger strikes was that a major thrust by the British government to defeat Republicanism was itself defeated. I think Gerry Adams best sums it up when he says that the British government tried to criminalize Republican prisoners, but Republican prisoners ended up criminalizing the British government.

As a Republican, and as somebody growing up in a very stable family environment, the last thing I ever wanted to do was to be part of an armed resistance in Ireland. But, as I said, there was injustice, and there was an inability to do anything about it, so therefore you fought in a war which was not of your choosing. It was something that was forced upon you. I think that inevitably people are going to negotiate a political settlement in Ireland. It's unfortunate that it took so long for the British government, which is not even grasping this present opportunity, to realise that.

Loyalist violence shows up the nature of Unionism, which has always painted anybody not loyal to the state as an enemy of the state; that's how they viewed Catholics right through Stormont; that's why they didn't trust the Nationalist Party, even though it was a very weak political party. So Loyalists have the idea that every time they shoot a Catholic they are shooting an enemy of the state. And they can claim that their victim bought the *Republican News*, or was seen on a march or whatever, but it's just

that they were Catholic. I think British violence in Ireland has always been of an oppressive nature, that the state armed itself well, and used its arms effectively to try and defeat resistance within the last twenty-five years, which led to Bloody Sunday, to the 'shoot to kill' policy, to the use of the SAS etc.

There's no doubt the Irish government abdicated its responsibilities. People in the North, right from 1969, saw that the Free State government was very weak in terms of the North. So pressure has always been applied to try and make the Dublin government see that it has a responsibility in the North, because – and it's written into the constitution – partition has been a failure. Fianna Fáil stands on that plank. Many Dublin governments tried to avoid their responsibility. But throughout the course of the last twenty-five years, under different types of pressures, Dublin started to realise that it too had a role to play in resolving this conflict, and now you can see some acceptance, a consensus, that the Irish government is going to have to be part of resolving the problem.

I was just getting out of jail at the time of the ceasefire. I think over the last four or five years you can see the emphasis that Gerry Adams and the leadership of Sinn Féin have put on trying to create this idea that there wasn't a military solution, that if the problem at its core is political, then the resolution of it will also have to be political and therefore political negotiation was going to have to take place. Perhaps Republicans in the past believed that they were a government in exile, that somehow they would fight the British to a standstill, and that the British government would then sit down across a table and have negotiations to pull out of Ireland. This was accepted Republican thinking for decades. Then the Hume-Adams Irish peace initiative came about. There were other voices saying, particularly the people in the secret negotiations with Martin McGuinness, that the history of Europe, the history of Ireland, was leading to a unitary state. Stop the armed struggle for a fortnight and you will be surprised how generous, how imaginative, we will be. They all claimed that the block to progress was the IRA armed struggle. So the ceasefire was no massive surprise. But what the last fourteen months have shown is that all those people who made these claims have now been found wanting by their silence.

If there is a consensus that all parties to a conflict have to be a part of its resolution, then the inevitable step is that there should be all-party talks. I think the British government was surprised by the ceasefire. I think the British are happier with an IRA campaign because they can justify their inaction, they can justify their repression while the armed struggle is continuing. The IRA called the ceasefire, and now the British government, since August 1994, has been looking for excuse after excuse. Other conflict resolution models have shown that it is the responsibility of the ruling government, in this instance the British government, to lay down the rules. So if it decides on all-party talks, and the Unionists don't come, then you have, as in South Africa, an empty chair. But what you will find is that once the British government becomes the mover, then it will be difficult for other forces, particularly Unionism, to ignore it because Unionism, in its most dynamic form, is underwritten by Britain.

I don't think it's an exaggeration to say that we now have the best opportunity in seventy years to finally resolve this problem. So I hope this opportunity will be grasped.

The last eighteen months, obviously with getting out of jail, have been a momentous time for me. I have watched this process evolve, and have been part of it on the street. I am now married, so I look to my own personal future with the hope that if this is resolved then that part of my life, which I am now thoroughly enjoying, will obviously be allowed to flourish even more. But hope isn't everything, and I have to say that there's a nagging doubt in the back of my mind that Britain isn't going to grasp this opportunity, that its record to date has been bad and there's nothing to suggest that it is going to change. Having been recently released from prison, I have watched the RUC making a very determined effort to put me back in jail. Most Republicans are subject to that harassment. The press ignore it at times, saying that it is *sub judice*. But I have experienced the RUC misrepresenting situations, and the John Major-day was a classic example. I was at the protest, and when I read some of the things now that they allege I said, it's just mind-boggling. But the RUC and the NIO have the power to take me off the street without any sort of judicial process. So for the future there's that sort of worry. Politically, there are obviously worries, though I'm hoping that the opposite is the case. But I don't want any false dawns.

Martin McGuinness

...the British government needs to demonstrate its commitment to the search for a just and lasting peace. It needs to give, publicly, clear specific and unambiguous assurances that negotiations will be inclusive, with no item on the agenda allowed to become an insurmountable obstacle to progress.

When I left school in the summer of 1965, I replied to an advertisement seeking an apprentice mechanic for a city-centre garage. The interview was abruptly terminated when I replied: "The Christian Brothers, Brow of the Hill" in answer to the second question: "What school did you attend?"

In those days, fifteen-year-olds didn't concern themselves with in-depth analysis of why and how this could happen. Satisfying myself with the thought 'they mustn't have liked the look of me', I trudged home to tell my parents. Reassuringly, my father rejected my theory telling me not to give the incident a second thought.

Little was I to know then that three years later, events in Derry would compel me to think again about that day in Great James Street when my religion disqualified me from finding employment in my own town.

By the time 5 October 1968 came, I was eighteen-years-old, employed and oblivious to the reality that the coming years would bring such incredible change to my life and the lives of the people of Derry. Asked, most people would say that the events in Derry on 5 October, flashed around the world by the new power of television, were the beginning of what has euphemistically become known as the troubles.

The full truth, however, is that the Northern state, artificially created under threat of immediate and terrible war by the British, for the Unionists has, from its inception, been a very troubled place, a state in which division, injustice, inequality and the denial of democratic rights reigned supreme. Therefore if we accept this as an irrefutable historical reality, the reaction of the state to the reasonable yet basic demands of the civil rights movement for equality in housing, votes and jobs was entirely predictable. The option of conceding these demands required a degree of sophistication far beyond the psyche of Unionist leaders. Change for Unionists was an alien concept and repression became the order of the day. Civil rights marches were banned, tension increased on the streets and conflict became inevitable. Student marchers were ambushed by loyalists with RUC assistance at Burntollet and Samuel Devenney became the first Derry victim of the troubles, dying as a result of injuries inflicted on him by the RUC in his own house in William Street.

The 12 August 1969 brought what has turned out to be one of the most defining moments in Irish history. From throughout the North came thousands of Apprentice Boys and their followers to strut through a city where the people had long been denied democracy and equality of citizenship. Finding this galling and unacceptable, the citizens of Derry rose from their knees in popular struggle against the injustices of the state.

For me, and I suppose for many others in the Nationalist community, it was a watershed. I joined the uprising and for almost two days played a small part in assisting the resistance to those who had denied our people justice and murdered Sammy Devenney.

For many of us involved in the 'Battle of the Bogside', the Apprentice Boys, the Orangemen and the RUC were the immediate manifestations of Unionist misrule.

During those few days the questions 'how can this be happening, who is really responsible for all this?' were foremost in my mind. No matter how many times I thought about it, the answer was always the same.

Those chiefly responsible were the British: it was they who had established and underpinned the Northern state; it was they who had stood idly by through almost fifty years of blatant injustice, discrimination and inequality. For me it was crystal clear; the blame lay in London with the British government.

The arrival of the British army onto the streets of Derry on 14 August 1969 did little to undermine the logic of my analysis. That night the people of Derry gathered in groups in or near the site of the historic 'Battle of the Bogside'. The events of recent days and the arrival of British soldiers were stoically assessed by a people revived, and whose resolve was stiffened by their defeat of the forces of the state, the RUC. Meanwhile in Belfast the Nationalist people were being attacked and murdered by the RUC and Loyalist gangs. Back in Derry, opinions were divided between those more highly opinionated, who thought the arrival of British troops was a good thing, and those who thought it ill-conceived.

The majority of people, including myself, didn't really know what the future held. I vividly recall listening to a group in conversation at the top of Fahan Street, and in particular the words of one man who exclaimed that 'they [the British army] haven't come here for our benefit'.

Marches and protests continued for an end to discrimination in voting, housing and employment, with both the Unionist government at Stormont and the political masters of the soldiers unable and unwilling to countenance that far-reaching change was essential if the slide into further conflict was to be averted. It was against this background that I decided to become an Irish Republican.

The murders of two young Derrymen, Seamus Cusack and Desmond Beattie, whom I witnessed dying at the bottom of my street, were a brutal confirmation that the British army's real purpose was the preservation of the *status quo* through the repression of the Nationalist people.

The killings of both young men did to the British army what the 'Battle of the Bogside' did

to the RUC – made them completely unacceptable and unwelcome in Nationalist areas.

From October 1969 to the summer of 1971, not one shot had been fired at either the RUC or British army, yet three Derrymen had been killed by the British army and the RUC. Coupled with events in Belfast, many could only come to the conclusion that in order to defend the corrupt nature of the Northern state, Britain's military forces had declared war on the Nationalist community.

The introduction of internment without trial completed the slide into open warfare on the streets of Belfast and Derry and throughout the six counties. I left my home in Elmwood Street on the morning of internment for the last time. Two months later, thirty British soldiers in a furniture van came down our street, broke in the front door and I was officially on the run from the British forces.

The IRA, which had lain dormant apart from the resistance of small ill-equipped groups resulting in incidents such as the tragic deaths of Joe Coyle, Tommy McCool and Tommy Carlin in an accidental explosion, in which Tommy McCool's two young daughters Carol and Bernadette also died, sprang to life. In doing so, it fulfilled the needs of that section of the Nationalist people who regarded resistance and struggle as the only credible alternative to British repression and occupation.

British repression and Republican resistance continued unabated. British soldiers were killed and Eamon Lafferty, the first IRA volunteer to lose his life in direct combat with numerically superior British forces, died a lonely and courageous death at Kildrum Gardens, Creggan.

The killing of civilians by the British army continued and increased with women and girls, such as Kathleen Thompson and Annette McGavigan, also losing their lives. Bloody Sunday visited the most appalling event of premeditated mass murder by the British army on peaceful protesters demonstrating against internment in Derry. Bloody Sunday was a desperate act perpetrated by a desperate British government unable to suppress the spirit of freedom which was by now imbued in the people of Derry.

Soweto, Gaza and the Bogside have for the past quarter of a century flashed their messages of injustice and struggle to a world prepared to recognise and embrace the need for change. The names of those who suffered and sacrificed for justice will long be remembered when the names of their oppressors have been forgotten. Names such as Mandela, Sands and the Irish hunger strikers will inspire future generations who may have to struggle for justice.

In this article I have, as is my responsibility, pointed to the suffering and injustice inflicted on the Nationalist community; I believe that it is important to do that. We have for many years lived with the power of British television and the print media, and the eagerness of the British who control them, to highlight the killings of people by the IRA. Even in death, inequality reigns. That said, Republicans have always been willing to recognise that no section of our community has a monopoly on suffering. The killing of British soldiers, members of the RUC and civilians by the IRA have also had a deep and profound impact on their families and communities. We have all suffered, we are all impoverished as a result of the cumulative effects of the past twenty-five years. It was in an attempt to end all this in a just and honourable way that we in Sinn Féin moved decisively to play our part in what the world now calls the Irish peace process.

Widespread media coverage of the events of the past two years has shown that Sinn Féin had been working to achieve a negotiated settlement long before the IRA called, to the surprise of the British government and the Unionists, their ceasefire in August 1994.

In our publication *Towards a Lasting Peace in Ireland* in 1992, we pointed out the need for inclusive negotiations led by both the Irish and British governments. We believed that if we were successful in getting both governments in particular to accept the importance of such a role, then we would provide all the people of Ireland and Britain with the first real opportunity in over seventy years to resolve this conflict in a deep-rooted and comprehensive fashion. We also recognised and accepted that for real and meaningful negotiations to take place, they would have to be conducted against the background of a peaceful situation.

Our dialogue with John Hume and Taoiseach Albert Reynolds was of crucial importance in that it achieved an agreement among Irish Nationalists that there could be no internal settlement in the North. It was also now common knowledge that Sinn Féin was in contact with representatives of the British government who were seeking to convince us that John Major was keen to see a resolution of the conflict.

Unconvinced by the British government's handling of this situation, we focused our attention on the building of an Irish Nationalist consensus supported by influential people in Irish-America. This consensus believed that an offer of talks, against the background of an IRA ceasefire, would provide an irresistible opportunity for all the parties to address and resolve all of the difficult issues which go to the heart of the conflict.

The IRA ceasefire was a traumatic experience for Irish Republicans, yet at the time I believed this was a wise and sensible decision; I still believe that. The IRA ceasefire, and the potential it created, was undoubtedly the best opportunity for peace we've ever had. History will show that it was an opportunity missed by John Major and the Unionist political leadership.

John Major's introduction of a new precondition, the decommissioning issue, five months into the ceasefire, effectively delayed and eventually smothered all hope that the British government would join with the Irish government in bringing all of the parties to the negotiating table. During the whole of 1995, I led Sinn Féin delegation after delegation in meetings with representatives of the British government. In these talks, our delegation asserted the right of all the people of Ireland to national self-determination and the need for the end to British jurisdiction in our country. These talks came to nothing as it became clear that the British government agenda was a single-item agenda – the surrender of the IRA. For months before the breakdown of the IRA ceasefire at Canary Wharf, we in Sinn Féin had warned both the Irish and British governments of our view that the peace process was in a perilous state. They were not listening.

For the eighteen months that the IRA cessation endured, Sinn Féin and others waited for the British government and the Unionists to come and take their seats at the negotiating table, to sit down with the rest of us to agree a new and peaceful future on this island. During those eighteen months there was not one word of negotiation.

The cumulative evidence of those eighteen empty and frustrating months points damningly to a British government strategy locked into a psychology of war; a mindset which demands victory over Republicans rather than agreement and compromise; a pursuit of victory by other means which sidelined the pursuit of peace.

At every juncture, the British government stalled and delayed the peace process. The demand for an IRA surrender, introduced by the British government as a new precondition to all-party talks five months after the IRA cessation, provided the British with their most effective weapon in their stalling strategy.

Only reluctantly, and under great pressure internationally, did the British government move at the end of November 1995 (fifteen months into the IRA cessation) to agree with the Irish government a twin-track approach, which had as its objective the removal of preconditions to all-party talks beginning in February 1996. The Mitchell International Body was established to tackle the arms issue while the political track was to prepare for inclusive talks.

Despite our grave reservations and doubts about British government intentions, Sinn Féin engaged positively and energetically in the twin-track process. We made a detailed written submission to the International Body. In this, and in several lengthy oral submissions, we outlined our view that the decommissioning demand was unrealistic and unrealisable and was a device introduced by the British government to stall, indefinitely, the commencement of inclusive peace negotiations. We pointed out that the commencement of peace talks was the absolute priority and the only way to an agreed and lasting political settlement. And that in the context of such a settlement, disarmament and demilitarisation would naturally and logically occur in a society at peace with itself and its neighbour.

Senator Mitchell and his colleagues conducted their task with energy, enthusiasm and dedication and they produced their report within a very short time.

In contrast, the political track was a charade, exposing again the British government's unwillingness to engage seriously. The Unionists refused to participate and the British made no effort to persuade them.

The Mitchell Report briefly rekindled the hope of August 1994. It recommended the removal of all preconditions, accepting that all issues should be dealt with in open, democratic negotiation. In our view this provided the basis for moving forward so that all matters could be settled to the satisfaction of all sides as part of the process. The Mitchell Report pointed the way into all-party talks.

We also welcomed the inclusion in the report of the many issues which Sinn Féin and others have argued are central to the advance of the peace process, but to which the British have shown intransigence and negativity. These include prisoners, repressive legislation, licensed weapons, the use of plastic bullets, the provision of a normal policing service and action on social and economic issues.

In contrast, the British response within hours saw John Major reject the Mitchell Report. He did so because he did not want all-party talks and because Sinn Féin had responded constructively to the Mitchell Report. He needed new excuses for reneging on his commitment to commence all-party talks by the end of February 1996. Tactically he opted for a series of new preconditions. By imposing an elective process, which is contrary to the Mitchell criteria of broad acceptability, and a Unionist forum, John Major succeeded in stalling talks for a further three months. So we had the ludicrous position where John Major ignored the report of the Mitchell body which in conjunction with the Irish government he had himself established.

As the last eighteen months have proven, peace in Ireland cannot be built without the positive participation of the British government. If we are to rebuild the peace process, and I believe we must, then the confidence which was missing, as a result of the negativity of the British government, must be found. We must all learn the lessons of conflict resolution. In the development of our peace strategy, Sinn Féin recognised that an end of conflict does not necessarily lead to a lasting peace. Irish history is full of instances in which hostilities have ceased only to reoccur at some future point because the causes of the conflict were not properly addressed.

As 10 June looms before us, few are certain that the British government and the Unionists intend this to be the beginning of real and meaningful peace negotiations.

It is my belief that the British government needs to demonstrate its commitment to the search for a just and lasting peace. It needs to give, publicly, clear, specific and unambiguous assurances that negotiations will be inclusive, with no item on the agenda allowed to become an insurmountable obstacle to progress.

The British government needs to herald publicly, through such assurances, the end of the old debate, an end to the failures of the past and the beginning of the new debate in which negotiations will provide the changes required to create peace. This means political and constitutional change, demilitarisation and democratic rights.

Negotiations must be an agenda for change; real, significant, substantive, comprehensive change. The British government needs to develop a peace agenda of peace making, of peace building and of peace talks.

Sinn Féin is willing to try again.

Peter McGuire

I honestly believe that the troubles were the inescapable result, and hopefully the last bloody climax, of Irish history. They happened because the people of this land, Protestants and Roman Catholics, have for generations been brainwashed, led by the nose by evil individuals, organisations and governments who all along had their own selfish power games to play.

Were the troubles justified? Justified by whom? By man, by the law, by God? I think the answer depends on your definition of justice. It is very easy for people to pass judgement on the 'other side'. I for one am not prepared to do that. The Republican/Nationalist communities were subjected to pressures, influences and circumstances that I have never experienced. But they are more than capable of telling their own story. I can only speak for myself and my own community.

When I became a Loyalist activist, I did so because I could genuinely see no other way. My community, my family, my friends, my people, were under attack. I grew up in Londonderry's Waterside and saw friends of my family and neighbours being murdered and maimed for no other reason that I could see apart from being Protestants and the so-called security forces were unable to deal with their murderers. I believed then as I do now that the security forces lacked the courage to crush this war with the full intensity it required; and as the war progressed I also believe that money became the motivating factor within the RUC to maintain the *status quo* at an acceptable level of violence. Well it wasn't acceptable to me. My community was without friends, betrayed and deserted by everyone. What else was there to do but fight.

I, along with many other young Protestants in Londonderry, joined what we call the Loyalist movement (Ulster Defence Association), which was then a legal organisation. Many of these young men are now incarcerated in Long Kesh, some are dead. Anything I myself took part in was only carried out after thinking long and hard whether it was justified. Of course there were many things I wasn't happy about, but a soldier in any war has to carry out decisions which are personally difficult. Taking everything into account, yes, I believe that I was justified in my actions, as were those around me. However, it must also be pointed out that the troubles also created an environment where evil people were able to masquerade as Loyalists and commit horrendous crimes against both communities. These people are scum and although they may well escape judgement in this world, they will certainly not in the next.

I honestly believe that the troubles were the inescapable result, and hopefully the last bloody climax, of Irish history. They happened because the people of this land, Protestants and Roman Catholics, have for generations been brainwashed, led by the nose by evil individuals, organisations and governments who all along had their own selfish power games to play. People in Ulster are born into tribal camps and then raised on a diet of 'us and them'. From day one you find yourself in a trap, pigeonholed as a Protestant or a Roman Catholic, Loyalist or Republican. It has always been a relatively easy task in this country to persuade uneducated working-class people that an 'enemy' exists and must be eradicated. Graves and prisons are full of these people who so badly needed to belong to some group, a group which kept them confined to sectarian boundaries. The only difference between these troubles and the hundreds of other previous sectarian wars and murder campaigns that have been fought in Ireland is that we can now kill our enemy and then go home in time to watch our latest 'victory' in colour on television. Given the circumstances which have always prevailed on this island, I believe there was absolutely no way of avoiding the bloodshed, hatred and violence which has blighted our home for the last twenty-five years. And each of us must be prepared to shoulder some of the blame.

As a young boy growing up in the Waterside, I constantly felt under fear of attack – the 'siege mentality' if you like. But it was an attitude based on personal experiences and one which continued to grow as I became more aware of what was happening around me. Although I have vague recollections of fleeing the cityside and moving to the comparative safety of the Protestant Waterside during the early 1970s, it was during my days at secondary school that I witnessed acts of violence and was subjected to influences which shaped my views, outlook and future. I attended Clondermot High School and during my time there I was frequently the target of sectarian attacks. The school was situated between the Loyalist Irish Street estate and the staunchly Republican Gobnascale area and on many an occasion my friends and I had to run a gauntlet of bricks and bottles going to and from school.

I have often heard various prominent individuals claim that Londonderry never suffered from sectarianism. I wonder where the hell those people were living. In fact it was whilst going to and from school that I witnessed two scenes that have had a major impact on my life. Walking to school one morning, I stopped to talk to a local bread deliverer with whom I was friendly. I said goodbye and continued down the road. I was only ten feet away when an IRA gunman jumped out of a car and shot him dead. The second scene was returning home from school. I turned a corner and saw the body of the local shopkeeper lying in the doorway of his shop. He had also been murdered by the IRA. No-one has ever been charged with these murders, and even then I knew that the RUC was incapable of ever catching anyone.

Remembrance Sunday has always been a major date in the Ulster calendar. As I watched Remembrance Day 1987 on television, feelings of cold hatred, extremely intense hatred for anything or anyone remotely associated with Irish Republicanism became entrenched in my being. Enniskillen devastated me, my family and the whole Protestant community. I'll never forget my decision that I had had enough. It was a very long time before I felt any compassion or sympathy for any member of the Nationalist community, regardless of age, sex or status.

Of course my chosen role as a Loyalist activist eventually brought me into contact with the RUC. And as you may already have gathered, I have never been too impressed by this force. However, after having to suffer the pleasures of their company on more than one occasion, my view has changed. I am no longer unimpressed, but utterly disgusted. They are without doubt one of the most undisciplined and corrupt forces I have ever come across. This is not from being in conflict with them but from what I have observed and experienced.

From late 1987 till the present day, my life has almost entirely evolved around being in prison or visiting comrades in jail. This experience, along with suffering a sustained and systematic campaign of harassment and humiliation at the hands of the RUC, has slowly broken down my hatred of the Republican/Nationalist community and caused me to rethink my previous beliefs. As distasteful as this comment may seem to some, I have come to realise that I have more in common with young Republicans living in Gobnascale or Creggan than I have with young RUC officers who live in large houses in the middle-class areas of Limavady and Coleraine and who can travel round the world on numerous holidays and drive the latest sports car and when on duty strut around my town with assault rifles like some modern-day SS.

The troubles robbed me of one of the best friends I have ever known. On 29 June 1991, Cecil McKnight was shot dead in his own home whilst in the company of two RUC detectives. Cecil was the first person I have ever met in the Loyalist community who tried to redirect my energies into community development work and politics. He had time for everyone and as a former Loyalist prisoner devoted a lot of his time to prisoners' welfare issues. Of all the targets the IRA could have chosen, Cecil McKnight must have been by far the most counterproductive.

When the Loyalist ceasefire was called, I felt as if a great burden had been lifted. But in truth I was also highly sceptical. After all, we've had ceasefires before. One year on I feel a great deal more optimistic. At least we seem to have a chance for a more permanent peace, but I still have niggling doubts that the IRA is not sincere in their intentions. If anyone thinks they can trick Loyalists into a united Ireland then they are very much mistaken. I pray to God that this is not the case.

To blame the troubles on a small minority within each community is sheer stupidity. The IRA/INLA and UDA/UFF are simply products of the sectarian attitudes widely held and deeply rooted within both communities. Terrorists were not imported. For twenty-five years our communities bred and raised them – thousands of men and women who took up the gun because they were encouraged to do so by communities fearful of the 'others'.

I think everyone has to ask themselves if they really want peace or not. And if the answer is yes, then they are going to have to be prepared to perhaps not forget, but forgive those memories. Only then can people in Northern Ireland begin treating each other as human beings.

Declan McLaughlin

There are different forms of violence. The way I look at it is that there is state violence, which is the RUC and the British army, and there is a kind of state-maintained violence, which is the UVF, UDA and any other names that MI5 and MI6 go under.

I think when you look back to before the emergence of the civil rights movement, you don't have to look too hard to see that things were unjust. Power, housing, gerrymandering, voting, the whole state was built upon discrimination. The demand for civil rights was emerging all over the world; the black civil rights movement in America and the student protests in Europe, particularly France. The civil rights movement here was a part of that general awareness. People weren't prepared to live in humiliating and degrading conditions any more; they weren't prepared to be second-class citizens. When you look at the way the civil rights movement progressed, to the point that the British establishment stamped on it, it was quite clear they weren't going to let this happen. So I think it was inevitable, from the early '60s onwards, that it was going to progress from a nonviolent protest to armed struggle. I don't believe people had an option; they weren't given an option. The British establishment wasn't prepared to give an inch, so people decided it was time to do something more than get shot off the streets.

In the history of this town, Bloody Sunday is very important because that day a lot of people wakened up to the fact that those in power, those given the role of looking after them, protecting them, were not fulfilling that role. They could see that this was the end of the line, that they were going to get shot off the streets, that they were going to be brutalised. I think everybody in Derry knows what happened, just from word of mouth. Bloody Sunday opened a lot of people's eyes to what the British establishment would do to keep the Unionists on board. The establish-

ment, as it is now, is not there to protect people; it is there to protect itself.

For me, the importance of Bloody Sunday is that it happened in this town and my family were there. My father was on the march and I was freaked-out that he had never told me he was there until I asked him many years later. I told him it was one of the most important events in modern Irish history, and he was afraid to even talk about it. I think he didn't want to expose me to what he had seen as a young adult; I think that is the case for a lot of people.

The Widgery Report was a whitewash; it was just the British establishment covering its own back. And what has happened since is that people have gone from being afraid to talk about it – afraid to say anything about it because it was so brutal, fourteen people murdered in cold blood – to demanding justice for it. And it has nothing to do with the national question or a united Ireland. It is about justice, working-class people getting the justice they deserve, and the British establishment being pulled across the coals. They were the people that were supposed to be there to protect us. We should not have had to live in bad housing; we should not have had to live in a gerrymandered state; we should not have had to put up with a corrupt, sectarian police force. Structures should be there to protect people, look after people, but the regime we live under, even now, does not do that.

When you look at things like internment, Stormont, power sharing, the Anglo-Irish Agreement, the Framework document, they are all attempts by the British government to get some kind of stability here, but still keep the Unionists on their side. After all these options, the last is going to have to be British withdrawal because none of the rest are going to work. As a people, we can't live under an establishment that doesn't treat us fairly and as an equal part of the equation. The Unionist parties will not sit down and talk to Sinn Féin. Why? They keep using this excuse that they are the IRA. But over the last eighteen months the IRA have been prepared to stop using violence and still the Unionists will not sit down.

I think all they did across the border was change the colour of the postbox from red to green. It is still a right-wing, conservative government in the Free State. They see up here as an embarrassment. They like to think of Ireland as the emerald jewel in the European crown. What the Free State government are trying to do now is to push things along slowly so that they don't offend the British, they don't offend the Unionists. But if they were in our position, they would see that they are going to have to put a lot more pressure on the British government to make the Unionists sit down and talk. I think they should be standing on our side, on the Republican side, because it is us who need the support. The Republican community has been demonised for the last twenty-five years. You can't stand up and say you are fighting a just cause when the media are portraying it as a murderous criminal conspiracy. And that's because it's been distorted by British censorship.

At the time of the hunger strikes the British government tried to break the IRA. They thought that by breaking the prisoners they could undermine the rest of the structure in which the prisoners are such a big link. But one of the things Britain doesn't appreciate is that they were not just fighting the IRA, they were fighting the whole community that supports them. They tried before the hunger strikes to take away political status. As we have seen through the recently-leaked document on Bloody Sunday, the British consider this to be a war. But when they talk about it in the media, it is only civil disorder; so the prisoners were going to be treated like criminals. They were not criminals. And they tried every other means of protest, the no-wash protest, the blanket protest, until they saw that the

prison system was not going to change. The only way they could deal with that was the hunger strike, which has been used in this country for centuries. The thing about a hunger strike is that it is nonviolent. The only person that you are inflicting any kind of pain on is yourself. You are not shooting or bombing. Ten people gave their lives for that issue; again, it wasn't directly involved with the national question, it was about the way the prisoners were being treated. We have seen that the hunger strike did, to an extent, work, but I think that it was a big watershed inside the Nationalist community. Once again, instead of trying to celebrate what we are, we ended up marching solemnly to remember our dead.

A lot of this is very negative whereas I would like to see us celebrating our identity. Things like the Gas Yard Wall Féile, the West Belfast Festival, all that is about celebrating our identity within an establishment which is trying to strangle it.

When you look at it, it is a kind of textbook struggle. It began with the civil rights movement when it was just about civil rights. Then people saw that in the British/Unionist establishment they were not going to get the justice they deserved, they were not going to be treated as equal citizens. So people thought if they were going to get shot off the streets, they would arm themselves and fight back. People went through that process and a political awareness developed. We are still going through that process, and we have come to the point where people in the Republican movement have made a decision to say that the armed struggle has taken them to the point where they now feel they can develop politically. One of the important things during the 1975 ceasefire was that Republicans didn't really have the political ideology to back up what was being demanded at that time, whereas now it is there.

There are different forms of violence. The way I look at it is that there is state violence, which is the RUC and the British army, and there is a kind of state-maintained violence, which is the UVF, UDA and any other names that MI5 and MI6 go under. I don't think the Republican community were left with any other option at the start of the troubles but the use of violence. Through the ceasefire they have shown that violence is just an option, not the ending and the beginning of the Republican struggle. They are prepared to use it when there is no other option, but if they see another way they are prepared to stop.

I think the ceasefire was great. It was really important that we, as a community, say to the rest of the world that we have suffered over the last seventy-five years, we have been dragged through the dirt, we have put up with the brunt of the discrimination, the bad housing, policing, the army, the raids, people getting shot. And if, despite all that, we can be stronger than the establishment, then that gives new hope.

What we have seen over the last eighteen months is British intransigence. They don't want to move because they are afraid of losing the Unionist backbone of the Conservative Party. They have tried everything: argued about permanency; argued about decommissioning; they just seem to be putting stumbling blocks on the path to peace and freedom. Decommissioning is not a real issue. It's John Major going through the dictionary looking for important-sounding words that he can pull out. Where there is a war going on you can't demand arms from one side. The British are looking for a victory, they want to be able to say to the Unionists 'look, we have beaten the Nationalist community into the ground, you can now do whatever you want with them'. I would like to see instead the British government saying to the Unionist parties 'you are going to have to sit down and talk, and talk until the thing is sorted'.

I don't want it to go back to armed conflict again. I have known nothing over the last twenty-six years but soldiers and armed police on the streets. I have hatred, but I would like to get to a point in my life where I don't have to live with that hatred because I hate the police, I hate the army, I hate the British establishment for what it has done here to me and to my family and to the community that I live in, and I think that can be really destructive. You should be able to look at the police and think: there is a copper, ask him the time; or if something happens you should be able to go to the police. In this society we can't do that because they are not a police force in any recognised sense of the term. They are a paramilitary organisation. I would like to see the disbanding of the RUC, I think that is very important. What we need in this country is a police *service*, something that *all* sections of the community can look to. I think if we had a police service that was accountable to the community they serve, that would be a big step forward.

A lot more prisoners should be released. I think the British are throwing crumbs to the media. There is this idea of 50% remission, but that was only removed in 1987. There have been numerous studies done on prisoners, and one of the findings is that most people who have gone to jail because of the political situation here, are not people who would normally be in jail. They don't come from deviant or anti-social backgrounds; they are there because of the political situation.

I am optimistic for the future because one of the important things about the process that we are going through – and the ceasefire now is part of that process – is that it's only going to make us stronger. So we can say that we have tried everything open to us and to me that's the important thing.

David Nicholl

Articles two and three will have to be rescinded if there is to be progress. I don't see the Irish government and the Irish people doing that. They have used it basically as a teaser, like a carrot to a donkey, to get Unionists around the table.

Around '68 and '69, there was talk of deprivation and civil rights and all this type of thing. Basically, what the civil rights movement was asking for at the time was also wanted by the Protestant community. It wasn't until later that sectarian divisions appeared in the campaign. We were poor, and they were poor. My understanding of it was that people were saying they were poor and they wanted better housing and they wanted this, that and the other and everybody shared those aims. But it was later on when things started to take a more sinister turn, when Republicans started to manipulate the situation into a confrontation for a united Ireland that problems arose. John Hume has been quoted the world over as saying it was 'a united Ireland or nothing'. We saw the riots in the Bogside and other disturbances and that's when the major division appeared because Protestants perceived that it was 'just that crowd at it again'. Nationalists saw Protestants doing something similar in the Shankill and they said the same thing about them.

As the street protests started to get out of hand, that was the starting point of the real violence. The two communities started to divide and take up their own particular positions and then the trust was broken down. The disturbances on the street got worse and worse, and just polarised the two communities, so there was no point in co-operating with one another.

Jack Lynch was responsible in my view for getting the Protestants' backs up straight away by saying 'we will not stand idly by at the border', and then we saw Protestant B Specials and the RUC being battered into the ground in Waterloo Street and places like that. Members of my own family were in those organisations at the time and they were coming home at night completely wrecked. We had good Catholic neighbours, we played with them, we did everything with them. It wasn't until the outbreak of the troubles that they drifted away. Personally I am disappointed that many of the friends I had when I was younger, around Strabane and around Ballymagorry where I was brought up, grew up to be teenagers like myself and took up arms and attempted to murder a few of our Protestant neighbours. Seeing those people put behind bars gave us no pleasure whatsoever, other than it prevented them from murdering anybody else.

I am still angry that the troubles happened, and like most ordinary Protestants I wish to God they had never happened. We have inflicted brutality on each other over the past twenty-five years, and there have been atrocities, innumerable atrocities. One of those that springs to mind is the La Mon House bombing where bodies were shovelled off the streets, charred to a crisp. I found it most distressing to see the pictures that appeared at that particular time, and again after the Enniskillen massacre. There have also been terrible atrocities committed by Protestants, and that's regrettable, but from a personal perspective, I can only say that I think that had there not been a reaction from the Protestant community it would have been worse for us. The IRA would have slaughtered a lot more than the 3,167 who have died during the troubles. Ultimately it was the IRA who were responsible for the onset of violence.

I felt frustrated during the troubles, frustrated that no-one, but no-one, seemed to want to do anything about it. You had guerillas on the streets inflicting psychological, mental and physical damage on the whole community, Catholic and Protestant, and I wish to God someone had sat down a bit earlier and convened talks where all parties could have come together and discussed a way to redress the economic and social issues which were affecting everyone.

From a very young age I thought 'I have to get the hell out of here, I can't live amongst this'. I had a six-weeks-old cousin who was slaughtered in his pram; and a brother kidnapped by the IRA, an experience that so personally and psychologically damaged him that he always thought they were coming back to get him, and he ended up committing suicide not long before the troubles actually ended. And then my own home was bombed on 16 December 1987, just after the Enniskillen massacre, when a device was placed on my doorstep at Tullyally. From then on I thought 'to hell with this, someone has to do something, and if they are going to try to kill me for doing nothing other than being a citizen living in this country then it's about time I started to speak out against it'; and that's when I became involved in politics.

I had already had some sort of warning, through the prison system, that there was going to be a ceasefire. The Loyalist prisoners were sending out word to the community that a break in hostilities seemed to be imminent, that the IRA would like to call a halt. The more talk there was about it, it didn't seem that it was ever going to happen, and then it did happen and we wondered was it permanent? Was it really over and done for good? We couldn't see why they had stopped, because they hadn't achieved their objectives. In fact they had failed by stopping. They hadn't obtained their united Ireland by coercion; and I don't think they'll ever achieve it by consent either, because most Catholics don't want it in my view. At the same time we felt elated that the death and the destruction had stopped.

I perceive that the Loyalist ceasefire was inevitable after the Republican one, because Loyalist violence was always reactive to IRA violence. It wasn't proactive for a great many years, and basically they never did go out intentionally, in my view, to slaughter Catholics wholesale. Any massacres, or what were perceived as massacres, like Greysteel, were basically as a consequence of war, and, unfortunate as they were, were basically a barometer of how the Protestant feeling was at that time after the Shankill bombing and those types of atrocities. I think that at the end of the day, this made both sides say 'this can't go on, it has to stop, or we will end up in a civil war'.

It would be wrong to say that there was no state violence. But when the state is set up, and they have structures of government to run which need protecting from insurgents, from whatever source, then you are going to have a counter-insurgency movement against those who are trying to overthrow the sitting government of the day. And it's understandable that the defensive forces used to do that will be seen as antagonistic by those who are insurgent. Protestants, and especially Protestant prisoners, have always felt that 'if you can't do the time, don't do the crime'. They see themselves as being part and parcel of those defending their state. On the other hand, the Nationalists see them as enemies. Therefore, when the police raid Nationalists' houses, you have situations where confrontations develop, and maybe people are injured, and obviously so, because in any conflict situation you are going to have casualties. If the state is against violence, from whatever source, then they will use tactics equal or similar to the ones deployed by those who are fighting the war.

For the past eighteen months now, the paramilitaries will have taken stock. They are not, on both sides, as unthinking as some people make them out to be. It has been claimed by many that these people are beasts and neanderthals, but there is a clear, cool, and calculated purpose in their actions. They are military-minded where the rest of us are not. But the situation now is not as stable as we thought it would be. There are several facets of the current stage of the process which we always knew we would come across. But what we didn't expect was that when John Hume declared the war was over and Adams and he and Reynolds had met at the Dáil, there would be a continuation of violence in another form, through petrol bombings and street protests. For the Protestant community, in my view, it was merely another IRA tactic, which they had already deployed in 1968-9, when they brought Catholics onto the streets to protest. Bloody Sunday, in particular, springs to mind, where for weeks they had hyped the whole situation, and had used the ordinary Catholic people as a battering ram with which to beat the army and the police and the government. They led innocent Nationalists onto the streets in large numbers, and then positioned their own people among them to open fire on the army, with the help, unfortunately, I must add, of elements from within the Free State army. What happened then was inevitable. People were going to be killed; and unfortunately it's the sort of thing that could happen again. It's the old tactic being deployed again; the IRA hyping up the situation so that they can return to an armed military campaign.

I think it would be better if everybody were to talk, but I also understand the Unionist anger at the thought of talking to people who have been out in the community for years and who are perceived as IRA men, not as Sinn Féiners, but as IRA men. In Protestant eyes Martin McGuinness was the chief of staff of the IRA. He's denied it innumerable times, but we have had Secretaries of State say he was, we have had the British government say he was; even Mates flew to the United States just after the ceasefires and said in the debate with Gerry Adams that Sinn Féin were the IRA, one and the same. The Unionist leaders in the Ulster Unionist Party and in the Democratic Unionist Party will not sit down at the same table where there is someone with a gun who's demanding 'right, you concede on this particular point or we'll blow your head off'. There could have been steps taken at this stage by the IRA to say that their arms are defensive only. The Combined Loyalist Military Command said that their arms are defensive, that they will never initiate violence, that it will only be reactive to IRA violence. The IRA could have stabilised the situation by saying that they would never initiate violence again on this island, or on these islands.

I believe talks will take place inevitably. The government will move towards that. Articles two and three will have to be rescinded if there is to be progress. I don't see the Irish government and the Irish people doing that. They have used it basically as a teaser, like a carrot to a donkey, to get Unionists around the table. What they are saying is 'you take your constitutional position and change it and allow our claim to your territory to be incorporated in the Act of Union under paragraph 75'. We are saying there will be no tinkering with the Union and the constitutional position will not change. But I think we can have a stable government in Northern Ireland which all parties can give their allegiance to, and which can work for the betterment of the people of all communities, of all ethnic origins. Personally, I would like to see former enemies sitting face-to-face at the table and addressing their grievances through dialogue rather than going back to violence where both communities would suffer needlessly. At the end of the day, the communities themselves cannot change constitutional positions without a referendum. I suspect it will take at least two generations before the old hatreds and animosities start to subside. Our hope is with the younger generation, and the children of tomorrow who haven't been born yet, who haven't got the old animosity inbred into them. They haven't been part of the troubles of the past twenty-five years, or seventy-five years, or even 300 years. But at the end of the day, we can't afford to let our historical past become an excuse for inaction.

The absence of physical violence over the ceasefire period had a very significant impact on the community as a whole in that people, while still apprehensive that the thing will re-emerge as before, are glad and happy that people are not killing one another on our streets. Unfortunately there are violent incidents coming from the IRA and from Loyalists, the punishment beatings which some people criticise but which others in the community condone. I have seen people coming on the TV and protesting the innocence of those who were beaten, but at the end of the day the local people in those communities knew they were nothing more than hoods and gangsters who were causing disruption to the community, and the people were scared to death by what was going on. The police didn't have the time or the experience or the power to deal with the situation, or couldn't deal with it because they couldn't get the evidence from the community. As a result, a rising tide of drugs and other criminal activities was rife in the community, particularly amongst the young, and action had to be taken. Unfortunately it was the paramilitaries whom the community chose to do it. I don't agree with taking people out and using baseball bats to beat them up. Policing has to be a matter for the civil forces of law and order, and basically we are not, the community is not, the police force of the country. I believe, with time, that we can establish a police force which can do the job in a reasonable manner. It will not always be perfect, but a police force such as the RUC can be reformable.

It's unfortunate that we have politicians on both sides who have stuck their heads in the sand and refused to budge. I think we need a whole new approach, with new people coming through from the grass roots. I would rather have a person from the community coming forward to meet the needs of that community in council than have a political party do it because the people on the street will tell you, irrespective of which community they come from, that the only time we see politicians is once every five years at a local council election, when they knock on everybody's doors promising us the sun, moon and the stars, and then disappear and are not seen for another five years. It has to come from the people on the ground because only they can initiate the change, and it's people-power at the end of the day which influences politicians.

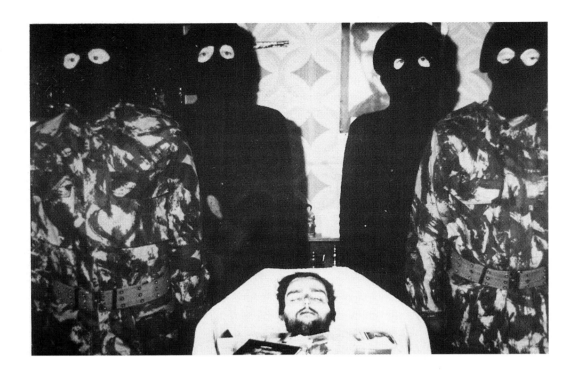

INLA colour guards in attendance at the coffins of hunger strikers Patsy O'Hara (above) and Michael Devine (below) in 1981. *(Photos: Willie Carson/Pacemaker Press)*

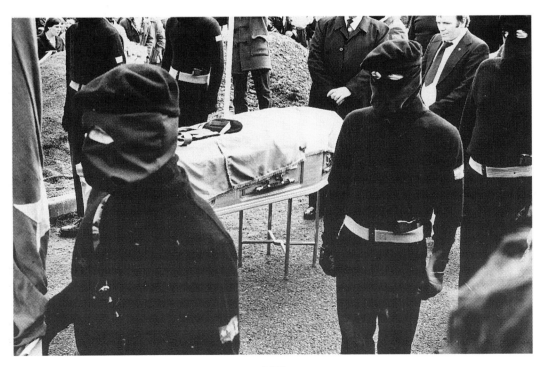

Ian Paisley and Sammy Wilson of the DUP attend a march for Prostestant civil rights organised by Gregory Campbell in the early 1980s. *(Photo: Willie Carson)*

DUP aldermen William Hay (front left) and Gregory Campbell (third left) and a number of their supporters protest against the city council name change from Londonderry to Derry in January 1984. *(Photo: Pacemaker Press)*

Riot police outnumber mourners at the funeral of IRA member Philip McFadden in Creggan in 1986. *(Photo: Jim Cunningham)*

An image from the Fountain circa 1992 highlights the feelings of Loyalists living on the cityside. *(Photo: Arlene Wege)*

Paul O'Connor

...I now regard it as the most important event during the troubles in terms of the carte blanche that it gave to the security forces to kill people – that if they could get away with Bloody Sunday they could get away with anything. I think that is the most important message given by Bloody Sunday ...

I grew up in a Nationalist family, my father was old IRA. It was a middle-class family. There was a lot of politics talked in our house, and I remember knowing what the word gerrymandering meant when I was only about eight or nine. We were all very aware of what was going on, very acutely aware of the political situation.

I think even to claim now, as some people still do, that the old Corporation was actually fair, that it did a good job, is one of the reasons why we still have to deal with the past, because there are people who are still unwilling to face up to what actually happened in those years. What really happened is there in black and white, it's there to be read. You just have to look at the employment figures within the Corporation, at the very nature of why Creggan was built, of why the Rossville Street high flats were built. It is important to make sure that these facts are documented because there are still a few people who would prefer to just put their heads in the sand and pretend it never happened.

I certainly believed totally in what the civil rights movement stood for. Growing up as a Catholic in Derry, and what I suppose would have been described as a Nationalist, the feeling was that we were emulating something that was happening elsewhere in the world, especially in America. People looked to the black civil rights movement in the US, and looked at what was happening here, and felt what we were doing was the very least that could be done. I think there was probably a certain sense of anger – that has not yet really been discussed – towards the previous generation, a feeling that they hadn't done

enough, that they had sat back and taken it, and there was a feeling within the generation growing up in the '60s that they were not going to take it any more.

I don't think that the civil rights movement ignored Protestant poverty, but I don't think there is a comparison. I think it is a waste of time to get into comparisons of poverty. There was no doubt that the Protestant working class were being treated badly just as the Catholic working class were being treated badly, but there were different levels of it. If you lived in a wee house in the Fountain but you had a job, or if you lived in a wee house in the Bogside and didn't have a job ... But my memories of the early civil rights movement are not memories of something that was exclusively a Catholic movement. It was very much a constitutional movement in a way. It wasn't challenging the very nature of the state, just demanding fairly minor reforms. There were Protestants involved in the civil rights movement; Ivan Cooper, Claude Wilton, Campbell Austin, were all involved in the early leadership of the civil rights movement

I think the responsibility for the violence at many of the marches lay completely with the Minister of Home Affairs at the time, William Craig; I've no doubt about that. They were looking for confrontation. It is important to remember that what actually led to the banning of the 5 October march was the Apprentice Boys last-minute announcement that there was to be a 'traditional' swearing-in ceremony and march on that day in Derry which gave the RUC an excuse to ban the original march. People forget that it was actually the Apprentice Boys who started off that chain of events.

At the beginning of 1969 I joined the People's Democracy march after it reached Derry. Walking past Irish Street on my way to meet the march I had seen the stones built up into a big pile on the banking, and the RUC were standing there with the young Loyalists who were getting ready to attack. What impressed me at that time was how people kept their dignity. Blood was pouring from marchers' heads – mostly people from People's Democracy who had been attacked in Burntollet a couple of hours beforehand – and no-one was fighting back. There were Loyalists in Shipquay Street and at the Diamond threatening to attack but the marchers weren't looking for trouble. They were looking for very simple, basic demands, and the irony is, and I think most people in the Unionist community know it now, that had those demands been granted, that would probably have been it, they would have effectively defused the movement.

Like most people, I certainly didn't have a clue what was coming. I wouldn't have had the slightest idea of what was on the cards, that the situation was going to get as bad as it did. But what moved me, and I think a lot of people of my age at that time in Derry, wasn't actually the events in Derry, it was the events in Belfast. I can remember going out to riot with other people because of what was happening in Belfast, or what had happened in Belfast, even half-an-hour or an hour beforehand. Probably one of the most important events for me growing up was the Falls curfew, and at the end of the Falls curfew seeing the Unionist MPs being driven around the Lower Falls in the back of an army landrover. For me that was just the end of it, I knew then that there was just no compromise with this government. I just felt that history was repeating itself, but repeating itself in an even worse form.

My memory of internment is one of a great sense of foreboding, that everything now was exploding, there was nothing normal left in our youth or in our future. The idea of just concentrating on exams or finishing school went completely out the window.

After Bloody Sunday I felt we were approaching a time when they would literally just take people out in the street and machine-gun them.

I would've hoped at that time that possibly the South was really going to come in behind Nationalists in the North. I don't think there has been any time in the last twenty-five years when Southern public opinion has been so moved; the events in Dublin, the burning of the Embassy. In Derry it was a shock that was just almost impossible to comprehend. I think the trauma of Bloody Sunday certainly hasn't been overcome yet because of what has followed on from it. I now regard it as *the* most important event during the troubles in terms of the *carte blanche* that it gave to the security forces to kill people – that if they could get away with Bloody Sunday they could get away with anything. I think that is the most important message given by Bloody Sunday, and I don't think that that is stressed enough. That's why I think it is important that Bloody Sunday still be dealt with, and that it be called for what it was, officially-sanctioned murder by the British government. Until that is faced up to, I don't think it is possible for us to move on.

The hunger strikes were again a case of history repeating itself, where once again you had an issue that could so easily have been resolved. All that was being demanded was what the prisoners already had until 1976. When Bobby Sands died, I think, for myself, as for a lot of people – it seems like a contradiction to say it – but it was yet again the last straw. But so much was the last straw; Burntollet was the last straw, August '69 was the last straw. And then the introduction of internment, and Bloody Sunday; but the death of Bobby Sands and the other hunger strikers certainly, emotionally, for me, fitted in to that category of total disbelief that the British government could be so arrogant. I don't think any other government in Europe could have handled the situation as badly as they did. I think the reason they handled it so badly was because of an inherent kind of racism and an inherent denial of what was actually happening on this island.

I think in years to come, when history is written that is not biased by the need to prove some kind of revisionist political point, then I don't think the Irish government will be very proud of its record over the last twenty to twenty-five years. As regards the British government, ironically it doesn't seem to have made much difference who was in power; in fact it seemed to be almost better if the Tories were in power than if Labour was in power. Some of the worst Secretaries of State we had were Labour. There was this denial that you could actually talk, and you still find it now, this total inability to actually sit down and talk about the situation, and try and work it out. It just seems like those twenty-five years didn't need to happen, but the will was not there in Britain to try and solve it until bombs started to go off in the financial area of London, and then they finally decided to grasp the nettle.

I would have to make a distinction between the three main types of violence; Republican, Loyalist, and state violence. But I would also include a fourth type – the structural violence, as it's called, that people here grew up with and still have to deal with. There is a spiral of violence which begins with the structural violence of the state we lived in. That structural violence caused people to go out on the streets and demand their rights in a nonviolent way, and that was met with violence. People who were peacefully demanding change then turned to violence, which brought on them more oppression from the state. I don't differentiate that greatly between Loyalist violence and state violence, because so much of the Loyalist violence has actually been led by the British state. If you look at the Amnesty Report from 1995, they are once again highlighting the issue of collusion, so I don't differentiate between the two of them.

I would not condemn in any way those people who decided that the only way to resist repression here was to use violence. I think that people took what was in many cases the only decision they could take, because sadly the British government seems to have shown over and over again that it won't listen to anything else. It had the chance during the civil rights era, and even then its response was almost zero, and the reforms came too little and too late. I don't think you can condemn the working-class people who decided there was only one way they could respond, by joining the IRA. Having said that, it does not contradict the fact that twenty-five years on, it was time to stop, time to find another way forward.

It was a very emotional moment for me when I heard the news of the ceasefire. I was on holiday in Spain, in an area where some people had hardly even heard of the North of Ireland, but there was such a lot of interest. There was massive media attention, there were pages and pages in the newspapers. I went into a bar and ordered a pint and watched it on the TV again because I couldn't sleep all night. I just sat down and cried.

I am glad that the ceasefire has lasted, and I think it is the only way forward, but I think that the response of the British government has been criminal. I don't think Republicans should hand any weapons over. I don't see why the Republican movement should have to make a gesture towards those who have been murdering people in our community for the last twenty-five years and never suffered the consequences. We are not talking about whether hundreds of members of the RUC and British army should be released from jail because of the murders *they* have committed. We are not talking about that because they are not in jail. I believe trust has to be built up, but I cannot for the life of me understand why, in a conflict that involved the British government, the Loyalist community and Republicans, why we are talking about only one side having to prove good faith? Why are we not talking about the need for trust to be built up within *our* community by those people who won't even admit that they murdered people on Bloody Sunday? Why should our political representatives be expected to talk to them without mutual trust first being established? They still have armed groups on the streets. They have broken limbs in this city very recently, they have fired over one hundred plastic bullets. Why is the trust one-sided? Everybody has got blood on their hands; everybody in the last twenty-five years has been involved in the violence.

I believe that people need to sit down and talk about starting up a new and acceptable police *service* on this island. I think there are a number of interim steps that can be taken before that can happen. One of them is the disarming of the RUC. People would argue with you that it's not realistic for them to be disarmed, but why is it not? There hasn't been a shot fired in this city in thirteen months. Why shouldn't they be disarmed? There is more violence on the streets of Dublin than there is here and the Gardaí are not armed. I think an independent commission needs to be set up to look at the history and human rights violations of the security forces. You may say, why? Why not look at everybody's human rights violations? Well, because I think there is a very clear consensus that there have been human rights violations by all sides. Many people from our community have gone to jail for long prison terms. The only human rights violations that have not been acknowledged in the last twenty-years have been those of the state, and that has to be acknowledged, not in order to extract revenge, but to set a marker that it's not possible for the state to kill people over such a period and then simply move on and say 'well, here's the people who did the killing, they are still in the same state forces, they still carry the same weaponry, and we all just have to accept it'. Well, that's not acceptable, clearly not acceptable, and it's very clear that people here and elsewhere are not going to accept the RUC. There can be levels of acceptance on minor issues, where people feel there is some issue in their community where by law they are forced to contact the RUC. That's fair enough, people will do that. But everybody accepts the fact that what we really need is a police service where a young woman or man who is Republican-minded, or is SDLP-minded, or whatever, could feel 'well, it's a career choice for me, to go and be a plumber, or go and join the police service'. That's obviously not the case at the moment and that's a situation we have to arrive at.

What I would like to see eventually may sound very simplistic, but what I would like to see in the future is that people within the Catholic community, whether they see themselves as Nationalists, Republicans or whatever, sit down and try to understand the nature of Protestantism in the North of Ireland. What does it mean to be Unionist? What are the fears of the Unionist community? What is it that they are afraid of? Does it always have to be the zero-sum game? Does one side always have to 'lose' for the other to

'win'? I have a very clear and firm belief that the people on this island of Ireland should self-determine what happens or not in this island.

Do British ministers really care about what happens here? In a year or two they are going to be back in Hampshire or Cheshire or wherever, playing their own wee political power games within the Conservative Party. They're not from here, they didn't grow up here, they don't care. For me that is what self-determination is about. I want the people who live here and who are going to be here in twenty years, and whose children's children are going to be here, and whose roots are here, and I don't care if they are Protestants or Catholics – if someone has been here for 300 years they are not planters, they are all of this country, however you might define it – those are the people I want to see determining what happens on this island. And that doesn't mean I want to see Catholics in charge, or I want to see Protestants in charge. In fact I want to see the Churches booted right out the door. I don't think they should be influencing laws, North or South. And it's not just the Catholic Church that has influenced laws; the Protestant Churches have also. The Christian Churches in general have had far too much malign influence on legislation on this entire island, and I want to see that stopped. I just want to see the people who live on the island determining what happens in it. I don't want London rule just to be supplanted by Dublin rule. One clique of people should not rule or determine what happens on the whole island. There could possibly be a second tier of government made up almost completely from the community and voluntary sector within our society who could help to determine what goes on. But that's what I would like to see further down the line.

I am firmly of the opinion that the British, whether Labour or Conservative, are the worst possible people to hold the reins of power in this society. I don't believe they are capable of really charting the way forward. I think the people who live and belong here are the only ones who can do that.

Fionnbarra ÓDochartaigh

Early on it was agreed that the Army Council gave total backing to the documents on social and economic policy. Before the civil rights movement was formed the Army Convention passed resolutions supporting the actions of all volunteers involved in social and economic issues in the North and called for the formation of a broad-based movement.

I first became politically conscious when a brother of mine was interned when I was thirteen, around about 1957. He was not a member of any branch of the Republican movement; his only activity was teaching Irish, and for that he was put in jail, which I found totally disgusting. I thought that if they can lock you up for teaching Irish you may as well do something decent, and oppose them politically as well as culturally. So I decided very early on that I would join the Republican movement. I was told at the time that I was too young and to come back the following year. And so for a couple of years after that I just went along to their headquarters, which was at the back of the Harps Hall in the Lecky Road.

I eventually got involved in the cultural and language side, and then, around 1962, a group of us younger people who felt the old crowd didn't want us formed Republican Volunteer Youth. The movement never recognised us, so we decided we would go out and collect door to door for the prisoners. Then we started smuggling in the *United Irishman*, which was banned, and we started selling it door to door. They had to bring us into the movement then and so we joined Sinn Féin. A lot of us were disgusted with Sinn Féin because we thought they were all just old men who saw themselves more as a commemorative committee than an active political party.

By that stage the IRA in Derry was smashed. We began a self-analysis of why we had failed in the past, and the conclusion was that it was because we had not put our roots down with the people on social and economic issues. But the old brigade, what *I* would call the old brigade,

the people in Sinn Féin here in Derry, they were for no new departure, they were pure traditionalists most of them.

From about 1964 the IRA in Derry began not so much to endorse the social and economic programme as discuss it inside the ranks. We were convinced of, and we endorsed, the left-wing position. By 1965 many of us were involved in the trade union movement in the BSR factory in Creggan. We had begun to read Connolly and Lenin and greatly admired the revolution in Cuba.

We formed the Derry Unemployed Action Committee. The DUAC then began to help people who had been evicted, such as the woman down in the Wells. They put her out in the street and we put her back in. It was not a pleasant sight, someone being evicted; and this was the so-called swinging '60s when the world was supposed to be changing. Already the bones of the social and economic programme were there but the muscle and the flesh were now going on it. Then we seriously began to analyse what the hell was going on in this country. We teamed up with Con McCloskey and his wife Patricia, in Dungannon. They ran the Committee for Social Justice in Northern Ireland. I began to realise that housing and unemployment and the electoral system were all linked, because you needed a house to have a vote and even if you had a vote there was still gerrymandering.

In 1966, a new publishing company based in Dublin, New Books, run by the Communist Party, began to produce a lot of Connolly's works which made their way into the movement, and rank-and-file members were encouraged to read them because they complemented the social and economic policy. Politics were always discussed. It wasn't just a matter of how many men have we got trained now; it was much more complicated than that. The Army Council had resolutions on social and economic issues. They were not just purely militarist and the volunteers were encouraged to think, to read. Early on it was agreed that the Army Council gave total backing to the documents on social and economic policy. Before the civil rights movement was formed the Army Convention passed resolutions supporting the actions of all volunteers involved in social and economic issues in the North and called for the formation of a broad-based movement. The idea was to bring together the unemployed, the homeless, the Campaign for Social Justice in Northern Ireland, small agitation groups and people who were fighting against ground rents. The other aim was to try and influence student groups, and anybody else who felt that the system was sick.

We were disgusted with the response from Derry. Even the so-called radicals didn't think that the civil rights movement was going to get anywhere. A lot of the old traditionalists didn't want anything to do with it. They saw the social and economic programme as a new departure. Instinctively I thought the Northern Ireland state would never be reformed, and after what my own family went through, and having seen how little progress we had made on a number of issues, I believed that the only way forward was to abolish Stormont. There were two distinct elements which I don't think the Dublin leadership fully understood. There were people like me who saw social agitation as a way of pushing the state to the limit so that it would react. There was another element who, incredibly, believed that through ordinary campaigning – leaflets, speaking, getting people elected – they could change the system. I fell into the first category.

It was just key people from the North who attended the Army Conventions, people the leadership knew were totally committed to the social and economic programme. The leadership wanted the most left-wing people to be there. The movement was very much influenced by the social and economic programme and by the works

of the Wolfe Tone Society and the Committee for Social Justice in Northern Ireland. So the demands of the civil rights movement were quite clear: the abolition of the B Specials and the Special Powers Act, and 'one man one vote'. People weren't really aware of the women's movement then; that it should be a call for 'one *person* one vote'. We kept the unemployed movement as part of the umbrella civil rights movement. We no longer saw the need for a separate unemployed movement, but we did stay active. We couldn't abolish the housing action movement, we couldn't say to the rank-and-file people that the civil rights movement would solve their problem. Then we called on the civil rights movement to hold a march in Derry. Belfast was very reluctant, and even on 4 October they were in the City Hotel arguing against the march. The bottom line was we were marching regardless of what anybody else was going to do. So Eamonn McCann and I became the main spokespeople.

I was arrested the morning after the 5 October march. I was delighted at that. I got up the next morning and I said to my mother: "They are going to come and arrest us this morning." I was taken to the barracks and McGimpsey asked me what was I smiling about. I was in great form. I told him: "Yesterday your batons were like magic wands, you have turned a small pressure group into a mass movement."

"Where's this mass movement?" he asked.

I said: "Wait and see, Ireland will never be the same again."

It was the happiest day of my life because the apathy was dead thanks to the RUC. Policemen came into my cell and agreed with me. They said they had known what was going to happen the day before, but that they were only carrying out orders. The Nazis used the same story when they put the people in the gas chamber, that was their yarn too.

During that period between 5 October 1968 and August 1969 there was a definite rift emerging between the leadership in Dublin and rank-and-file leaders like myself. People's Democracy was founded, and a number of influential leading Republicans here in Derry saw it as a genuine expression of working-class politics. We didn't see the line coming from Dublin fitting into that category. People's Democracy had our support, and of a lot of working-class people. You had Michael Farrell coming to the fore and Bernadette Devlin later on. The democratization argument came up again and increasingly the national question and Stormont were being debated. We joined the Republican movement to end partition but now we were being told by our leadership in Dublin that we must democratize the very institution which was set up against the wishes of the Irish people, 72.5% of whom voted for Sinn Féin in 1918. Partition was enforced literally by the British government and by Loyalist pogroms, armed by Britain with guns coming from Germany. Long before the actual split took place I, like Farrell, genuinely wanted the civil rights movement to be as nonviolent as possible. But the reaction of the people at the grass roots was to meet violence with violence. Violence, you must remember, was used by the RUC on 5 October, they were the people who opened that can of worms. I began to realise that if we continually used the nonviolent argument we would have the moral high ground, but on the other hand the violence at grass roots level would bring the national question up anyway.

I was very much involved in the defence of the Bogside. I was on the streets for almost seventy-five hours, and I took a bus to Letterkenny to appeal for arms, shotguns, anything, because the shooting was starting in Belfast. That was the day the British army came in. The crunch came inside the movement when Roy Johnston came up to Derry while the fighting was going on, and there was a meeting which about three or four leading members attended. He told us to stop attacking the RUC. We said the RUC were attacking us. He said that we had influence, so get the movement to disengage. We told him it wasn't organised by the movement, that it was a popular uprising. What had happened was that the people had taken over. The Republican movement could either stand aside and be rejected by the people or take part, and we took part. Those who wrote on the walls in Belfast 'IRA = I Ran Away' didn't understand what was happening. The IRA did not run away. They did not run away

in Derry, and they did not run away in Belfast.

When the IRA split in 1970, I went with the Officials because I didn't think the older traditionalists, the Provisionals, had done a lot for the civil rights movement. I can understand why the Provos were created. The leadership in Dublin had been told often enough by people like myself that the bubble was going to burst. We had joined the Irish army in the '60s because we knew we were going to need some sort of defence. The Dublin leadership did not support us joining the Irish army.

I wasn't in Derry on Bloody Sunday. I wanted to go to the march but Cathal Goulding wanted me to remain in the South. At the time a number of Republican leaders commented that the paratroopers were coming in, and that that was very ominous. They thought something serious was going to happen. From my understanding, it had been agreed that there wouldn't be any IRA presence on the streets that day. I have heard all the arguments that the IRA fired first. There was a report that one particular man fired shots *after* the first shots were fired by the British army. I think Bishop Daly made a similar statement, that one man was seen, but that would hardly excuse what happened on Bloody Sunday. Let's face it, at the end of the day, as John Lennon's song says: "Not a soldier boy was bleeding when they nailed those coffin lids."

I was the last one to speak outside the British Embassy in Dublin before it was burnt, and again Republicans were actively involved in that expression of anger. They were the only real organised force in Dublin that could have done it.

But that period is all history now. The future? Well, whatever way this Mitchell commission goes is going to be important. I believe there are elements in the English ruling class who would like to see the Republican movement split. Within the Republican movement many say we cannot disarm because we can't leave the people in Belfast and Derry and elsewhere defenceless. We don't know what the future is and we can't go back to the situation we were in in 1969. It would be ironic for the current leadership to totally disarm now. We could have a repeat of history.

It has to be an institutionalised peace. It has to deal with fundamental questions like parity of esteem, turning it from a slogan into an actual program. There must be equality for the Irish language. There is a real bias within the civil service that must be removed. There must be a strong affirmative program on employment. We are in many ways still fighting for the same demands as in 1968, so on the repressive legislation side we have made no progress. I would actually call for a war crimes tribunal. Every Republican who was caught went to jail, but there are at least 150 disputed cases, including about seventy or eighty children under eighteen. The RUC have never accounted for Sammy Devenney and the British government has yet to apologise for Bloody Sunday and declare that those people were innocent. There has to be a tribunal. Those war crimes, Britain's war crimes, have never been fully exposed.

There has to be a new agenda if peace is going to last, a new mass movement, built again on reformist demands. If Republicans reject a new form of Stormont as a transitional measure then they have to put up some alternative. They want all-party talks but nobody has yet spelt out what the agenda for those talks is. The Unionists hold a key card because Major is in such a weak position.

There is a big gap in policy that the broad radical elements have not yet tried to fill. Calls for working-class unity are just slogans. I don't believe that there will ever be working-class unity in this country while partition remains because a large section of the working class in the North have a vested interest. They had a vested interest in the old system, and they have a vested interest in the continuation of the various forms of discrimination.

Many Republicans in Belfast and Derry have become quite apathetic just because the Brits are off the streets. But they are not off the streets in south Armagh, they are not off the streets in many other parts, in fact they are not off the streets in those areas the British and Irish governments believe are the real traditional Republican strongholds. So that's not a very good sign.

There's need for a whole new thinking. I'm not advocating the return to armed struggle, I

actually do believe that at the end of the day the IRA and the British army have fought themselves to a stalemate, and the people who have suffered most through the last couple of years have been ordinary working-class people in the ghettoes, and I'm including the Shankill Road in that. There has to be some kind of British disengagement. Nobody ever talks any more about 'troops out', it's not 'respectable' now. In my opinion, the Provos could rethink their federal policy as a stopgap measure, because it could well be that a large section of the Unionists are now opening up to new ideas.

If the Provos sell out, and I'm not saying they will, but if they do, now anyone who has got their ear to the ground will note that on 1 January 1996 a new headquarters was opened in Dublin by Republican Sinn Féin. There were six members of their movement locked up recently, including their general secretary, Josephine Hayden, and if there was a sell out, a new movement has already been created.

The fundamental issue still remains – partition. Britain is still occupying Northern Ireland. Without its financial support the Northern Ireland state could not have existed. The end product has to be British withdrawal. It has to be a solution worked out by Irish men and Irish women, Unionists and Nationalists, left and right wing, the whole lot. My view is that there might well be some kind of transitional institutions set up. I think at the back of every Loyalist's mind is the fear that sooner or later there is going to be a united Ireland. And I would argue that economically Ireland is already united. Britain does not have to pack up and go overnight, that would be a disaster, we don't want another India situation. Let them declare their intention to leave within ten years. Ten years is nothing, and there are Republicans who would condemn me for saying that, they want them out now, but that's not practical. All the issues have to be tackled, the role of the police etc, but nobody has spelt out that agenda. When these issues come to be discussed, by both governments, and by the various party leaders North and South, and changes begin to take place, there will be elements within the Loyalist community who will see this as a major threat to their own supremacy. They see every Catholic as Republican, every Republican as a member of Sinn Féin, and every Sinn Féin member as an IRA member. That's the simplistic, moronic way they look at it. Because of this it logically follows that the IRA must keep its weapons and the Republican movement must remain intact. In fact I would like to see a new Republican congress aimed at reuniting the Republican grass roots.

It's about time everyone was told what the agenda is going to be because that agenda is going to put a lot more strain on the peace process, particularly from the Unionist elements. They are the people who are going to have to give because what have the Nationalists got to give? In 1967 the Nationalist worker was 2.7 times more likely to be unemployed, and almost thirty years later the figure is still 2.5, so in all that time we have not moved very far on the economic front.

What we have been through in the last thirty-odd years was inevitable. The bubble had to burst. If we hadn't tackled the issues in the '60s, the Springtown camp might have been refurbished, but it would still be there. We would never have had a majority council in the city. What happened was a logical conclusion of the struggle for basic reform which the Northern state resisted. The people in turn had to resist oppression. The oppression lasted, it's still here, the infrastructure of repression is still here, that's why I say the questions about new institutions, British occupation, partition etc are still here. They won't go away.

I would support the idea of a new federal Ireland. There was a time when I wasn't sympathetic to the proposals contained in Eire Nua, I thought it was a sop to the Unionists. But now I think the Unionists need a sop to bring them into some kind of a new reality. One central government, four provinces – they will still have their majority on a nine-county basis, and they will have power over all things except, say, foreign affairs and the economy. So I think there is a lot of sense in the federal argument. Republicans have to go back to the drawing board. If they don't accept the federal principles contained in Eire Nua the only other transitional institution that will emerge is a new Stormont, and then we are back to square one.

Eamon O'Kane

The most obvious effect of the troubles hit home when, against everyone's advice, my brother joined the RUC. Now, I admire what was a brave decision for a Catholic; then, it seemed tantamount to suicide.

I have two strong memories of the ceasefire. The first is of the futile attitude of the hardcore activists who were shouting about victories and sellouts. I despair to think what view these people hold for the future of Northern Ireland. The second, more prominent memory, is of a middle-aged man who was a member of the audience in one of the endless media postmortems of peace. When his turn came to speak, he vilified all those who had been behind the troubles and accused both terrorists and politicians of having robbed him and his family of twenty-five years of their lives. To some it may have seemed an off-the-cuff remark, but to me it was a comment that could apply in some degree to everyone who had endured the previous twenty-five years.

I was born in November 1970 which I suppose made me a child of the troubles. However, I still see myself as one of the luckier ones. No-one in my social circle was blown up, no-one was gunned down in front of their family, no widows, no orphans. That said, I can't say we weren't affected. But who wasn't? For that matter, who cares?

I lived in a small mixed community in the rural North West, and to all intents we had an 'average' troubles childhood. My friends were mixed. Religious difference was more a curiosity than an obstacle. Perhaps we saw less of our Protestant friends around the twelfth of July but that was accepted as one of those things. We played at war games, and were more excited by the sight of soldiers than annoyed. They were nice to us and we were nice to them. Many of us wanted to be like them. I remember every time they had a checkpoint nearby we went to show

them our toy guns and they would give us their ration biscuits. They seemed to enjoy our company and we felt awed by them. I remember once tripping over a well-camouflaged one who was covering a checkpoint. He almost wet himself laughing but gave me a piece of chocolate for my trouble. In retrospect, I suppose they were glad of a friendly face. As I got older, I couldn't understand their being killed, they'd always been dead-on to us.

But you can sense things too as a child. I always remember an air of tension at airport security screens and whilst queuing to be searched at Shipquay Gate. You could see the hostile looks and off-hand manner afforded to troops in town and you were aware of the bored look of resignation on department-store security guards.

When I grew older my perceptions changed little. I felt the police were only doing a job and the soldiers didn't want to be here anyway. Why defend people who didn't like you? The obvious answer seemed to be stop killing them and they'd gladly go home.

The most obvious effect of the troubles hit home when, against everyone's advice, my brother joined the RUC. Now, I admire what was a brave decision for a Catholic; then, it seemed tantamount to suicide. The stress on the family showed almost immediately. On his third day at police college we received the first threatening phone call '...leave the cops or else'. It was New Year's Day and it's one we won't forget. My mother took the call early in the morning and like any concerned mother she freaked. The calls continued long after my brother had relented from pressure on all sides and emigrated to America eleven months later. He had only wanted to make a living, someone else had other ideas. The police had told us they were probably made by someone local. Admittedly, we soon got used to it. The calls were wordless. The caller would ring and say nothing. He must have been a really sad individual. This was their contribution to the 'cause'. A fireside terrorist.

It was a time for true colours. Some people stopped using my father's business, others stopped talking. Others became confused and thought my father had joined the police. He shared the same Christian name as his son. It wasn't healthy that he worked in a Nationalist town.

These events were to influence my plans for the future. On several occasions I had toyed with the idea of taking up a graduate commission in the forces or graduate entrance to the RUC. I was officer material and it was a career for life. I applied on several occasions but never went through with it. It would have been harder on my family than me. I would also have had to stop seeing my girlfriend; she lived in Donegal. The cons narrowly outweighed the pros but it is a decision I often regretted, especially since I have had only one year of employment since leaving law school in 1992. I blame the trouble-makers; they have done nothing for me.

With age, I developed greater animosity for the troublemakers and sympathy for the peace-keepers. If a soldier or policeman hassled me it wasn't his fault. It was because some other toss-er had led him to tar everyone in this country with the same brush. Better safe than sorry. When I travelled to college in England I filled out numerous Prevention of Terrorism question-naires because some unenlightened moron had decided it was feasible to bomb 'heavily-armed' marching bands and school children. My first month in Leicester they bombed the army re-cruitment office. It was not a good place to be Irish, especially if you'd only arrived.

My English classmates were also enlighten-ing. The troubles meant little to them. Some couldn't tell the difference between Belfast and Dublin, many wanted to know if I'd ever been

shot at and were disappointed when I said no. Sometimes too disappointed. Others felt if the SAS were given a free hand it would all be over in a week. And one drunken ex-para decided I was covert IRA. (He didn't scare me, much, but he did apologise when sobered and couldn't be nicer from then on.)

All that is in the past now and the future is meant to be brighter, but I'm still undecided about that. I hate to see antagonists of the past being hailed as heroes of peace by foreigners who don't know better. I dislike politicians who talk 'straight from the shoulder' when they should be talking from higher up. These are the men we rely on, men who bang shins on obstacles that aren't there; don't they realise that the tide turns at low water as well as high? People need to bear in mind the old proverb 'one enemy is too many, and a hundred friends too few'.

What was it all for anyway? Am I the only one who struggles to name half-a-dozen people who died since it all started? Ask their families what it was all for. I sure don't know. If the me-dia are to be believed, it has returned already in different clothes.

Recently we had a US presidential visit and I was naively inspired by his diplomacy and the goodwill that seemed to flow in his wake. Two days later I was dismayed to hear people who had used the opportunity to press his flesh and bend his ear, misquoting him and regressing to narrow-minded bigotry. Clinton did his best, but how do you talk to people who don't see preju-dice is a weakness and don't realise that the dawn will only appear to those who are awake?

My sister recently gave birth to her first child, the first member of our family to be born to 'peace'. I sincerely hope that for his sake and the sake of others like him that we, the people he trusts, will see the error of the past and put things in perspective.

It shouldn't matter *where* we live, but *how* we live. Stop watching the pictures and start lis-tening to the sound. It may be a longer road than we'd hope, but as someone once said 'the curve that can set a lot of things straight is a smile'. You have to start somewhere.

Geraldine O'Neill

...it was a great disappointment because I thought maybe the Labour government would have been better than the Conservatives. But as it has turned out, the Conservative government have actually been responsible for more happening here than the Labour government. Every British government did as little as they could. They have never done enough. In other words, the Orange card was always played, preventing anything positive happening.

Before the civil rights campaign, there was a lot of unease and tension below the surface. There wasn't 'one man one vote' then; people who owned businesses were allowed multiple votes. Many ordinary people in the street had no vote and they felt helpless because they didn't seem to be able to do very much about it. The civil rights movement was just ordinary people coming out and trying to do something positive. Before that, people talked about it but no-one seemed to do anything about it.

There were activists in the community and they channelled the people, but it was the ordinary people who decided. And it was peaceful protest. The problem was that they were not allowed to walk in certain parts of the city; if they went to walk on the main thoroughfares they were told they weren't allowed to. They were allowed to walk in the Bogside and Creggan, but once they came near the Diamond or Guildhall Square, or any of the main thoroughfares, then the police were there in force to prevent them, even though they were walking peacefully. But when they *were* prevented people got angry and a few hotheads started trouble. It eventually led to the Duke Street confrontation, and that's history now.

Bloody Sunday was a dreadful event. On that day there was a peaceful march coming down from Creggan, down William Street and into Rossville Street, where Bernadette Devlin and the other speakers had positioned themselves on a lorry they were using as a platform. I wasn't actually on the march, but myself and a few others decided we would go down and see what was happening. This was before the march had gone far. We came down into Rossville Street and William Street where the army were lined up with their shields, and there was an eerie atmosphere; I can always remember that atmosphere.

We decided then to go on up to Fahan Street, intending to go down Waterloo Street and around that area, just out of curiosity more than anything else. As we came up to the steps to Fahan Street the police were up on the Walls and there were a few civilians with them. Suddenly, a hail of stones came down on us. My husband and myself weren't sixteen or seventeen, so they had no reason to think we were out to cause trouble. I can always remember that, and it was before the march came into William Street at all. There were a few boys I noticed who had stones at the end of Rossville Street and William Street but that was normal for the time. When the march came into William Street and on over Rossville Street I was standing at the lorry talking to Bernadette Devlin. Then we heard the shooting. Everybody was just standing listening and all of a sudden we heard shots. I went over to the bottom of the New Road and into a flat. Myself and ten or fifteen other people crowded into the flat just to get out of the way; we were terrified; everyone was in shock; we were just sitting there. The shooting seemed to go on and on. We were there for about two or three hours.

That was my experience of it. People say there was a shot fired first before the army fired back but that is absolutely untrue; I was there and saw what happened. And when I heard afterwards about the deaths it was an awful feeling. I had no idea so many people had been killed; it was dreadful to think that all those young people were killed. I knew one or two of them. One of them in particular used to run messages for me when I lived in Tyrconnell Street. He was a very quiet boy, Michael McDaid, a very quiet boy. I went to the funerals in Creggan and it was the most awful thing to see, all those coffins in a line. The Widgery Report made excuses for it and said the soldiers only retaliated because they were in danger. That was completely untrue.

When Stormont fell everybody felt the civil rights movement had achieved something at long last. There was relief that something was going to happen and everyone felt it. For a while everyone thought the two sides of the community were going to work together and power was going to be shared. Everyone felt that was good, and I would say a lot of the Protestant people would have been quite happy as well, with the two sides in government and power being shared. But the Irish dimension was brought into it then and unfortunately a very violent reaction came from the Protestant side. They just couldn't take the two sides together. So I would say that it was a mistake, bringing in the two at the one time. That violent reaction led to the strike. Wilson was too wishy-washy, I think. If he had come down very firmly against the UWC strike it would have fizzled out; but he held back and a lot of people who weren't involved at the beginning suddenly decided to become involved and it became stronger as time went on.

I remember Callaghan coming down to the Bogside. I was there when he went into a house and started telling the people there that things would be different in the future; that they were going to do something positive about power sharing. But they did absolutely nothing. I must admit it was a great disappointment because I thought maybe the Labour government would have been better than the Conservatives. But as it has turned out, the Conservative government have actually been responsible for more happening here than the Labour government. Every

British government did as little as they could. They have never done enough. In other words, the Orange card was always played, preventing anything positive happening.

People outside prison say people inside shouldn't do this and shouldn't do that. But when prisoners are being abused and their families are being strip-searched – it was an awful thing, women going up to visit being strip-searched every time – they were frustrated and they couldn't see themselves getting anywhere. So I suppose somebody came up with the idea of a hunger strike, thinking that Thatcher would have to do something positive. No matter what you think about it, they were very courageous people. Bobby Sands is the one everyone knows best because he died first, but each one in turn, including O'Hara and Devine from Derry, achieved something. They didn't achieve all that they wanted and Maggie Thatcher never really backed down. She allowed them to die which was dreadful. I have mixed feelings about the hunger strike. I don't believe that people should die for a cause and for a piece of ground, but it was their principles they fought for and I do believe they were very courageous.

The troubles were a dreadful time. If you had a family it was awful; if they were out late at night you felt something had happened to them, that they were arrested or the army had stopped them, or something had happened to them. It was a time of worry and that's what I remember most vividly.

When the ceasefire came I was absolutely delighted. I was telling people long before the ceasefire that there was going to be one. When you become involved in politics you listen to what people are saying. You hear from all sides: you know people from different parties; people in Sinn Féin; people in the SDLP; Unionist people you are friendly with and you can gauge some of what is happening. So I knew there would be a ceasefire before it happened.

Now, over a year later, I'm a bit frustrated, I suppose, like a lot of other people. Alright, some things have happened, the roadblocks have been taken away and of course you are not going to hear of anybody having been shot when you put the radio on in the morning. I was very optimistic for a while, but nothing positive has been happening recently.

Talking doesn't hurt anyone. I think the twin-track approach really should be followed. There is too much talk about decommissioning. All these words, 'permanent' and words like that, have been brought in to delay the process because Major has to take the Unionists' votes at Westminster into account as well. So while I can understand why he is doing this, I still think we have to be positive and move forward, even if very slowly.

They keep talking about minority and majority, but never spell out that it's a 60/40 split at the moment and that's not very far off 50/50. Catholics are the people who have suffered while living here in Northern Ireland because any good jobs that were available in the past have always gone to the Unionist side. It is changing slowly, not quickly enough. I would like to see the power-sharing concept coming back again, and that, at least, we could all live together.

I was brought up in the Waterside and my friends were nearly all Protestant, and at that time everyone was friendly; but that was when I was a child. As I got older I realised the extent of the discrimination that existed. A school friend of mine, a girl who was top of our class, was sent for a job on one occasion. Her name happened to be Wilson, so the employers thought she was a Protestant, and of course they gave her the job. But just before she started work, they discovered she was a Catholic and they made some excuse that she wasn't suitable and gave the job to someone else. These things were happening behind the scenes all the time. We have to do away with all that now. Everyone should be treated equally.

Peace and Reconciliation Group

...we have the UDP calling for the IRA to decommission its arms, but there was no call from the UDP for the UVF or the UFF to decommission their arms. All the arms should be taken out of the whole situation but not as a precondition for establishing the grounds for peace.

Jimmy Duffy and John McCourt

JMcC In 1968 I had just left the local Technical College. I was naive politically, but my education was to be completed very, very quickly. I think the state, from its inception, was unfair, and the way the state was set up did not give consideration to the views of all the people. It was something forced on the Catholic people of Ireland. I would make a difference between Catholics, Nationalists and Republicans. The Catholic population of Northern Ireland got a raw deal from the Unionist government of the day which manipulated legislation to ensure that it would be guaranteed a majority and maintain control.

I was sixteen at the time when civil rights became the new buzz word in Derry. I remember hearing of civil rights marches, of Martin Luther King, of street protests in America and other parts of the world. There was an attempt to keep them peaceful, but, nevertheless, these peaceful protests ended up being dealt with in Northern Ireland as they were in the southern states of America. I think we wouldn't have had to go through the twenty-five years we have just come through if the government of the day had seriously decided to take on board the complaints of the Catholic population of Northern Ireland.

JD I remember the civil rights marches very well and I think they were one of the most productive phases of the start of the troubles because we did get 'one man one vote' and other rights. A lot of people had to suffer to get that. But Catholics were definitely being treated unfairly; everybody in the world saw that.

JMcC The violence that broke out in many parts of Northern Ireland at the end of the 1960s actually took a bit longer to appear in Derry. While we were still talking about civil rights, while we were still talking about protests, in Belfast people were actually dying on the streets. Between October 1968 and August '69 the violence, to an extent, was in reaction to the force that the state had used to quell the protest. I come back again to the point that if the state had taken on board the protests and the issues of the Catholic population, then the whole situation that we have just come through could have been avoided.

JD I think it has been proven, without a doubt, that the people killed on Bloody Sunday were murdered. There were no guns seen. The British government kept bringing out these statements that there was gunfire before the soldiers opened fire. But everybody knows that the fourteen were murdered, and to this day all that it would take is an apology, a simple 'we were wrong'. They still won't admit it, and if you don't admit the thing at the start, if you don't say 'I'm sorry, we were wrong', things can only get worse. They can never get better until someone says they're sorry.

JMcC I think what they have done with Bloody Sunday is they have left a festering sore, something that isn't going to get any better until the government turns around and says it is prepared to open another enquiry and take a look at what happened on the day, and on the three or four days previous to it. One of the things that is overlooked is that people who were shot were specifically targeted. If you examine the Bloody Sunday monument and see the age group of those who died, all are between sixteen and about forty-two or forty-three. They specifically targeted people who could have been, or through the media could have been portrayed as being, members of a paramilitary organisation, or involved in some type of subversive activity. There were also covert operations and propaganda that have to be dealt with and need a lot of owning up to by Britain. I am not saying that we Catholics, or we the people of this city, can stand back and say our hands are lily-white. Many people have died, but Bloody Sunday caused a lot of those deaths, and not just the fourteen who died as a result of the shooting that day. In 1990, a young boy from Strabane on a Bloody Sunday commemoration march died as a result of a bomb going off on the Walls. People were still dying up until August of 1994, and people are still in prison as a result of becoming involved as their way of venting their anger against what happened on Bloody Sunday.

JD Bloody Sunday drove a lot of people into the paramilitaries to get revenge. Without that massacre, without Bloody Sunday, the paramilitaries would not have been as strong as they became. The greatest recruiting officers for any paramilitary group in this or any city in Northern Ireland were the security forces, without a doubt.

JMcC The movement of the Protestant population from the cityside to the Waterside is a very visible effect of the troubles. The perception would be that the Protestant people of the west bank of this city were intimidated out of this area. That's not the truth. Protestants perceived a threat. But nobody went to every Protestant house in the cityside and told them they had to get out because they were Protestant. As members of a community, as members of a specific Church, people themselves felt under threat. They felt that maybe they were not going to be able to practise their faith, or the traditional rights they treasured, and felt threatened. I suppose for some who would have been members of the B Specials or the security forces, or who would have done work for the security forces, there would have been an implied threat. But the reason that 15,000 people from the cityside moved to the Waterside or further up the country wasn't as a

direct result of intimidation. That's something that we daily, weekly, have to work with, trying to bridge that gap, saying to people that while there may be a river between us, that's not the barrier we have to cross. We are trying to get people to cross the barrier of the mind. As a whole community, as all of the people of this city, we can make this place a better place to live in.

I remember in 1972, when I was, I suppose, a vigilante, one of our duties was to go around and assure the Protestant families living in Creggan, in the Bogside, living within the Free Derry area, that they were OK, that people weren't going to come and put stones through their windows. To be honest, I don't remember very many incidents of Protestant families living in Creggan being physically intimidated out of their houses in the middle of the night. I think what happened was that if the rest of their family had gone to the other side of the river, people then went because it suited them to follow. The fact is that it can be politically expedient to say that there was a mass evacuation of Protestants; it is a card that has been played on numerous occasions.

On the day the IRA called a ceasefire, I thought of the people who had died, the people who had suffered, the people who will continue to suffer as a result of what happened. But, although it might be strange to say it, there were gains in those twenty-five years as well. Some of the most modern housing in Europe is in this city, and the only reason it's in this city is because it was brought about by pressure; it was a political trade-off. The only thing they couldn't give to the people who were protesting for civil rights was more jobs. But they got the vote. I suppose internment ended, but the fact that it has been replaced by more repressive legislation now makes you question whether anything was actually won there.

Voting, housing and jobs are something. I suppose if we couldn't have 'one man one job', at least everybody had no job. I think it has shattered the belief that being a member of the Protestant community *per se* meant that you were privileged because there are people living in the Fountain area who were, and are, every bit as deprived as the people who were out protesting on the 5 October 1968. People who were as deprived in a community that is still as deprived.

JD I was highly delighted when the ceasefires were called. Highly, highly, delighted. People came and said to us: "That's you lot out of a job now." Actually we have been busier since the ceasefire than we were pre-ceasefire. But hearing the news of the ceasefire was absolutely wonderful because every morning I got up and there hadn't been a shot fired, or somebody seriously injured through terrorism, then I thought it's going to be that wee bit harder to break, because the people are getting used to it. Paramilitaries are certainly not stupid people, on either side. Far from it. They know that people are far happier, so every day there is no death, no terrorist action, they are going to find it all the harder to even think about breaking the ceasefire, hopefully. I'm fairly optimistic that this is going to hold.

JMcC I remember on the day of the ceasefire thinking back to the Enniskillen bombing. Around that time there was a lot of emotion, there was a lot of feeling that maybe this is the one that's going to make them call it off. But within a couple of days we discovered that it wasn't going to be and we wondered why it was still going on. I felt it was because people hadn't suffered enough, and hadn't shouted loud enough 'this is the end, let that be it'. More people had to die to make it stop. Greysteel and the Shankill Road bombing – bringing it home to people on that sort of scale is a very, very painful way to make a nation realise that the cost of war, the cost of violence, doesn't make war worth it, that there has to be something to put in its place. And if the reaction from that created the breathing space where the Godfathers, the people who were in control of the violence, of the strategies, sat back and said 'this time we have gone as far as we can go' ... I am not saying that those deaths – even though the violence ended I believe as a result of the whole community's reaction to those deaths – were worth it. I don't think that. I would hate to think anybody would read that into what I am saying. But that was when some people, people who would have for-

merly supported violence, turned round and began to think the price had now become too high.

JD The peace is absolutely marvellous, but there are people still suffering out there. I think over 300 people have died from this area alone. Those people are dead and gone, but they've left maybe four or five of a family, so if you multiply that 300 by five, for an area of this size it is a lot of people who will suffer for the rest of their lives. The suffering is going to go on, and it will take decades to get back to peace in our land. But every day has helped, and is certainly helping people out there. Because people like myself have had enough and can't take much more.

JMcC A year on there are definite problems, but none that can't be looked at, discussed, and negotiated around. I suppose the issue of the decommisioning of weapons is going to be a hot potato. I suppose the ridiculous thing about it is that we have the UDP calling for the IRA to decommission *its* arms, but there was no call from the UDP for the UVF or the UFF to decommission *their* arms. All the arms should be taken out of the whole situation but not as a precondition for establishing the grounds for peace. I believe those things can be negotiated and resolved once we put in place a mechanism to resolve the problems, the political problems, that we have here. I think that it is an entitlement, a right, for all of the people of Northern Ireland, all of this island, to be able to say 'tomorrow, nobody is going to die so that somebody can say they are scoring a political point in my name'.

JD My opinion on the guns issue is that they first of all get round the table and talk. OK, they still have their guns but they haven't been using them for the past year or so. So why not just talk first, and then talk about handing in guns? But start talking first.

One thing I would like for the future is more work. Young people need work because if a young person is out working and he gets paid on a Friday the last thing he is going to think about is terrorism. He will look forward to getting his pay and enjoying himself. At the moment all I want is to see nobody being killed and people getting on with their lives and getting on with their new jobs, and then, down the line, let's talk about what we want to do and decide who wants to be in an all-Ireland or who wants to be in an Ulster. But that's up to politicians and governments. Today and tomorrow all I want to see is nobody being killed, people getting happier, and more jobs for the young people. And that can only be good.

JMcC It's part of a whole healing process. I think we all have to stand back and ask ourselves what we have contributed during the last twenty-five years first of all, and have we sat back and allowed it to happen, watched it happen, or maybe even been part of it, or supported it? And then look at the last twelve months and ask 'what have I done to ensure we don't go back to that?' But I think we have a lot of people at the minute sitting on their hands. There is a gap between the Protestant and Catholic communities in this city that politicians could be helping to heal, that the Churches could be helping to heal. But the only people who seem to be doing anything are community workers, people who are out there working day and daily with the disadvantaged, with the under-privileged, with the homeless, the unemployed, with single mothers. They are the people who are building the bridges, while the politicians, the councillors, the MPs and the Churches, I believe, have a lot more to do. But I think there is a lot more for the ordinary lay-people of this city to do as well. They should be promoting cross-community contact, they should be promoting a development that ensures that if an opportunity comes around again for violence to start up, that the support isn't going to be there for it. Resources have to be directed towards ensuring that young people are not going to get angry and bitter and become lured into violence. We have just had a political war. I don't want to see a drugs war, or a criminal war, or a territorial turf-war taking its place in this city, as it has in other cities throughout the world.

I am optimistic. I think we have everything to look forward to, but I can't look forward without learning from what we have just come through. And I think if we all are to learn the lessons of the last twenty-five years of violence, and the last year without violence, I think we can be optimistic. I think we do have a future, but it is something that isn't going to happen, it's something we all have to work for.

During the peace process Loyalists and Republicans campaigned for the release of political prisoners – with little success. These murals reflect the sentiments of Nationalists in Creggan (above) and in the Bogside (left). *(Photos: Jim Cunningham)*

A Sinn Féin march passes through the Brandywell on its way to meet marchers from other parts of the city on the first anniversary of the IRA ceasefire, 31 August 1995. *(Photo: Jarlath Kearney)*

Decommissioning of IRA weapons is a major issue in the peace process, and here unknown artists have customised an advertising hoarding in the Bogside to illustrate another viewpoint. *(Photo:Jim Cunningham)*

Maureen Shiels

Even after a year of the ceasefire my attitude towards Britain has not changed at all because as far as I'm concerned, what the British have done in the past year they could have done in two or three weeks. I don't believe they have done anything meaningful. I think everything they are doing is a stalling tactic.

I'm just twenty-six, so any ideas that I have about what it was like here before the troubles would be based mainly on what I heard at home. Obviously there was never equality here, and there wasn't enough employment. My father was lucky enough to have a job, and he would say that all the time, that he was lucky to have a job, but he was surrounded by people who didn't. My father's generation would say that the Protestant community had everything and they didn't care what we had.

I think the civil rights movement was a peaceful way to try and change things. There was nothing wrong with people asking for better houses and better jobs. The British should have tried to understand their problems instead of looking on people coming onto the street and asking for a better situation and for equality in the place where they lived as a threat. They should have thought 'let's sit down and talk to these people, we are responsible for them, we are the government, we are ruling the six counties, surely they deserve to be listened to and deserve to be heard'. Instead, they looked on it as a threat and took action.

I certainly don't see the violence as the fault of the civil rights movement. It was women getting out of work and going to marches because everybody wants what's best for themselves and their children. There is nothing wrong with wanting human rights, there is nothing wrong with not wanting to be second-class citizens, it's quite normal, quite human.

People have described the day of the Bloody Sunday march as a beautiful day, the atmosphere quite carnival, which would indicate that these people were not out to start any sort of trouble. They were just out to have their voices heard. There certainly wasn't any violence intended from the marchers that day. Women had brought along their children, which is always a key thing in my mind. If people expected to start trouble, or if they thought there was going to be trouble, they certainly wouldn't bring children with them.

The Widgery Report was absolutely ridiculous. Fourteen people were murdered, and five of them were my neighbours. Five people within a hundred yards of where you lived is a lot of people to die in one street. To see five coffins and not knowing which funeral to go to, all that dilemma I remember my parents going through.

All the people who were shot dead were men, so the British knew exactly what they were doing. There was no indiscriminate shooting, there were no random shots. People were on their hands and knees, people were waving handkerchiefs, people came out with their hands up, people were shot in the buttocks, they were shot in the back, they were shot under their arms. To set Gerald Donaghy up and plant nail bombs on him was a disgrace. Then bring in a British army lawyer, who flew into Eglinton in a British army helicopter, surrounded by British army soldiers, stayed in a British army base that night, and then came to a Catholic/Nationalist community, which at that time didn't know how to deal with lawyers, it was the first time anything like this had happened. Nobody had expected to go out and see fourteen people shot dead, not to mention the many that were injured. This community was numb. I actually received a letter from a British soldier who was in the Royal Anglians at the time. He said he was very sorry for what happened on Bloody Sunday and he believed that the order to go ahead came from above because the Anglians were moved out to the army base at the Old City Dairy on the Letterkenny Road. They were told that by no means were they to interfere with what was to happen on Bloody Sunday, that the parachute regiment, which had just arrived in Derry four days previous, was here to sort us fenians out and sort us out once and for all, to ensure we didn't feel that we could just get up and protest whenever we liked.

So I think that Widgery came at a time when people were numb. You didn't know what to do, and people turned to the Catholic Church for help because that was the pillar of their community. The Catholic Church advised them to go along and talk, and listen, to Widgery, but with hindsight the community, and the bereaved, say now that they never should have done it. It was a whitewash. His name is dirt. You just don't mention that man's name in this community even now, especially not to the relatives of the dead.

I think the prison protests were necessary because of what was happening to those in jail. These people were political prisoners, and they didn't deserve to be treated the way they were. The British had the Special Powers Acts and the special prison categories and all the rest – they were calling them special prisoners, yet they were treating them like common criminals. So I think the protests were necessary in that people throughout the world, and the media, needed to be made aware in order to spread the word about what was happening within the prisons. As a tactic they were very important, they were quite necessary.

During the hunger strikes was when I first felt that something was wrong here. I was ten and I remember going to school and everybody talking about it. I remember sitting down and thinking 'oh, my God, why? Why starve yourself to death? That must be a really horrible, hard thing to do'. Now looking back at it, I have nothing but, obviously, admiration for the hunger strikers and their strength, and the same for their families. The families had to take to the streets and protest because at the end of the day

their hands were tied, what else could they do? They had to support their loved ones. It was a very traumatic time. For Britain to sit back and watch people starve themselves to death, it makes you think. You just realised what exactly the British think of Irish people's lives. They just don't matter, they are less than nothing to them. And if Irish people chose to starve themselves to death then ...

I think the fact that violence needs to happen is a horrible thing. For a human being, having to sit down and rationally decide that they have to take up arms and defend themselves can't be an easy thing to have to do, nor can it be a very pleasant thing to have to do. Republicans are portrayed as thugs or monsters, but in reality they are just ordinary people you have known all your life, that you have grown up with. You know they are rational, clear-thinking, kind-hearted people who have had to make that choice.

Bloody Sunday set the precedent for violence in this state anyway. It set the precedent for the British to believe they could kill Irish people with impunity, without any sort of punishment. Lee Clegg's release still proves that to this day. Twenty-five years on you still have paratroopers being allowed to shoot people. I don't condone violence but at the end of the day Bloody Sunday said to people 'they're just going to keep shooting us off the streets, every time we go onto the streets they're going to keep shooting us', so some people decided they had to take up arms and fight back.

I could understand Loyalist violence if they went out and fought as soldiers, as a paramilitary organisation, and they had a specific target, as in a uniformed target, or another paramilitary target, but the content of their violence is pure bigotry, and it is just sectarianism towards Catholics. I think the fact that you know the RUC and the British security forces are backing these people up, and indeed arming them and allowing them freedom to operate within the communities, is another very scary factor. It has always frightened me.

It was obvious for a few weeks there was going to be a ceasefire called, and I was very shaky and unsure about how I was going to feel about it. What I was toying with in my head was 'what's going to happen to us now?' I have never had any reason to trust the British, not for over 800 years in this country have Irish people ever had any reason to trust the British, so why suddenly now, after twenty-five years of seeing exactly what they can do and being faced with the harassment of the RUC and the British army on the street. Is it going to go right back to the way it was in 1968, before the troubles?

Even after a year of the ceasefire my attitude towards Britain has not changed at all because as far as I'm concerned, what the British have done in the past year they could have done in two or three weeks. I don't believe they have done anything meaningful. I think everything they are doing is a stalling tactic. They should stop playing politics and start talking. Irish people's and British people's lives are important, and they are very valuable, and they just don't see it. The release of Lee Clegg, the demand for decommissioning of arms, and the fact that they have not released any political prisoners, all show they are just stalling the whole process. It is just ludicrous. I think to demand the decommissioning of arms when the reasons those arms existed in the first place haven't changed is wrong.

Nothing has changed here. The RUC are still here. They still exist as a paramilitary police force. They still discriminate within my community. I still can't walk out the door, or open my curtains in the morning, and think it's really nice living here now, it's different. I still expect a house raid. I still expect an arrest. I still expect to be stopped in the street and searched. I still expect my children to be given abuse going to and coming from school because I chose that they learn to speak the Irish language.

What I would like to see in the future, what I would like to see now, is for all political parties to sit down and talk. There are a lot of fences to mend and I know it won't be easy for everyone involved, but it has to happen. I don't think this whole situation is going to move any further forward if they don't sit down and talk. What I would like to see is my representatives being allowed to use their electoral mandate as I voted for it. The British government said at the beginning of this that they would use imagination and initiative. I haven't seen any evidence of that. Should it take three years, should it take five years, the talking needs to happen.

I would also like to see more women going forward, and more women being *allowed* to go forward. I would just like a better place to live for me and my children. I would like to feel equal. I would like to feel like a first-class citizen and no longer feel like a second-class citizen. I would like to feel that I don't need to be embarrassed any more about my politics, that I don't need to be afraid to say I am a Republican, and that the people in this island can live together. Peace needs to bring about change.

William Temple

When civil unrest came onto the streets, Protestants felt threatened and they were nervous going through some of the barricades. It was only natural they would think about moving to a safer environment.

In the years immediately before the start of the troubles I was living in Abercorn Road, which is between the Fountain and the Bog, although I was brought up in what is now commonly known as the Bogside. So I have a fair idea of some of 'he perceptions of the people there before the troubles. I blame the outbreak of the troubles on bad housing, high unemployment, and a lack of understanding between two divided communities. I can't see how the troubles could have been avoided. We have paid a heavy price, but at least we have made progress in community relations.

It must be said that there were a lot of Protestants who supported the demands of the civil rights movement. Unfortunately, as far as I'm concerned, a Republican element hijacked the civil rights movement and once Republican banners appeared, a lot of Protestants moved away from it and two opposing factions came into being.

Protestants have mixed feelings about Bloody Sunday. They regret the loss of life, but they have a feeling that tension was heightened before the march and they felt insecure. They relayed this to the authorities who took measures which were probably excessive. Intelligence gathering was misinformed and paid too much attention to the wilder elements of society. So there was a reaction, it was overplayed, and we had the unfortunate killing of people. This is regretted, and Protestants have a lot of sympathy with the victims of that day.

The cityside was made up of small enclaves of Protestants surrounded by a large Catholic population. When civil unrest came onto the streets, Protestants felt threatened and they were nervous going through some of the barricades. It was only natural they would think about moving to a safer environment. The barricades around the periphery of the Bogside meant Protestants in the Northlands, in the Glen, and even Ballymagroarty would have had to go through them. If they were collecting children from school and taking them through the barricades, they would have feared for the children's safety. With the tension on the streets, sides were being taken and Protestant children felt threatened on the streets, even by their former playmates.

The violence affected us all. There was always the risk, especially in business, that you were going to be blown up; I have been robbed at gunpoint. These were unpleasant experiences, and if I hadn't money invested I'd probably have moved away as well from Abercorn Road.

The feeling during the troubles was one of anxiety rather than anger; wondering what would happen and how I would get through the day, especially if there were protests. The burning of Magilligan, and when Frank Stagg died on hunger strike were periods of very high tension and there was a lot of apprehension and anxiety. Once you got over the crisis you settled down again, but crises were always happening so you never really had peace of mind.

My own experiences of the troubles included, as I said earlier, being robbed at gunpoint; I have also had thirteen windows smashed within two days; I've had my door kicked in; I have been called at and insulted in the street. I now live in a Protestant enclave, and after 1986 we had a hard time with the security forces, especially the Mobile Support Unit, and this went on from '86 right up until '94.

All the major events of the troubles, the UWC strike, the hunger strikes, the Anglo-Irish Agreement, brought tension onto the streets. As I work in an area that's in between the two communities, these events left me anxious and fearful for my own property. They were unpleasant experiences, but you live through them. At the time it was not pleasant, but eventually you begin to forget about the tensions and fears. Nature has a way of overcoming these traumatic events and when I look back on them now it is hard to say how they really affected me. At the moment I have no tension or prejudices; I just feel I'm back to normal.

I believe in peaceful protests, and I believe they were necessary to effect civil rights. Violence has done a great deal of harm by creating victims who find it hard to forgive, thus impacting on future political progress. No violence is ever justified and that includes violence used by the forces of the government. Diplomacy and dialogue are the way to further any cause if it is going to have any meaningful conclusion.

In the Fountain you feel absolute safety; the problem with the Fountain is getting to it if you are approaching it from the west bank. If you're approaching it from the Waterside there are no difficulties; you can live in the Fountain just as handy as the Waterside. Within the Fountain there's really no great fear or tension; once you're in you feel safe.

I was brought up amongst Catholics, and socially and recreationally all my contacts were with Catholics, so I would view Catholics differently from most Protestants who have had no contact with them. As far as I'm concerned, the friendships I had as a child have remained and I have no problem in identifying with Catholic people.

Hopefully, the troubles are over and lessons have been learnt. But at the moment it's hard to gauge whether they have been learnt or not. We still have the threat that violence could come back. I would hope people realise that violence really is nonproductive, and that there are other ways of settling differences and injustices without resorting to it.

I was relieved when the IRA ceasefire was called. It was as if we had overcome an obstacle and were coming now to easier times. The unfortunate thing is there is still a threat that violence could return. We wonder is the ceasefire really permanent. There is also the fear of intimidation that seems to be still there.

I think that we went about it the wrong way, believing peace had come with the cessation of military attacks. We should be talking, all-party talks, about how to get permanent peace. I think more progress could have been made. That would have sorted out issues like decommissioning, attacks on property and attacks on persons. We didn't do it the right way. We should have gone on to talks regarding the evolution of the peace process.

The release of prisoners is something that has to be negotiated and could have been negotiated as part of the peace settlement.

I would like to see new faces and fresh thinking brought in on the peace process. And it is happening; people are being replaced at the moment. The Unionist Party now has a new leader, and I would say this is only the start of replacing older politicians who are set in their ways.

People have got to sit down and work out their position, and base their opinions objectively on what is right, rather than on what they want to happen from a party point of view. I think for a period we will have the division of community, political divisions, but as time goes on I can see people coming together. In spite of twenty-five years of strife the Protestant and Catholic communities have a greater understanding of each other. This understanding, and the dispelling of misconceptions, can only be helpful to the future, a future where we can sit down and openly discuss the various problems we have.

If the situation starts to move too close to a united Ireland, the Protestant community will form themselves into a monolithic pact and will work within their own community. Rights would not need to be negotiated once established by law. We at the moment feel we have to negotiate everything. I think we should have a set of principles recognised as basic human rights, and when the basic human rights are there nobody should have to be humiliated by negotiating with either a community or a government. They are their rights, and they should be incorporated into some charter.

There are a lot of historical reasons for people having a constitutional stance. It's up to people to make up their own minds. I wouldn't try to influence anyone to change their political opinions just because it would suit me economically, or increase my prestige, or I felt that I was right and they were wrong. I think we've got to approach this with an open mind, and work out honestly what is the best way forward politically, whether it be within a united Ireland or the United Kingdom. Whatever happens, I would agree with what is best not for Northern Ireland but for people generally. I'm more concerned about people than any territorial claim.

I would hope we are moving into permanent peace where people can sit down and study their relationships with their constitutional allies and with their neighbours. I hope we don't return to the old days where we would just divide and have no understanding of the other group whatsoever. I believe that we need openness, we need dialogue, and we need more integration as communities.

Updates

Ancient Order of Hibernians

The all-party talks due to start on 10 June must be exactly as described with *all* parties invited to take part. Preconditions should not be imposed on any party as an excuse to prevent their presence at the talks. Decommissioning of the arms held by Loyalist paramilitaries is not being demanded by Nationalists so it is totally unreasonable for Unionist leaders and the British government to demand the decommissioning of the arms held by Republican paramilitaries as a precondition to inviting Sinn Féin to take part in the all-party talks. The Anglo-Irish Agreement was not accepted by Unionists as they had not been involved in any discussions prior to the announcement of the Agreement. Surely, Unionist leaders should understand that any agreement reached in the absence of Sinn Féin would not be accepted by their supporters. We feel that Sinn Féin must be present at the talks without any preconditions. Loyalist delegates must also be present and, again, without preconditions. We are not saying the input of paramilitaries should be greater than other delegates at the talks. Indeed, none of the parties taking part should think their input is greater than others. This attitude is important to prevent any *prima-donna* walkouts. It is our fervent hope that all the delegates will realise from the outset the importance of the talks and that they should do their utmost to bring about an agreement that will enable the two communities to live together in peace. *(3/5/96)*

Glen Barr

We have not made enough strenuous efforts throughout the ceasefire period to find a solution to the problems that created the situation in the first place. I have said from day one that whatever is part of the problem must be part of the solution. I think the only people that can come out with any credibility in this must be the Loyalist paramilitaries, they are the only ones who have been attempting to find a solution to move the thing forward and who were prepared to shift their positions in order to accommodate a solution. Therefore, I am extremely critical of all the parties concerned. They haven't put Northern Ireland first, they only want to put their own position first, give their own positions priority, and were more concerned about how they were going to come out in the opinion polls. So I think that very few people can claim any laurels during the ceasefire period. There was an opportunity to try and find a solution, but unfortunately people were not prepared to take that opportunity. If we really return to violence again then I believe it will probably be a lot worse than we had in the last twenty-five years. *(2/5/96)*

Jimmy Cadden

The breaking of the IRA ceasefire was as sad and shocking as it was sudden. In years to come, people will talk of 'where were you when the ceasefire collapsed?' However, since then the IRA have stuck mainly to small bombs, letting the British government know they are still there and still possess a real threat to life. It matters little that the IRA have abandoned their ceasefire. There was no real peace for all the time the IRA were supposed to be observing a ceasefire. Try talking in terms of peace to the many people whose legs were broken and whose faces were battered with hammers by Provo terror gangs.

But what for the future? Will the forthcoming elections and subsequent talks resolve our many problems? In short, no. The past few months have only served to further underline to me that we live in the middle of a problem which is unsolvable. Elections will come and go; talks will rumble on – if they ever really get started. At the end of the day the IRA will either get what they want or they won't. Either outcome leaves us in a terror situation, only the identity of the terrorists changes. Sad, solemn and pessimistic, yes. But then, this is also a statement of reality. *(25/4/96)*

Gregory Campbell

In terms of the central issues nothing has changed, and the positive outlooks at this stage just about outweigh the negative ones in terms of a genuine understanding across the community divide. *(29/4/96)*

Tony Crowe

Recent events have vindicated my reservations about the variety of processes. This community can only prosper when there is true accommodation of all traditions. *(18/4/96)*

Diane Greer

I was in the former East Germany when the IRA ceasefire ended. Not having access to newspapers until the next day, I spent a long night feeling numb, hoping that it was all a mistake, that the bomb had been planted by some obscure terrorist group from the Middle East. Coming through Heathrow two days later, I knew and felt it was over, I accepted it at gut level. However, to this day, I refuse to accept it at the level of my heart or my head.

In the coming election on 30 May, I will stand as a candidate for the Northern Ireland Women's Coalition, and whatever happens I am committed to the right of women to participate when the future of Northern Ireland is being worked out. After all, we have sustained families and communities throughout the 'war', and therefore we have a valuable contribution to make to the discussions and a vested interest in seeking a solution. *(9/5/96)*

Cecil Hutcheon

As I mentioned, I live beside an army barracks with a seventy-five-foot watchtower outside the homes of people around it. Residents of the area fought a long hard campaign for two years and nine months to have this tower removed. After peaceful protests for that length of time, and members of the group going to Westminster to lobby MPs, the RUC finally gave in to the residents' protest and removed the tower from the midst of this small community. To me this was a great victory for the campaigners and the people of Rosemount who stood by them. It just proved to me that if you stay with something, you will finally get a result.

The people of this area will continue their protests to have security cameras that have been placed around the barracks removed, as we feel this is still an invasion of our right to privacy in our own homes.

I also think that if people from other areas have any grievances, they should get together and stand up for their rights. It only takes a small number of people to form a campaign and, if they stay with it, they will win, as the people from Rosemount proved. *(1/5/96)*

Paul Laughlin

Regrettably the space opened up by the ceasefires was not used creatively. Other contributors to this volume will advance complex and conflicting analyses of why this happened. The simple truth is that politicians have shown themselves to be unimaginative and incapable of moving beyond the politics of failure and stagnation. The existing political elites are manifestly unwilling to address constitutional issues and questions of human rights and economic dignity in open debate. This, however, merely confirms the need to redefine the vocabulary of politics and to elevate the voices of precisely those who have been marginalised and silenced. *(29/4/96)*

Donncha MacNiallais

Like everyone else, I was pretty shocked when the news came through of the bomb explosion in Canary Wharf. Having said that, it was quite evident for some months previously that the complete cessation of military operations declared by the IRA in August 1994 was in serious difficulty. It wasn't the case that Republicans weren't happy because things weren't going their way, it was that things weren't going *anywhere*, either for or against any objectives the Republican movement

162

had. It had got to the stage of ridicule as far as I was concerned. The process had been stonewalled from day one, and while you expected that in the initial months of the ceasefire, you didn't expect it to last for almost eighteen months. I think the responsibility for that breakdown lies totally and absolutely with the British government; they encouraged the Unionists to become even more inflexible and intransigent than they had been previously. What has to happen now is that the peace process has to be rebuilt. I don't know how long that is going to take, but there is obviously a complete lack of trust, in the British government in particular. Even if they were to do a complete U-turn and decide to engage positively the whole process of reaching agreement, it is quite obvious that Major would probably be unable to deliver that type of British government engagement. *(7/5/96)*

Pat McArt
I am really disappointed at the end of the ceasefire and I don't think the IRA are justified in renewing the campaign because I feel it's just not going anywhere. It only means more bombings, more sectarian killings and more community division. I am not absolving either the British government or the Unionist parties, because they also have to share the blame. Some people are suggesting they don't, but they do. The ceasefire needed to be worked at, but what it got from the British was prevarication and from the Unionists, negativity. *(24/4/96)*

Raymond McCartney
In the months since I did this interview, the nagging doubt has become the reality. A glorious opportunity to resolve this conflict in a lasting way has been squandered. I have no doubt in my mind that John Major and his government did not live up to the expectations of people who wanted peace. People in this city, and throughout Ireland and beyond, are now faced with uncertainty. This could have been avoided, and perhaps, if the will is there, can still be avoided. *(23/4//96)*

Declan McLaughlin
I feel sad that the best chance of working towards a lasting resolution has been destroyed by the British establishment. But it is part of the process, a learning process, which will help us identify the issues and deal with them in what I hope will be a nonviolent way. *(25/4/96)*

David Nicholl
The state of the present peace process is as I previously predicted, the IRA have as usual returned to the armed campaign which I and others described as purely tactical. However, they have effectively neutralised Sinn Féin and have prevented them entering all-party talks on 10 June 1996.

Until there is a realisation that Unionists cannot be coerced into a united Ireland and that Sinn Féin is required to persuade the Unionist community of the legitimacy of their argument, the political *status quo* will remain.

For our part the intentions of the Loyalist community have proven to be entirely honest and open in our deliberations.

The statement of the Combined Loyalist Military Command remains intact. However, there is increasing pressure on the Loyalist community to respond to the actions of violent Republicanism. Discipline remains the key to our survival and having an earnest desire to pursue peace through a process of conflict resolution, Loyalists will not easily be drawn into a renewed conflict by provocative and violent Republicanism.

There is a realisation that the present situation regarding Northern Ireland's position within the union is going through a very testing period but we have been there before and emerged intact. We have no doubt that when it comes to compromising and accommodation that Unionists will prove themselves to be willing partners in the search for parity of esteem. *(10/5/96)*

Paul O'Connor

One person, more than any other, has typified why the ceasefire broke down and how confidence in the whole process was lost – that's Paddy Kelly, the prisoner who's suffering from cancer and is dying. The whole edifice didn't collapse because of Paddy Kelly, but the attitude of British Home Secretary Michael Howard to prisoners in general is a metaphor for the arrogance and the cold indifference of those in charge of the peace process on the British side. It has been said a thousand times – the end of the ceasefire was depressing, but hardly surprising. *(29/4/96)*

Fionnbarra ÓDochartaigh

Partition and peace can never coexist. We are in a political twilight zone which does not offer much towards creating a sense of optimism. Real peace based on new structures is possible, but we need a lot more new thinking. Federalism, if properly debated, could well prove to be a popular way forward. It would give greater democracy and clout to all those at the grass roots, be they orange, green, pink or blue. *(9/5/96)*

Eamon O'Kane

So, memories of the troubles has become memories of a ceasefire. I suppose we should know by now that Northern Ireland demands cautious optimism. Our elected representatives have learned the limit of their abilities. It is said that the master key to success is in everyone's hands at the start. There must be a lot of lost keys littering our country. Responsibilities have to be shouldered on all sides. It's time for a one-eyed man to infiltrate the ranks of the blind. Only in Northern Ireland, it seems, can stupid men be as dangerous as intelligent ones. The lies they tell haven't a leg to stand on but have no problems getting around.

It annoys me now that things have resumed their usual futility. Winston Churchill said that you can't please all of the people all of the time. Never was it more true than here. I believe that some people here, given their rights, would complain about being deprived of their wrongs. We are being more heavily taxed by the ineptitude of individuals than by any Chancellor of the Exchequer.

More infuriating is that we know the people of this country have no wish to tolerate another lifetime of violence. Peace would always be an acquired taste for some, but many have found it more than palatable and yet their nation is again held to ransom. I only hope that for the first time in their history the antagonists will finally listen to those they claim to represent. How long will it take them to realise that tolerance is the only ticket to a decent future?

It isn't easy to remain optimistic in the light of present events. All sides have agreed to run in the forthcoming elections but how many will be satisfied by the reality of the results? It isn't easy to teach an old dog new tricks. Meanwhile, in time-honoured fashion, we keep our fingers crossed in the hope of a satisfactory resolution and a future worth waiting for. *(1/5/96)*

Geraldine O'Neill

I was very disappointed when the ceasefire broke down. I think everyone was. Looking at it from both points of view, the British government kept putting up obstacles, so I can understand the frustration of Republicans, but violence solves nothing. Now that the date for negotiations has been finalised as 10 June, I hope the IRA will call another ceasefire and allow the talks to proceed with the inclusion of Sinn Féin, because unless everyone is involved, it won't work. My vision of the future is where people can live and work together irrespective of religion or politics, where each person respects the other point of view and different cultures have parity of esteem. I would like to see a time when unemployment, health and education are the most important topics. *(9/5/96)*

Peace and Reconciliation Group

John McCourt – I think in the first interview in September last year we were optimistic, and I still feel we were right to be optimistic, I think we had everything to look forward to. We had hoped there would be some kind of agreement reached where we could have seen the end of this conflict, and the causes of this conflict. But February, literally, blew that all away. We were saddened by the deaths, and saddened by what we lost as well. We lost the vision of hope, I think. It took the heart back out of the people. And we still felt that a week after the explosion in Canary Wharf when we were in the Guildhall Square and thousands and thousands of people came and signed statement books just wishing it had never happened. Having the opportunity to be the channel for people's feelings after that was a moving experience for us. We didn't realise how much people had appreciated the absence of war and the peace we had become accustomed to, and it left us feeling how fragile it really was. I think it's time now to look towards a real settlement and towards real accommodation, and towards putting our history and our past behind us and look forward to what we could have built on through the seventeen months of the cessation of violence.

Jimmy Duffy – I would echo everything John has said. I am also optimistic. Every morning that I waken up and I don't hear of a bomb going off is great. The people in our city were always smiling during the ceasefire until Canary Wharf. But the smiles are starting to come back. The people are hopeful, every day they are hopeful there will be another ceasefire, and I feel the same. People are starting to get back to normality, and it will happen as long as there are no bombs and the Loyalist paramilitaries continue to hold their ceasefire, and they are doing a first-class job by holding back. Something has to give. They have to get round the table. I don't know how, that's for the politicians, but common sense tells you they must. Nobody can go through again what we have been through, it's just impossible. Something has to give. *(23/4/96)*

Maureen Shiels

When I heard the news about Canary Wharf, my reaction wasn't of shock but of disappointment; I felt a deep sadness. I don't believe anyone could have been shocked as it was an inevitable consequence of Britain's attitude towards eighteen months of the IRA ceasefire.

Why can't John Major and his government stop playing politics and instead take a human attitude towards Irish and British lives? Maybe if *his* children had to live through what *I* have lived through, or what my children may have to live through, then maybe he wouldn't be so worried about buildings, money or power.

If you were to ask me what my vision of the future is, it's to watch my children grow old; for them to have the same opportunities as anyone else on this island; to own their own home, to have a job; and for the areas they live in not to be deprived because of religious beliefs. That's all the civil rights movement wanted.

Ask me do John Major and the Unionists instill confidence in me that I will see this happen. Ask me do I believe that I'll not see another Canary Wharf and civilian lives lost; and just ask me do I believe I'll not see any more Edward O'Briens ... *(26/4/96)*

William Temple

When the ceasefire was announced, I was suspicious it was on the basis of a promise or assurance given by the government to the demands of the IRA. Or, it could have been on the assumption by the IRA that enough hurt had been afflicted on any opposition to their designs for their peace terms to be accepted. To me, if this was the case, the peace process was going to be a gamble, as trust in the government could be misplaced or misunderstood, and the gauging of opposing positions could have been misjudged. Originally, I had hoped there would be a conditional ceasefire by all involved in the conflict; with a cooling-off period of three months followed by three months of talks between the paramilitaries and the government discussing the expectations for peace, with firm assurances entered into regarding protection of individual and cultural rights by law. If this ever comes about, a permanent peace may evolve enabling the future to be more conducive to resolving what are now serious and major problems. *(19/4/96)*

Notes on Contributors

Born in the Fountain, **Jack Allen** (54) is a member of the Orange Order, the Apprentice Boys and the Royal Black Preceptory. He was first elected to the old Corporation in 1966 and was mayor of the city in 1974-75. He was a member of the NI assembly between 1982 and 1986 and is currently treasurer of the UUP. Interview date – 14/9/95.

The modern-day **AOH** was founded in the 1830s and is organised in divisions. Its traditional parades, complete with banners and sashes, take place on 15 August and on St Patrick's Day. Written submission – 25/9/95.

The Apprentice Boys of Derry was founded after the siege of Derry in 1689 to commemorate the actions of the thirteen guild apprentices who closed the city Gates against the army of King James II. Their main parades are held in the city on 12 August and 18 December. Written submission – 6/5/96.

Glen Barr (53) has always lived in the Waterside. After an early involvement in trade union politics, he joined the Vanguard movement in 1972 and was elected to the assembly in 1973. He was a member of the Loyalist Association of Workers, and was chairman of the co-ordinating committee of the Ulster Workers' Council strike in 1974. Interview date – 12/10/95.

Jimmy Cadden (51) is editor of the Londonderry Sentinel where he started working in 1984 as the paper's sports editor. He is not a member of any political party. Interview date – 16/10/95.

Gregory Campbell (42) is the leader of the DUP on the City Council. He is also the party's spokesman on defence. Interview date – 26/9/95.

Originally from Cookstown, **Joe Cosgrove** has lived in Derry since 1944. A doctor since 1940, he has been a member of the Alliance Party since its foundation in 1970. Interview date – 24/11/95.

Tony Crowe (47) is a member of the Apprentice Boys and the Walker Trust, and is also chairman of the Diamond Project Trust. As a historian, he has written many articles and journals. A member of the City Council's Cultural Sub-committee, he has a 'keen interest in the preservation of Ulster culture'. Interview date – 18//9/95.

Kathleen Doherty, Harriet Hippsley and **Eileen Semple** are three of the original five Derry peace women whose public protests after the killing of Ranger William Best in Derry in May 1972 are widely believed to have contributed greatly to the OIRA decision to call a permanent ceasefire. Interview date – 4/4/96.

A former Republican prisoner, **Tony Doherty** (32) is a spokesperson for the Bloody Sunday Justice Campaign and a member of the Bogside and Brandywell Development Association. His father, Patrick Doherty, was one of those shot dead on Bloody Sunday. Interview date – 17/10/95.

Born in Belfast and raised in Derry, **Diane Greer** (38) is a counsellor at Derry Well Woman. She is also a member of the Protestant Women's Group set up in 1993 to give Protestant women a 'voice in politics'. She will stand in the 30 May elections as a candidate for the Northern Ireland Women's Coalition. Interview date – 2/11/95.

John Hume, MP, MEP, first appeared on the political scene during the civil rights agitation of the 1960s. A founder member and leader of the SDLP, he has been MP for the Foyle constituency since the seat was created in 1983. Interview date – 4/4/96.

Cecil Hutcheon (41) is a resident of the Rosemount area and was actively involved in the campaign to remove the Rosemount watchtower. Interview date – 22/9/95.

The **IRSP** was formed in December 1974 as a breakaway group from Official Sinn Féin. It is a 'revolutionary Socialist organisation which believes that the establishment of Republican Socialism in Ireland is the best means by which the working class in Ireland can be liberated from both imperialism and capitalism'. Interview date – 12/4/96.

Marlene Jefferson (62) is a member of the UUP and was mayor of the city in 1980-81. She was patron of the group Widows' Might which was set up to give a voice to the widows and families of security force personnel killed in the troubles. Interview date – 25/4/96.

Brian Lacey (46) was born in Dublin and moved to Derry in 1974. A former lecturer in history and archaeology at Magee College, he is currently in charge of Derry City Council's Museum Service. Written submission – 7/11/95.

A native of Derry, *Paul Laughlin* (39) is an active trade unionist and secretary of Derry Trades Council. He has contributed articles and short stories to a number of periodicals, magazines and radio programmes. Written submission – 2/1/96.

Donncha MacNiallais (37) is a former Republican prisoner. He is currently a member of the Bogside Residents' Association, the Bogside and Brandywell Residents' Association, and Conradh Na Gaeilge – the Irish language group. Interview date – 20/9/95.

A native of Donegal, *Pat McArt* (42) has lived in Derry since 1981. Having previously worked in RTE, he is currently the Managing Editor of Journal Group Newspapers. Interview date – 7/11/95.

Born in the Bogside in 1944, *Nell McCafferty* now lives in Dublin where she works as a freelance journalist and author. Interview date – 13/3/96.

A prominent civil rights activist in the 1960s and early 1970s, *Eamonn McCann* (52) was one of the main organisers of the march in Derry on 5 October 1968 and is currently a member of the Socialist Workers' Party. A journalist and author, McCann has written two major books about events in Derry during the troubles – 'War and an Irish Town' and 'Bloody Sunday in Derry – What Really Happened'. Interview date – 22/9/95.

Raymond McCartney (40) is a former Republican prisoner who was OC of the IRA prisoners in the H-Blocks and took part in the first hunger strike in 1980. He has been a member of Sinn Féin since his release from prison in 1994 and is currently the party's Press Officer for the six counties. Interview date – 25/10/95.

Martin McGuinness (45) is a member of the Sinn Féin Ard Chomhairle and the party's chief negotiator in its meetings with the British government.

Peter McGuire was born in 1967. An ex-Loyalist prisoner, he became involved in community work after his release from prison in 1994. Written submission – 9/10/95.

Declan McLaughlin (26) is a singer with local band 'The Screaming Binlids'. He is also a muralist, responsible for a number of wall paintings in Nationalist areas of the city. Interview date – 21/11/95.

David Nicholl (34) is currently the leader of the UDP in Londonderry and North Antrim, and intends to stand in the elections on 30 May. He is also the Londonderry co-ordinator for Ulster Community Action Network (UCAN) and is on the board of the Waterside Area Partnership. Interview date – 7/9/95.

Paul O'Connor (40) has worked in the Pat Finucane Centre for the past five years. The centre, set up to explore nonviolent and non-political responses to injustice, is named after solicitor Pat Finucane who was killed in 1989. O'Connor is not a member of any political party. Interview date – 4/10/95.

Fionnbarra ÓDochartaigh (51) was involved in the civil rights and Republican movements in the 1960s and 1970s, and has written his own account of that time in his book 'Ireland's White Negroes – From Civil Rights to Insurrection'. He was a member of the Irish Republican Socialist Party until 1984, but is not currently a member of any political party. Interview date – 24/1/96.

A law graduate, *Eamon O'Kane* (25) currently works for the Waterside Development Trust. He is not a member of any political party. Written submission – 5/1/96.

Geraldine O'Neill was born and raised in the Waterside but has since lived on the cityside. She is not a member of any political party, but is 'inclined towards labour politics' and stood as a candidate in the local government elections in the early 1970s adopting the stance of 'taking party politics out of local government'. Interview date – 17/10/95.

The Peace and Reconciliation Group was founded in 1976 as part of the Peace People but split from them, amicably, in 1978 to concentrate their efforts on work within the city. Jimmy Duffy (59) is the group's chairman and John McCourt (46) its co-ordinator. Interview date – 19/9/95.

*Originally from Creggan, but now living in the Brandywell, **Maureen Shiels** describes herself as a Republican although she is not a member of any political party. She worked as a researcher on Eamonn McCann's book about Bloody Sunday interviewing relatives of the victims of that day. Interview date – 25/9/95.*

***William Temple** (58) spent twenty-eight years living in the Bogside before moving to Abercorn Road and then to the Fountain. He is a member of the UUP, the Orange Order and the Apprentice Boys, as well as the Wapping Community Association and the Diamond Project Trust. Interview date – 13/9/95.*

List of Deaths in the North West – 1969-94

Year	Month	Date	Name	Age	Status
1969	July	14	Francis McCloskey	67	Catholic civilian
		17	Samuel Devenney	42	Catholic civilian
	September	25	William King	49	Protestant civilian
1970	June	26	Thomas McCool	40	IRA
			Bernadette McCool	9	Catholic civilian
			Carol Ann McCool	4	Catholic civilian
			Joseph Coyle	40	IRA
			Thomas Carlin	55	IRA
1971	February	28	William Jolliffe	18	British army
	July	8	Seamus Cusack	27	Catholic civilian
		8	Desmond Beattie	19	Catholic civilian
	August	10	Paul Challoner	23	British army
		13	Hugh Herron	31	Catholic civilian
		18	Eamon Lafferty	20	IRA
		18	Eamon McDevitt	24	Catholic civilian
		19	James O'Hagan	16	Civilian
	September	6	Annette McGavigan	14	Catholic civilian
		14	Martin Carroll	23	British army
		14	William McGreanery	43	Catholic civilian
		18	Robert Leslie	20	RUC
	October	11	Roger Wilkins	32	British army
		16	Joseph Hill	24	British army
		27	David Tilbury	29	British army
			Angus Stevens	18	British army
	November	6	Kathleen Thompson	47	Catholic civilian
		9	Ian Curtis	23	British army
		19	Bridget Carr	24	Catholic civilian
	December	10	Kenneth Smyth	28	UDR
			Daniel McCormick	29	ex-UDR
		12	John Barnhill	65	Protestant civilian
		18	James Sheridan	20	IRA
			John Bateson	19	IRA
			Martin Lee	19	IRA
		29	Richard Ham	20	British army
1972	January	27	Peter Gilgun	26	RUC
			David Montgomery	20	RUC
		30	Robin Hankey	35	British army
		30	John Duddy	17	Catholic civilian
			Bernard McGuigan	41	Catholic civilian
			Patrick Doherty	31	Catholic civilian
			Kevin McElhinney	17	Catholic civilian

		Gerald Donaghy	17	Catholic civilian
		John Young	17	Catholic civilian
		Gerald McKinney	35	Catholic civilian
		Hugh Gilmore	17	Catholic civilian
		Michael McDaid	20	Catholic civilian
		Michael Kelly	17	Catholic civilian
		James Wray	22	Catholic civilian
		William Nash	19	Catholic civilian
		William McKinney	26	Catholic civilian
		John Johnston	59	Catholic civilian
February	16	Thomas Callaghan	45	UDR
	25	Gerard Doherty	16	OIRA
March	4	Marcus McCausland	39	ex-UDR
	14	Colm Keenan	19	IRA
		Eugene McGillan	18	IRA
	20	John Taylor	19	British army
	28	Joseph Forsythe	57	Protestant civilian
		Robert McMichael	27	Protestant civilian
April	10	Eric Blackburn	24	British army
		Brian Thomasson	21	British army
	16	Gerald Bristow	26	British army
	16	Martin Robinson	21	British army
May	13	John Starrs	19	IRA
	19	Manus Deery	15	Catholic civilian
	21	William Best	19	British army
June	8	Edward Megahey	44	UDR
	21	Kerry McCarthy	19	British army
	24	Christopher Stevenson	24	British army
		David Moon	24	British army
		Stuart Reid	26	British army
	26	James Meredith	20	British army
July	11	Terence Jones	23	British army
	16	Tobias Molloy	18	IRA
	19	Alan Jack	5mths	Protestant civilian
	24	James Casey	57	Catholic civilian
	31	Daniel Hegarty	16	Catholic civilian
	31	Seamus Bradley	19	IRA
	31	Catherine Eakin	9	Protestant civilian
		James McClelland	65	Protestant civilian
		David Miller	60	Protestant civilian
		Elizabeth McElhinney	59	Catholic civilian
		Joseph McCloskey	38	Catholic civilian
		William Temple	17	Protestant civilian
August	* 3	Rosemary McLaughlin	51	Catholic civilian
	* 8	Joseph Connolly	15	Catholic civilian
	* 12	Arthur Hone	40	Protestant civilian
	25	Arthur Whitelock	24	British army
	28	Anthony Metcalfe	28	British army
September	15	John Davis	22	British army
	17	Michael Quigley	19	IRA
	18	John Van Beck	26	British army
	27	George Lockhart	24	British army
October	28	Thomas McKay	29	British army

* Injured 31 July 1972.

170

	November	22	Samuel Porter	30	UDR
		22	Liam Shivers	48	Catholic civilian
		28	John Brady	21	IRA
			James Carr	19	IRA
		28	Paul Jackson	21	British army
	December	20	George Hamilton	28	UDR
		20	Michael McGinley	40	Catholic civilian
			Charles McCafferty	31	Catholic civilian
			Bernard Kelly	26	Catholic civilian
			Francis McCarron	58	Catholic civilian
			Charles Moore	31	Protestant civilian
		27	Eugene Devlin	22	IRA
		29	James McDaid	30	IRA
1973	January	1	Oliver Boyce	25	Catholic civilian
			Breige Porter	21	Catholic civilian
		4	James Hood	48	UDR
		14	David Dorsett	37	RUC
			Mervyn Wilson	23	RUC
	February	1	William Boardley	30	British army
		25	Gordon Gallagher	9	Catholic civilian
	March	3	David Deakin	39	UDR
		17	Lindsay Mooney	19	UDA
	April	11	Keith Evans	20	British army
		27	Anthony Goodfellow	26	British army
		28	Kerry Venn	23	British army
	May	3	Thomas Crump	27	British army
		22	Thomas Friel	21	Catholic civilian
	June	12	Francis Campbell	70	Protestant civilian
			Dinah Campbell	72	Protestant civilian
			Elizabeth Craigmile	76	Protestant civilian
			Nan Davis	60	Protestant civilian
			Robert Scott	72	Protestant civilian
			Elizabeth Palmer	60	Protestant civilian
		21	David Smith	31	British army
		21	Barry Gritter	29	British army
		26	Noorbaz Khan	45	Civilian
		26	Robert McGuinness	22	Catholic civilian
	August	24	Patrick Duffy	37	Catholic civilian
	September	22	James Brown	26	Catholic civilian
	October	3	Lindsay Dobie	23	British army
		28	John Doherty	31	RUC
	November	14	Kathleen Feeny	14	Catholic civilian
		18	Charles Logan	26	UVF
		25	Heinz Pisarek	30	British army
		25	Joseph Brooks	20	British army
	December	3	Joseph Walker	18	IRA
1974	January	11	Cecilia Byrne	53	Catholic civilian
			John Dunne	46	Catholic civilian
		21	John Haughey	32	British army
		25	Howard Fawley	19	British army
		29	William Baggley	43	RUC

	February	24	Patrick Lynch	23	IRA
	March	15	Adam Johnston	34	Protestant civilian
	April	14	Anthony Pollen	27	British army
		18	Seamus O'Neill	32	Catholic civilian
	May	31	Alfred Shotter	54	Catholic civilian
	June	24	Gerard Craig	17	IRA
			David Russell	18	IRA
	July	23	John Conley	43	UDR
	October	5	Asha Chopra	25	Civilian
		23	Michael Simpson	21	British army
		30	Michael Meenan	16	IRA
	November	12	Hugh Slater	29	Protestant civilian
			Leonard Cross	19	Protestant civilian
		12	Joseph Elliott	21	Catholic civilian
	December	7	Ethel Lynch	22	IRA
		7	John McDaid	16	IRA
1975	February	24	Brendan Doherty	23	Catholic civilian
	May	10	Paul Gray	20	RUC
		24	Noel Davis	22	RUC
	July	26	Robert McPherson	25	RUC
	October	2	Samuel Swanson	28	UVF
			Mark Dodd	17	UVF
			Robert Freeman	17	UVF
			Aubrey Reid	25	UVF
		6	David Love	45	RUC
		10	David Wray	18	British army
		21	Bernadette Friel	22	Catholic civilian
	November	25	Robert Stott	22	UDR
	December	2	Charles McNaul	55	Protestant civilian
			Alexander Mitchell	46	Protestant civilian
		18	Cyril McDonald	43	British army
			Colin McInnes	20	British army
1976	January	5	Clifford Evans	30	RUC
		17	Mark Ashford	19	British army
		22	John Arrell	32	UDR
	February	12	William Hamer	31	RUC
		17	Colin Lynch	18	Catholic civilian
	April	1	John McCutcheon	48	UDR
		2	Robert Lennox	60	UDR
	May	17	James Gallagher	20	Catholic civilian
	June	2	Linda Baggley	19	RUC
		30	Bernard Coyle	17	IRA
	July	3	William Miller	19	British army
		21	David Evans	20	British army
	August	3	Alan Watkins	20	British army
		11	Michael Quigley	33	Catholic civilian
	October	3	Kevin Mulhearn	33	Catholic civilian
		8	Arthur McKay		RUC
		8	Robert Hamilton	25	Prison officer
		8	Edward Boyd	29	Protestant civilian
	November	7	Ronald Bond	53	UDR

		9	James Speers	45	UDR
		11	Winston McCaughey	33	UDR
		18	William Kidd	37	UDR
		22	John Toland	35	Catholic civilian
		23	Joseph Glover	60	Protestant civilian
		25	James Loughrey	35	Catholic civilian
		27	Frank McConnellogue	46	Catholic civilian
	December	11	Howard Edwards	24	British army
		22	Samuel Armour	37	RUC
1977	January	14	James Greer	27	RUC
		27	Patrick McNulty	30	RUC
	February	2	Jeffrey Agate	59	Civilian
		23	Peter Hill	43	UDR
	March	15	David McQuillan	36	UDR
		16	Alexander Watters	62	Protestant civilian
	April	6	Gerard Cloete	46	UDR
		8	John McCracken	22	RUC
			Kenneth Sheehan	19	RUC
		15	William Edgar	34	British army
	November	2	Walter Kerr	34	UDR
	December	12	Colm McNutt	18	INLA
1978	February	8	William Gordon	39	UDR
			Lesley Gordon	10	Protestant civilian
		28	Charles Simpson	26	RUC
	March	17	David Jones	23	British army
	June	10	Dennis Heaney	21	IRA
		16	Robert Struthers	19	RUC
	August	11	Alan Swift	25	British army
	September	28	Brian Russell	30	Protestant civilian
	November	24	Patrick Duffy	50	IRA
1979	February	14	Steven Kirby	22	British army
	May	20	Stanley Wray	50	RUC
	August	10	Arthur McGraw	29	Protestant civilian
1980	January	18	Graham Cox	35	Prison officer
	May	14	Roy Hamilton	22	Protestant civilian
	July	19	Christopher Watson	20	British army
	November	11	Owen McQuade	31	British army
	December	27	Heather Pollock	53	Protestant civilian
1981	January	20	Christopher Shenton	21	British army
	February	10	David Montgomery	27	UDR
	April	7	Joanne Mathers	29	Protestant civilian
		19	James Brown	18	Catholic civilian
			Gary English	19	Catholic civilian
		25	Paul Whitters	15	Catholic civilian
	May	21	Patsy O'Hara	23	INLA
		22	Henry Duffy	45	Catholic civilian
		25	Thomas Ritchie	28	UDR
		28	Charles Maguire	20	IRA

			George McBrearty	24	IRA
	June	3	Joseph Lynn	60	Catholic civilian
	July	21	John Hazlett	43	Protestant civilian
		25	Cecil Stewart	17	Civilian
	August	20	Mickey Devine	27	INLA
	September	12	Alan Clarke	20	UDR
		14	John Proctor	25	RUC
	October	5	Hector Hall	22	ex-UDR
		28	Edward Brogan	28	Catholic civilian
	November	18	James McClintock	57	ex-UDR
		19	John McKeegan	49	UDR
1982	January	19	Deborah Rowe	17	Catholic civilian
	March	28	Norman Duddy	45	RUC
	April	1	Michael Ward	29	British army
			Michael Burbridge	31	British army
		19	Stephen McConomy	11	Catholic civilian
		20	Noel McCulloch	32	Protestant civilian
			Wilbert Kennedy	36	Protestant civilian
		27	Leslie Hamilton	37	UDR
	May	4	Samuel Caskey	21	RUC
		12	Thomas Cunningham	23	ex-UDR
		24	Anthony Anderson	22	British army
	June	11	David Reeves	24	RUC
		15	Hugh Cummings	39	UDR
	July	16	Colm Carey	28	Catholic civilian
	August	25	Eamon Bradley	23	IRA
	October	5	Charles Crothers	54	RUC
	December	6	Stephen Smith	24	British army
			Neil Williams	18	British army
			Stephen Bagshawe	21	British army
			David Murray	18	British army
			David Stitt	27	British army
			Shaw Williamson	20	British army
			Philip McDonagh	26	British army
			Terence Adams	20	British army
			Clinton Collins	20	British army
			Paul Delaney	18	British army
			David Salthouse	23	British army
			Ruth Dixon	17	Protestant civilian
			Carol Watts	25	Protestant civilian
			Angela Hoole	19	Civilian
			Patricia Cooke	21	Catholic civilian
			Valerie McIntyre	21	Protestant civilian
			Alan Callaghan	17	Protestant civilian
1983	January	18	John Oliphert	39	RUC
	February	2	Eugene McMonagle	24	INLA
	May	10	Alice Purves	47	Catholic civilian
	August	23	Ronald Finlay	32	UDR
		24	William Young	52	Protestant civilian
	October	15	Alan Stock	22	British army
		28	John Hallawell	35	RUC

	December	17	Brown McKeown	40	UDR
1984	March	27	David Ross	31	British army
	April	22	Richard Quigley	20	IRA
		23	Neil Clarke	21	British army
	December	6	William Fleming	19	IRA
			Daniel Doherty	23	IRA
1985	February	23	Kevin Coyle	24	Catholic civilian
		24	Douglas McElhinney	42	ex-UDR
	August	6	Charles English	21	IRA
	September	22	Martin Patten	18	British army
	October	7	Damien McCrory	20	Catholic civilian
	November	18	Robert Boyd	55	UDR
		21	Kurt Konig	38	Civilian
1986	February	18	Francis Bradley	20	Catholic civilian
		22	Anthony Gough	24	IRA
	August	28	Mervyn Bell	22	Protestant civilian
	October	24	Kenneth Johnston	25	Protestant civilian
1987	March	23	Leslie Jarvis	62	Protestant civilian
		23	Austin Wilson	35	RUC
			John Bennison	41	RUC
	April	21	Harold Henry	52	Protestant civilian
		23	Thomas Cooke	52	RUC
	August	30	Winston Finlay	44	RUC
	October	28	Patrick Deery	31	IRA
			Edward McSheffrey	29	IRA
	December	16	Gerard Doherty	68	Catholic civilian
1988	March	21	Clive Graham	25	RUC
	August	10	Samuel Patton	33	UVF
		31	Sean Dalton	55	Catholic civilian
			Sheila Lewis	60	Catholic civilian
			Gerard Curran		Catholic civilian
1989	February	14	John Davey	61	Catholic civilian
		22	Norman Duncan	27	British army
	March	8	Miles Amos	18	British army
			Stephen Cummins	24	British army
	July	1	Norman Annett	56	RUC
	October	9	Thomas Gibson	28	British army (TA)
1990	January	28	Charles Love	16	Catholic civilian
	October	24	Patrick Gillespie	42	Catholic civilian
			Vincent Scott	21	British army
			Stephen Beacham	20	British army
			Stephen Burrows	30	British army
			Paul Worrall	23	British army
			David Sweeney	19	British army
	November	12	Alexander Patterson	31	INLA
	December	1	Hubert Gilmore	49	ex-UDR

		3	David Shiels	30	Protestant civilian
1991	May	25	Eddie Fullerton	56	Catholic civilian (Sinn Féin)
	June	6	Ruairi Finnis	21	IRA
		29	Cecil McKnight	32	Protestant civilian (UDP)
	August	9	Gary Lynch	28	Protestant civilian (UDP)
		16	Thomas Donaghy	38	Catholic civilian (Sinn Féin)
	September	16	Bernard O'Hagan	37	Catholic civilian (Sinn Féin)
		17	Erik Clarke	37	RUC
	November	6	Michael Boxall	27	UDR
1992	April	2	Danny Cassidy	40	Catholic civilian (Sinn Féin)
	November	21	Gerard Holmes	35	Catholic civilian
	December	13	John Collett	36	Catholic civilian
1993	January	23	Michael Ferguson	21	RUC
	March	25	James McKenna	52	Catholic civilian
			Gerard Dalrymple	58	Catholic civilian
			Noel O'Kane	20	Catholic civilian
			James Kelly	25	IRA
	May	31	Christopher Wren	34	RIR
	October	30	Steven Mullan	20	Catholic civilian
			Moira Duddy	59	Catholic civilian
			James Moore	81	Catholic civilian
			John Moyne	50	Catholic civilian
			Joseph McDermott	60	Catholic civilian
			Karen Thompson	19	Catholic civilian
			John Burns	54	Protestant civilian
1994	April	20	Gregory Pollock		RUC

Glossary

Adams, Gerry
Born 5 October 1948 in Belfast, he was working as a barman when he became embroiled in the troubles. He spent some time in prison in the 1970s accused of membership of PIRA and for escaping from internment. He has been president of Sinn Féin since 1983, and was MP for West Belfast from 1983-92.

Alliance Party
Launched in April 1970, it attempts to draw support from both sides of the community. Its current leader is Dr John Alderdice.

Anglo-Irish Agreement
Signed by Margaret Thatcher and Garret Fitzgerald on 15 November 1985, it set out to establish peace and stability in Northern Ireland and encourage co-operation in a variety of areas, including security. Nationalists welcomed it while the Unionists were totally opposed to the Republic having any say in the internal affairs of Northern Ireland, especially the creation of a permanent secretariat near Stormont as support for joint ministerial contact between Britain and Ireland.

Army Council
Term applied to the leadership of the IRA.

Battle of the Bogside, Derry
In the afternoon of 12 August 1969, a parade by the Apprentice Boys of Derry led to a riot as the marchers passed the Bogside. The RUC entered the Bogside in large numbers to quell the rioting with water cannons. In response, the rioters formed barricades and attacked the police with petrol bombs and stones, forcing them back. The riot lasted for three days and only ended when the British army was brought in to replace the RUC on 14 August.

Blanket Protest
With the ending of special category status in 1976, Republican prisoners immediately made it apparent that they were not going to co-operate by refusing to wear prison clothing. Instead they covered themselves with blankets, hence the description of prisoners as being 'on the blanket'.

Bloody Sunday
On 30 January 1972, thirteen unarmed men taking part in an anti-internment march through Derry were shot dead and seventeen wounded by soldiers of the First Parachute Regiment; another man died later.

Boundary Commission
Commission set up by Britain to ratify the borders of Northern Ireland. When it delivered its report in 1925 Nationalists expected it to change the existing boundary in their favour, but it didn't and the borders of Northern Ireland remained as they are today.

B Specials
Section of the Ulster Special Constabulary, a 100% Protestant auxiliary police force set up in 1920 and disbanded in 1970.

Burntollet
The area in County Derry where the People's Democracy march from Belfast to Derry was ambushed on 4 January 1969. The seventy or so marchers were attacked by about 200 Protestants, allegedly with B Specials among them. Many of the marchers were injured.

Callaghan, James
British Labour Home Secretary in charge of Northern Ireland affairs, 1967-70, and Prime Minister, 1976-79.

Clegg, Lee
Member of the British Parachute Regiment jailed for life in June 1993 for the murder of Karen Reilly in Belfast. He was released in July 1995 and allowed to rejoin his old regiment.

Craig, William
Minister for Home Affairs in O'Neill's government, he banned the civil rights march in Derry in October 1968. He was sacked from the cabinet in December 1968 and then became a strong critic of what he saw as O'Neill's appeasement policies to the enemies of Unionism. Head of the Ulster Loyalist Association 1969-72 and the Ulster Vanguard movement, he was also one of the planners of the UWC strike in 1974.

CSJ – Campaign for Social Justice
An organisation formed in Dungannon in January 1964 to fight discrimination in housing, employment and electoral practices.

Devlin, Bernadette
Leading member of People's Democracy and MP for Mid-Ulster, 1969-1974.

Duke Street March – 5 October 1968
A civil rights march planned for 5 October was banned because of fears that it might clash with an Apprentice Boys' parade, but it went ahead, attended by 200-400 people. The march was stopped by the RUC in Duke Street in the Waterside, and in the ensuing trouble several people were injured including MPs Gerry Fitt, Eddie McAteer and Austin Currie. The march and subsequent trouble received worldwide media coverage, putting Northern Ireland firmly in the headlines.

DUP – Democratic Unionist Party
Right-wing Unionist party founded in September 1971 by Rev. Ian Paisley MP, MEP, who is still the party's leader.

Enniskillen Remembrance Day Bombing
Eleven civilians were killed and sixty-three injured when an IRA bomb exploded close to the Enniskillen war memorial as the annual Remembrance Sunday ceremony was about to begin. The IRA admitted the bombing in a statement that expressed 'deep regret'. It suggested that the bomb could have been triggered by a security force scanning device, a claim rejected by the RUC.

Faulkner, Brian
The last Stormont Prime Minister, in office 1971-72. He introduced internment without trial in August 1971.

FF – Fianna Fáil
One of the two main political parties in the Republic, it originated from the members of old Sinn Féin who were opposed to the Anglo-Irish Treaty in 1921. It first came to power in 1932 under Éamon de Valera and has been the governing party for most of the state's existence.

FG – Fine Gael
An important political party in the Republic, FG emerged from the pro-Treaty faction of old Sinn Féin. It was known as Cumann na nGaedheal in the 1920s and formed the first government of the Irish Free State. It has often been regarded as taking a softer line on Northern Ireland issues and unification than Fianna Fáil.

Greysteel Massacre
On 30 October 1993, six Catholics and a Protestant were killed and thirteen others injured in a UFF gun attack in the Rising Sun Bar at Greysteel, County Derry. The UFF claimed it was in response to the Shankill bombing.

Hunger Strike (1980)
Began on 27 October 1980 with seven Republican prisoners in the H-Blocks refusing food and demanding the right to wear their own clothes. The no-wash protest was suspended to concentrate public and media attention on the strike. On 12 December, three women prisoners in Armagh joined the hunger strike and two days later another twenty-three Republican prisoners joined. The strike ended on 18 December amid rumours there might be a positive move towards political status.

Hunger Strike (1981)
On 25 January 1981, the newly-elected leader of PIRA prisoners in the H-Blocks, Bobby Sands, claimed that moves for co-operation between the administration and the prisoners had broken down. On 1 March, the fifth anniversary of the phasing out of special category status, he began a hunger strike. This marked the beginning of a campaign that was to last seven months and result in the deaths of ten men, seven from PIRA and three from INLA. During this time, Sands was elected MP for Fermanagh-South Tyrone and another prisoner, Kieran Doherty, was elected TD for Cavan-Monaghan. Sands was the first to die on 5 May and almost 100,000 people attended his funeral. Nine others died in the succeeding four months. Throughout the strike, Thatcher refused concessions and once more there was an upsurge in Nationalist feeling. The strike ended on 3 October. Three days later, the Secretary of State announced that prisoners would be allowed to wear their own clothes and protesters would have 50% of lost remission restored.

INLA – Irish National Liberation Army
Republican paramilitary group set up in 1975 as the military wing of the IRSP. Among its initial members were ex-OIRA men opposed to the ceasefire in 1972 and it is also believed to have attracted some PIRA members during their ceasefire in 1975. It attracted world attention when it killed the Conservative Party's Northern Ireland spokesman Airey Neave in March 1979. It was declared illegal in July 1979.

Internment – Operation Demetrius
Internment was introduced in August 1971 by Brian Faulkner, then Prime Minister of Northern Ireland. In a series of dawn raids, the army attempted to arrest over 400 men they believed were connected with the IRA. However, their intelligence was completely outdated and very few of those arrested had any association with the current Republican movement. This policy of internment without trial led to a major upsurge in violence.

IRSP – Irish Republican Socialist Party
Formed in December 1974 as a breakaway group from OSF and made up largely of members unhappy with the Official Republican movement's (OIRA and OSF) ceasefire.

La Mon House Hotel
On 17 February 1978, fire bombs were used by the IRA to attack the hotel near Comber, County Down, while it was crowded with 400-500 people. Twelve people died instantly while twenty-three others were badly burned.

LAW – Loyalist Association of Workers
The group that organised the 1973 strike protesting at the internment of two Protestants in connection with the murder of a Catholic man. Its leader was Billy Hull, formerly a member of the Northern Ireland Labour Party. At its full strength it claimed about 100,000 members. The organisation broke up soon after the strike and most of its support was transferred to the UWC.

Londonderry Corporation
Unionist-controlled body which administered Derry until 1969 when it was replaced by a Development Commission, which lasted until 1973 when the present Derry City Council took over.

Lynch, Jack
Fianna Fáil Taoiseach from 1966-73 and 1977-79.

NICRA – Northern Ireland Civil Rights Association
Umbrella organisation established in January 1967 to bring together the various groups campaigning for civil rights in Northern Ireland.

No-Wash Protest
An intensification of the blanket protest which began in March 1978 after the British government refused to make any concessions. The prisoners involved numbered more than 300. They refused to leave their cells to wash or use the toilet because of the brutality of the warders, and began to smear excrement and food on the walls of their cells and smash up the furniture.

ÓConaill, Dáithí
Leading member of the Provisional Republican movement in the 1970s and early '80s, but left in 1986 and was one of the founders of Republican Sinn Féin. He died in 1991.

OIRA – Official Irish Republican Army
Dates from the end of 1969 with the split in the movement and the formation of PIRA. It represented those who remained loyal to Cathal Goulding as Chief of Staff. In Northern Ireland the 'Officials' are often called 'Stickies' after their habit of sticking Easter lilies to their lapels to commemorate the 1916 Easter Rising. The OIRA seems to have been largely inactive since it declared a ceasefire in 1972.

O'Neill, Terence
Unionist Prime Minister of Northern Ireland from 1963-69, O'Neill's reformist policies failed to satisfy Nationalists and angered Unionists. Caught between the two, he resigned in February 1969.

OSF/WP – Official Sinn Féin/Workers Party
A section of the Republican movement which agreed with dropping the policy of non-recognition. It had a strong Socialist content and changed its name to the Workers Party in 1982 in an attempt to distance itself from paramilitarism.

Paisley, Ian
Born in Armagh on 6 April 1926, the son of a Baptist Minister. In 1951 he founded the Free Presbyterian Church in the Ravenhill area of Belfast. His interest in politics was ignited in 1963 when he organised a march to protest at the lowering of the Union flag at Belfast City Hall to mark the death of Pope John XXIII. He formed the DUP in 1971 and has been its leader ever since. He has been MP for North Antrim since 1970 and a Northern Ireland MEP since 1979.

PD – People's Democracy
Left-wing group formed at Queen's University, Belfast, in October 1968. Its most famous members were Bernadette Devlin and Michael Farrell.

PIRA – Provisional Irish Republican Army
The most dominant force in the troubles. It originated in December 1969 when a split occurred due to the 'old' IRA Army Council voting in favour of giving recognition to the parliaments of Dublin, London and Northern Ireland. This was against traditional policy and the more militant elements opposed to this broke away and formed PIRA, normally referred to as the IRA.

PSF – Provisional Sinn Féin
Political counterpart of PIRA formed in 1970 after a split in the Republican movement over the policy of non-recognition of the Dáil, Stormont and Westminster, with those in favour of keeping the policy creating PSF. Its current leader is Gerry Adams, former MP for West Belfast.

PTA – Prevention of Terrorism Act
Rushed in after the Birmingham pub-bombings in 1974, the PTA declared the IRA illegal in Great Britain, allowed suspects to be held without charge for up to seven days, and permitted the expulsion of people either to Northern Ireland or the Republic.

RSF – Republican Sinn Féin
Emerged after a split in PSF in 1986 over the issue of abstention from the Dáil. Those opposed to ending the policy of abstention broke away and became known as Republican Sinn Féin.

SDLP – Social Democratic and Labour Party
Largest Nationalist party in Northern Ireland, formed in August 1970. Its current leader is John Hume MP, MEP.

Shankill Bombing
On 23 October 1993, an IRA bomb at a fish shop on the Shankill Road in Belfast killed nine people, including one of the bombers; another person died later. The IRA later claimed the upstairs room of the shop was being used by Loyalist paramilitaries at the time of the bombing.

Special Category Status
This was the special status given to paramilitary prisoners by William Whitelaw, Secretary of State, in June 1972 after a hunger strike by Republican prisoners in Belfast. Those sentenced to over nine months for offences related to the civil disturbances in Northern Ireland were not required to do prison work, could wear their own clothes and were allowed extra visits and food parcels. In 1975, the Gardiner Committee came out against special category status claiming it meant the loss of disciplinary control by the prison authorities and Merlyn Rees, Secretary of State, announced its phasing out from 1 March 1976; no-one convicted of an offence committed after that date would get special category status. Prisoners would now be put in cells instead of compounds, and eight new cell blocks were built at the Maze Prison, also known as Long Kesh. These became known as the H-Blocks because of their shape.

Stormont
Seat of the Northern Ireland government set up under the Government of Ireland Act of 1921. The regime, which lasted until the introduction of direct rule in 1972, enjoyed the support of the majority Unionist population, but caused great resentment among the minority Nationalist people.

Sunningdale Conference/Agreement
The conference, held in 1973 at Sunningdale Civil Service College, Berkshire, between the British and Irish governments and the SDLP, UUP and Alliance, set up a power-sharing executive made up of Unionists, led by Faulkner, the SDLP and the Alliance Party. The conference was also designed to establish the 'Irish Dimension', ie the role of Dublin, with a Council of Ireland.

UDA – Ulster Defence Association
The largest Protestant paramilitary group, it was launched in 1971 as an umbrella body for Loyalist vigilante groups which had sprung up around Belfast and surrounding areas amidst the growing violence at that time. In many Loyalist districts it was seen as a replacement for the B Specials and was organised very much along military lines.

UFF – Ulster Freedom Fighters
Allegedly a component group of the UDA used to claim responsibility for acts of violence against Republicans/Nationalists/Catholics.

Ulster Vanguard
Unionist pressure group launched in 1972 and led by William Craig, former Northern Ireland Minister for Home Affairs.

UUP – Ulster Unionist Party
The largest political party in Northern Ireland, the UUP governed Northern Ireland through Stormont from 1921 until March 1972 when direct rule from London was introduced. Its current leader is David Trimble, MP for Upper Bann.

UVF – Ulster Volunteer Force
An illegal Protestant paramilitary group which allegedly also uses the cover-name Protestant Action Force (PAF). It emerged in its present form in 1966, reviving the title given to the Ulster/Protestant force which fought against Irish Home Rule in 1913. It was made illegal after a Catholic barman was shot dead in 1966 by one of its members, Gusty Spence.

UWC – Ulster Workers' Council
The body that organised and ran the Loyalist strike in May 1974 which led to the fall of the power-sharing executive in Northern Ireland. It operated through a co-ordinating committee led by Vanguard assembly member Glen Barr, and had strong backing from the Loyalist paramilitaries.

UWC Strike
The strike was organised as a protest against the Sunningdale Agreement, especially the power-sharing executive and the Council of Ireland. It began with power cuts and factory closures. Many workers, including those in shipbuilders Harland and Wolff, went on strike. On 27 May, the British army took over twenty-one petrol stations across Northern Ireland only to be faced with the UWC stepping up its strike action by threatening further power cuts. The chaotic situation, which had developed after fourteen days, caused Unionist members of the executive to resign, rendering it ineffective.

Widgery Report
The report into the events of Bloody Sunday was released in April 1972 and named after Lord Chief Justice Widgery who was head of the tribunal of enquiry. Widgery held that there would have been no deaths if the march had not gone ahead illegally. He also found that none of the dead or injured had been armed, but that the soldiers must have been fired on first or else they would have had no reason to shoot at the crowd. An open verdict was passed on the deaths. The report was strongly condemned by Nationalists as a whitewash.

Whitelaw, William
First Secretary of State for Northern Ireland after the introduction of direct rule in March 1972, an office he held until November 1973.

Reference Sources

Bew, Paul, and *Gillespie, Gordon,* Northern Ireland: A Chronology of the Troubles 1968-93, *Gill & Macmillan, DUBLIN 1993.*

Bruce, Steve, The Edge of the Union – The Ulster Loyalist Political Vision, *Oxford University Press, OXFORD 1994.*

Campbell, B., McKeown, L., and *O'Hagan, F. (Eds),* Nor Meekly Serve My Time – The H-Block Struggle 1976-1981, *Beyond the Pale Publications, BELFAST 1994.*

Carson, Willie, So This Was Derry, *Wholesale Newspapers Marketing Ltd., DERRY 1994.*

Curran, Frank, Derry – Countdown to Disaster, *Gill & Macmillan, DUBLIN 1986.*

Egan, Bowes and *McCormack, Vincent,* Burntollet, *LRS Publishers, LONDON 1969.*

Flackes, W. D., and *Elliott, Sydney,* Northern Ireland: A Political Directory 1968-1993, *Blackstaff Press, BELFAST 1994.*

Grimaldi, Fulvio and *North, Susan,* Blood in the Street, *People's Democracy* and *Lotta Continua, DUBLIN 1972.*

Lacey, Brian, The Story of Derry and Londonderry, *Blackstaff Press, BELFAST 1990.*

Limpkin, Clive, The Battle of the Bogside, *Penguin Books, ENGLAND 1972.*

McCann, Eamonn, War and an Irish Town, *Pluto Press, LONDON 1993.* Bloody Sunday in Derry – What Really Happened, *Brandon Books, KERRY 1992.*

McKittrick, David, The Nervous Peace, *Blackstaff Press, BELFAST 1996.*

ÓDochartaigh, Fionnbarra, Ulster's White Negroes: From Civil Rights to Insurrection, *AK Press, EDINBURGH 1994.*

Sutton, Malcolm, Bear in Mind These Dead ... An Index of Deaths from the Conflict in Ireland 1969-1993, *Beyond the Pale Publications, BELFAST 1994.*

Index